THE MANY ROLES OF STEVE McQUEEN

ACTOR

"Every line counts. If it doesn't, then how come I'm out here in my funny hat making a damn fool of myself... trying for truth?"

WORLD-CLASS RACE DRIVER

"Racing is worth all the risk and the hassle because it keeps me human."

LOVER

"He was an absolute wild man." *(His first wife)* "Steve is into *basics*." *(His second)* "Steve cares." *(His third)*

FATHER

"Terri's into prelaw now. Chad's a lot like me, likes dirt riding...Christ, I was stealing cars at his age!"

LONER

"I'd rather run a fast bike over clean desert than do anything else in the world."

McQUEEN

WILLIAM F. NOLAN

BERKLEY BOOKS, NEW YORK

McQUEEN

A Berkley Book/published by arrangement with
Congdon & Weed, Inc.

PRINTING HISTORY
Congdon & Weed edition published 1984
Berkley edition/February 1985

ISBN: 0-425-06566-9

A BERKLEY BOOK ® TM 757,375
Berkley Books are published by The Berkley Publishing Group,
200 Madison Avenue, New York, New York 10016.
The name "BERKLEY" and the stylized "B" with design
are trademarks belonging to Berkley Publishing Corporation.
PRINTED IN THE UNITED STATES OF AMERICA

To Donna Seebo
for extraordinary reasons

Contents

Introduction

Steve McQueen never trusted writers. He refused to reveal himself for the printed page. He felt threatened or (as he called it) "spooked" by the press and avoided, whenever possible, all magazine and newspaper interviews. In fact, during the final decade of his life, McQueen gave *no* in-depth personal interviews at all, instructing his press agent to keep journalists away from him. They could write about the films he was making, that was public business, but the man behind the actor's mask retained a fierce, well-guarded privacy.

Steve let that guard down to me. No other writer knew him as I did. Each time we met he revealed more—about his early, troubled childhood, his rational (and irrational) fears, his near-mystical love of cycles and cars (and, finally, biplanes), his early struggles in New York, his feelings about love, friendship, family, marriage. He was a man of shifting moods and passionately expressed opinions—and he shared many of these opinions with me.

Why me? Why am *I* able to tell his story as no one else could?

The answer takes us back more than two decades, to the fall of 1959, when I was watching Steve in a scene for *Wanted— Dead or Alive,* the television series that launched his career.

On the interior studio set, at Four Star Productions, a large tank had been filled with water and edged with mud and brush to resemble a river bank. The plot gimmick involved an offbeat bank robbery engineered by a character known as "Bartolo the Baffling," a crooked escape artist who (in this scene) was entertaining a crowd at the river, having lured the local sheriff and deputies there to watch his act while his outlaw companions knocked over the town bank. McQueen, in his role of bounty hunter Josh Randall, had been tracking Bartolo and would ride in to arrest him in the middle of his carnival act.

This scene held special interest for me because I'd created it (in collaboration with John Tomerlin, a regular writer for the series). John and I had written this particular episode, "Vanishing Act," and I had been invited along that afternoon to watch the shooting and meet McQueen.

I had arrived late, with the scene already in progress, and I was frankly apprehensive. This was my first script assignment, and I had heard that McQueen could be rough on writers. If he didn't like your work he was quick to say so—feeling that *he* knew more about Josh Randall than any beginning writer. He would explode into sudden anger over dialogue he considered out of character and would change his lines within a scene if the words failed to meet his standards. This did not endear him to directors, and the atmosphere on a *Wanted* set was often tense and explosive.

I watched McQueen ride into the background, over a fake grass-covered hill built by studio carpenters behind the "river." He dismounted, unslung his weapon, and walked up to the escape artist. The script called for him to poke the sawed-off muzzle of his rifle into the crook's back, using the line: "Just raise those arms of yours, Bartolo, and don't turn around."

The camera was rolling when McQueen approached the actor, gun in hand. He hesitated. I saw the skin tighten along his jaw. He lowered the rifle and killed the scene with a single word: "Shit!"

The director walked over to Steve, looking upset, frustrated. "Okay, *now* what's wrong?"

"That line is flat," said McQueen. "Dull. It stinks. What

kind of idiot would write a line like that?"

I suddenly found myself stepping forward. "I'm the idiot."

Dead silence on the sound stage—as McQueen leveled his frost-blue eyes on me. It was like looking down the barrel of a gun.

"Who the hell are you?" he asked.

"I'm Nolan. I wrote the script with John Tomerlin—and that line happens to be one of mine." Before McQueen could reply I added: "But you're right, it stinks. I've got a better one."

"Let's hear it," said McQueen.

"Bartolo is into his act," I said, talking fast. "He's holding up both arms, above his head, waving to the crowd. You walk up, poke him with the gun, and say, "Long as you got 'em up, *keep* 'em up.""

McQueen's cold expression didn't change. The silence deepened as he continued to glare at me. Then he nodded tersely.

And that's how the scene was shot.

Not a great line by any means, but it saved the moment. McQueen shook my hand after the scene was finished, smiling thinly. "Sometimes I get spiky. They say I'm nuts to worry about every line of a show like this. Just a cheap western series. Grind 'em out. Assembly line stuff, right? Wrong, I tell 'em. You do a thing, you go all the way. Which means I give every scene my best shot. Every line counts. If it doesn't, then how come I'm out here in my funny hat making a damn fool of myself?"

I told him I respected his kind of dedication.

"Lotta people don't," he said with a shrug. "They just want to slam-bang it through and to hell with trying for any kind of truth. To me, Josh is real. He's alive. He's a part of *me*. So I look out for him when no one else does. That make sense to you?"

It made sense.

I didn't talk to Steve McQueen again for 11 years—not until the spring of 1970, when we met to discuss a racing profile I wanted to write on him for *Road & Track* magazine. Our careers had progressed far beyond *Wanted—Dead or Alive* in those 11 years; Steve had achieved world stardom—and I had written and sold more than a dozen books. (Among them my first novel, *Logan's Run,* which became a major MGM film and a CBS television series.)

On the phone, when I finally got through to McQueen, I asked if he remembered our meeting in 1959.

"Yeah, I remember." He chuckled softly. "Come see me at the Springs. We'll talk a little."

He meant Palm Springs. And we talked more than "a little." A lot more.

We established a relationship that has finally led me, here and now, to write his full story.

We were going to write it together. Steve had told me many things, talked at length of all he had been and done, what he called "the whole wild scam"—from the farm in Missouri through the New York years into the Hollywood era. But we never did the book. He was busy, I was busy, and it never got written.

"You should do it," he said, late in 1980. "I'll never live to write the damn book, and you know it all, how it really was...the racing...what bikes have meant to me...and now, flying the Stearmans...the whole scam." A silence on the phone, then: "You *do* it, okay?"

I never talked to Steve again. But I told him, okay, I would do it.

Tell how it really was. The whole scam.

Here, then, the book that really began, for me, on a twisting mountain road in Palm Springs, California, in the spring of 1970.

When I believe in something, I
fight like hell for it.

Steve McQueen

1...

Top
of the
Mountain

Rimcrest. A snake of narrow black asphalt off the main highway between Palm Springs and Cathedral City. Leading, first, to a gate guard, then on up, winding higher, to a scattering of plush, ranch-style homes spread out along the ridges like glittering box toys, each with its flower-filled patio and bluewater pool overlooking the sunheated expanse of California desert. Beyond the houses, the road continued to climb, steeply twisting, to the mountain's crest, shimmering above me in a haze of noon heat.

McQueen had said, "Look for me on the road beyond the gate. The gateman knows you're coming. Mention my name." I had done that, and the guard waved me past. I motored upward a mile or two, eased around a long looping curve to find McQueen, unsmiling, looking wary (not trusting me yet), his arms folded across his tanned, shirtless chest, leaning against his Jeep, waiting for me.

No ordinary vehicle, this Jeep. Custom paint job. Foam-padded double rollbars. Tooled leather bucket seats. Oversize wheels.

"My place is full of production people," he said, nodding toward a low, flat-roofed home to the right. "Park your car here and we'll take this up top where nobody can hassle us." McQueen slid behind the wheel of his Jeep, and I climbed into the seat next to him as he gunned the engine to thunderous life.

"What have you *got* under there?" I shouted, pointing toward the hood.

"Five-fifty Traco Chevy," he shouted back above the din. "Long wheelbase. Full-race suspension. Light chassis. She can step."

And she did. McQueen's boot on the accelerator sent the 550-hp vehicle forward in a raw surge of power that snapped my head back.

I have raced sports cars, and I know something about speed. I am not easily impressed by fast road driving—but McQueen was in a class by himself as he blasted the powerhouse Jeep around each curve, eating up the short straights between turns at high throttle, slinging the hard-sprung vehicle up Rimcrest with the skill of a professional racing driver.

Which, in part, he was.

"She's earned silver at Ascot," he said, when we'd reached the top and he'd shut down the brutal Chevy power plant. Meaning he had won trophies competing with this Jeep at Ascot Stadium in Los Angeles.

I had not seen him race there, but I'd watched him at Santa Barbara and Riverside.

"Saw you run the Porsche 1600 and the Lotus Eleven at Santa Barbara," I told him. "That Lotus was one swift little machine."

He nodded. "Network executives made me sell her. Figured I'd bust my melon. She sure was swift, an' that's a fact."

McQueen often personalized his machinery.

The antique Stearman biplane he flew during the final year of his life was, to him, "A real sweet lady...but she can bite when you get sloppy!"

We talked about his bikes, the fast two-wheelers he took so much joy in riding. Motorcycles remained Steve's prime passion. The sports cars and the off-road specials and the antique planes were all great, but the cycles were something else, and his eyes would soften when he talked about what they meant to him.

"I'm out there, alone, on a fast bike—just me and the desert and a slice of clean blue sky, with the wind around me and the cactus and the sound of that engine at high revs...It's pure. It's freedom—maybe the only *real* freedom there is."

"Hemingway felt that way about the Gulf Stream," I said.

"Yeah, well...he had *his* sea and I've got mine." McQueen nodded downward.

We were on a flat rock plateau at the mountain's crest. Below us the dazzling white sand stretched away for miles in heat-rippled waves.

"I live here for a reason," McQueen told me, striding to the edge of the rock, surveying the horizon, eyes narrowed against the reflected sunglare. "I can drop down into the Gorgonio wash and run a bike for 40 miles, balls out, all the way to Indio. There's nothing better than the smell of puckerbushes and cholla in the early morning. I'd rather run a fast bike over clean desert than do anything else in the world."

He was silent for a moment; then he swung his head toward me, lionlike, challenging. He probed my eyes with his own, reading sign. "I don't talk about myself to many people. Especially writers. The talk gets twisted. Half the time I end up sounding like an asshole in print. Sometimes they really work me over." He shook his head. "I just can't figure writers."

McQueen was sizing me up; the top of the mountain was his personal testing ground. I felt the hot weight of the sun pressing against my head and shoulders.

"I'm not a butcher," I said quietly. "I don't butcher the people I talk to. You've won some races. *Road & Track* hired me to write about them. I'll do a good job. Fair and accurate."

"I hear you've raced," he said.

I nodded. "Some. Not a lot. I ran an Austin-Healey Le Mans 100-M at the Hourglass near San Diego. Even got a trophy."

His eyes were intense. "Then you know. About racing. About how it is."

"I know."

Another silence. I was passing his test; I wasn't just another writer, I was a fellow competitor, and that meant a lot to McQueen. He began to relax. I could see the mistrust and the hard-edged wariness dissolving. He shot me a crooked smile. "How 'bout a beer?"

"Sounds great."

He flipped open a small ice chest in the back of the Jeep, took out two cans, tossed one to me.

"I drink more of this stuff than I should, but that's okay because I sweat it all out on the bikes," he said, opening the can. He took a long swig, patted his flat stomach, and belched heartily. We exchanged grins.

As the sun slipped down the western sky, we sat in Steve's Jeep, talking about cars and racing and women and films and acting and how it was to grow up in the Midwest.

We had more than racing in common. We'd both been born in March, just two years apart— me in 1928, Steve in 1930—and had both spent the early years of our childhood in Missouri. Me in Kansas City, Steve in Slater, a rail town roughly 100 miles northeast of K.C. We'd shared the same humid summers and snowbound winters.

There was one major difference. My parental environment was solid, but Steve's father had deserted the family when the boy was just six months old. As an adult, Steve tried for years to locate William McQueen, ex-stunt pilot and barnstormer.

"I finally traced him to a small town here in California," Steve related, "but it was too late. He'd died three months earlier—so we never got to see each other. His friends told me he used to watch me on TV and that he was real proud of me. But maybe they just said that because they figured I wanted to hear it." He stared at the shadow of the Jeep, inked against the flat gray rock. "He probably didn't give a damn about me. If he had, he coulda found me easy enough."

He nodded, rubbing a thumb slowly along his cheek. "I wanted to just stand in front of him, just face him square and ask why he left us the way he did. It hurt my mother at the time, and it hurt me later. But . . . I guess he was just a bastard who didn't give a shit."

Steve lapsed into silence.

We talked for four hours that day on the mountain—and we talked in his Studio City office at Solar Productions, between cycle races at Indian Dunes, on film sets, in coffee shops, and over the telephone.

I noticed an odd fact about McQueen: when he talked to reporters and interviewers his speech was often "formal." He was careful in his selection of thoughts and phrases. But when he talked to me, and to others he trusted, he would use street slang, racing jargon, profanity, often dropping the "g" in many words (*racin'* for *racing*, *pushin'* for *pushing*). He was never entirely comfortable around the press, even in the days when he granted many interviews; sometimes he would be short-worded and curt, at other times expansive, with the words machine-gunning out at a rapid clip.

Steve was pleased with my racing profile in *Road & Track* (October 1970: "Out Among the Puckerbushes with Steve McQueen"). I'd won his trust because I had kept my promise; the writing was fair and accurate.

I was never one of Steve's close friends, never part of his inner circle of racing buddies or film pals or flying companions, and I never got to know his family—but I was the one writer he'd talk to in depth.

That was our special bond.

Steve McQueen's life was never dull. From early boyhood, to his death some seven months beyond his fiftieth year, he constantly challenged the system. He was a true rebel who hated to be tamed, a stallion who wore no man's bridle. He made many mistakes during his tumultuous life, and got into what he termed "plenty of hairy scrapes" ("Had my nose busted three times in fights before I was twenty!"). As a result, the McQueen years were a wild patchwork of edge-of-the-cliff failures and successes, personal and professional.

I'd ask him: "What was your first cycle race like? Tell me about it."

Or: "How did you meet Neile, back in New York?"

Or: "Just how tough was it, on location in Taiwan for *Sand Pebbles*?"

Or I'd ask him: "What was it really like for you on that farm back in Missouri when you were a kid?"

And he'd tell me.

2...

Time of Trial

He was wary about discussing his childhood.

"A lot of reporters have asked me about the early years," McQueen told me, "but I always shut down on that period. Lotta pain there . . . yet some happy times along the way. Guess you could call it a *mix*—of the bad and the good."

Lillian Thompson, Steve's maternal grandmother, was from St. Louis, Missouri. She married Victor Crawford, a local businessman, and they had a daughter, Julia. Shy, blonde, petite, Julia Crawford was a teenager when she met an older man she later described as "dashing and very romantic."

He was William McQueen, soldier of fortune and stunt pilot attached to a "Flying Circus"—and he dazzled the young girl with his tales of hazardous, death-defying aerial exploits performed at county fairs across the nation. When he left St. Louis he took 18-year-old Julia with him to Indiana as his wife.

7

"She was still a teenager when I came along," Steve related. "Small and slim . . . like a little girl. Looked real young to be a mother. She gave me a first name I never used, Terrence. My father supplied the middle one, Steven. He liked to gamble, and he named me after Steve Hall, a one-armed bookie pal of his." The birth date was March 24, 1930, and the place was Beech Grove Hospital, in a suburb of Indianapolis.

William McQueen hated the idea of parenthood; it didn't fit his devil-may-care image, and just six months after Steve was born he deserted his family. "Just flew over the rainbow," as Steve put it.

> He was a sky gypsy. Between air shows he'd hedge-hop the States, crop dusting a farm for his gas and the price of a meal. Always on the move. I heard he was with Chennault's Flying Tigers in China during the Second World War. For a long time I hated him for leaving us, but later—after I had kids of my own—I got to feeling sorry for him because he missed seeing me grow up. He never had the special kind of kick that being a father can give you.

In shock at being abandoned, Julia McQueen turned to her mother's side of the family for help, to Steve's great-uncle Claude W. Thompson, who owned a farm in Slater, Missouri. She moved there with her baby son, to the Thompson farm, and remained long enough to earn a bit of money. Then she returned to Indianapolis, obtained a job, and tried to raise young Steve. "Things didn't work out," he related. "After a couple of years she took me back to Uncle Claude's place, left me there, and headed west. So, for the next six years, I lived in Slater."

Claude Thompson was known throughout Saline County as an expert farmer and cattleman, and his labors never failed to garner a comfortable annual profit. "He really loved the land," Steve recalled.

> And he taught me a lot about farming. I milked cows, worked the corn field, cut wood for the winter . . . There was always plenty to do. And when I'd get lazy and duck my chores he'd warm my backside with a hickory

switch. I learned a simple fact. You work for what you get. Uncle Claude had no use for slackers.

Steve had a small room of his own, near the attic, under the eaves of the tall wooden farmhouse. He was up by sunrise— and his favorite job was hog herding.

Slater was a rail town, a link on the main line to St. Louis, and Claude Thompson shipped his prize hogs to market from the local depot. "We'd get up extra early when it was still dark," Steve recalled. "An' me an' Uncle Claude would start the hogs toward town."

The trip was three and a half miles, over a gravel road, from the farm to the railroad loading pens in Slater. En route, young Steve liked to imagine himself a cowboy, handling a trail herd, as he urged the sleepy animals along the road with a sharpened stick, watching the sun come up over the trees, listening to the early morning birds. He never failed to enjoy these outings.

As a special reward, Thompson would treat the youngster to a movie each Saturday, at the Kiva, Slater's only cinema house. Steve recalled seeing his first motion pictures there; his favorites were westerns, and he'd bring along his toy cap pistol to fire at the villains.

At the age of four, he received an exciting birthday present: a bright red tricycle. McQueen claimed that it started his racing fever. "There was a dirt bluff behind the farm, and I'd challenge the other kids in the area. We'd race up it for gumdrops. I usually reached the top first. Got some skinned knees—but I sure won a lot of gumdrops!"

Steve attended the Orearville School, a white frame, single-room building in Slater. He was not a good student. Lessons bored him; he much preferred playing catch with his pals in the open field behind the schoolhouse. But when the other youngsters would brag about their father, Steve would lapse into pained silence. He felt insecure, abandoned, as if life had cruelly selected him for special punishment. His subsequent rebellion against all forms of organized authority originated in these early school years.

The semideafness that would plague him for the rest of his life also began during this period. At five, McQueen suffered a mastoid infection, an inflammation of the temporal bone behind his left ear. No antibiotics were available in 1935, and the infection spread to the boy's middle ear before it could be contained.

Otherwise, young McQueen was in fine health. Farm life agreed with him. He had a special affinity for the animals under his care ("In some ways, I felt they were superior to human beings!"), and he enjoyed fishing the local creeks and game-hunting the woods. A favorite story involved hunting:

> When I was eight Uncle Claude would let me use the family rifle to shoot game in the woods. But he never gave me more than one shell. I either hit something first shot, or I came back empty-handed. Well, one day I came back carrying *two* dead pigeons. I said that I'd waited in the woods for them to line up, just right, side by side, and that I'd calculated things like wind angle and muzzle velocity—and that I killed 'em both with a single shot. He was amazed. Bragged about me to all his hunting cronies back in town. I never did tell him the truth, which was that I'd gone into a neighbor's silo and shot at some nesting pigeons. The bullet hit one, went right through him, glanced off the side of the silo, and hit another. To his dying day, Uncle Claude remained convinced I was a miracle marksman with a rifle!

Julia McQueen shattered this idyllic period by returning to Slater when the boy was nine, announcing that she had re-married and intended to establish a home for Steve with her in Indianapolis. Therefore, young McQueen was again uprooted for a new and unsettling life in a strange city with a mother he no longer loved "and a stranger who called himself my Daddy."

McQueen retained a special memory of his leavetaking: "The day I left the farm Uncle Claude gave me a personal going-away present: a gold pocket watch, with an inscription inside the case." The inscription read: "To Steve—who has been a son to me."

The move to Indianapolis was traumatic, and McQueen failed to adjust. He joined a street gang of young toughs who sought nightly thrills by breaking into local shops. Steve admitted that his main ambition, at this troubled stage of life, was to become the gang leader, to show that the "hick farmboy" could be tougher than any city kid. He later recalled mastering two basic skills, in Indianapolis: "How to steal hubcaps and shoot pool."

By his twelfth birthday they had moved again, to the Silver Lake area of Los Angeles, where his mother married (in Steve's words) "a creep named Berrie." Steve was bitterly unhappy. "It was a rotten scene. I didn't like my new stepfather and he didn't like me. He was a bully—a prime sonuvabitch—and I was no prize package myself. We locked horns from the day we met."

Feeling rootless and unloved, fired by an active hostility toward his new stepfather, Steve resumed his lawless street activities. He fought in a violent gang "rumble," was arrested, brought to court, and released with a stern warning from the judge that a second offense could result in a jail sentence.

"Berrie used his fists on me," Steve angrily recalled. "He worked me over pretty good—and my mother didn't lift a hand. She was always weak, and I guess that's when I really began to despise weakness in people. I had a lot of contempt for her. She wanted my love, but she sure never tried to earn it."

McQueen's escape was fast driving and drag racing—a release for his tension and frustrations. At 13, working with an older buddy who shared this new passion, Steve built a potent street dragster, mating a modified Ford 60 engine to a Model-A frame. "We used an Edelbrock manifold, and we could accelerate with a J-2 Allard, which was *the* going sports machine at the time. She didn't handle worth a damn, but when the engine held together that rod of ours had *stark* acceleration."

McQueen was beginning to feel the pressures of adolescence. Other boys his age were dating, attending parties and dances, had girlfriends. But not Steve. He felt cut off from such normal pursuits. Having lost Claude Thompson, the one loving influence in his life, he was victim to a desperate sense of personal desolation. Steve's fumbling efforts at sex were crude, unsatisfactory, and he turned back to the streets.

When he was arrested again (for stealing a set of Cadillac hubcaps) his stepfather became enraged and in the course of a beating, threw Steve down a flight of stairs. At the bottom of the stairway, blood flowing from a cut on his mouth, the 14-

year-old boy glared up at the man he hated. "You lay your stinkin' hands on me again—an' I swear I'll *kill* you!" Berrie called in the authorities, declaring that the boy was "totally incorrigible and beyond parental control."

In the fall of 1944 McQueen's mother and stepfather signed a court order that sent Steve to the California Junior Boys Republic at Chino, in San Bernardino County, optimistically described as "a home for wayward boys" but which was actually an honor-based reform school.

But unlike the more extreme examples of its type, Chino had neither walls nor fences to hold in the troubled youths who were sent there. "Trust is the operative word," said Frank Graves, then the principal. "We encourage our boys to learn solid vocational skills and to become trustworthy members of society. When a boy breaks our trust in him and runs away, he is brought back by the police, and we start over again."

That is precisely what happened to McQueen. He felt no obligations of trust. As he put it: "That stuff seemed stupid to me. So after three months of doin' classes each morning and workin' afternoons in the laundry, I got bugged and split. But I sure didn't get far. I was hiding out in a stable when the cops grabbed me."

Steve spent that night in the local jail. The next morning he was taken back to Chino and told that he had a choice: Either settle in and serve his term there or be shipped off to a much tougher reform school. He agreed to cooperate but secretly planned another breakout.

"I still remember my number at Chino," he recalled. "I was 3188. For skipping out, Graves turned me over to the Boys' Council." At Chino, punishment was meted out to boys *by* boys—and Steve was assigned to a series of dirty, exhausting jobs: uprooting tree stumps, digging ditches, mixing cement... "They even had me cleaning out the urinals."

All this punishment failed to deter McQueen in his plans for escape. He was in the midst of planning another breakout when one of the school's older superintendents took up his case. "This man's name was Mr. Panter," Steve related. "And he reminded me of my Uncle Claude. Stern but just."

Panter spent many hours with Steve in long, quiet talks; he knew that threats of corrective action would not be effective with such an angry young man. Punishment merely stiffened

McQueen's bitter resistance to authority. Instead, Panter used logic, demonstrating a basic sympathy and understanding that drew a positive response from Steve. "He was saying some straight things—and I began to listen, to soak in what he was trying to get across."

Panter's message was clear: If McQueen continued to fight the system at Chino, he would lose everything—dignity, freedom, respect. But if Steve would channel his energy—the same energy that fueled his rebellion—he could win both respect *and* freedom. "He said he saw that I had something special, that I could really be *somebody* in the world if I gave it a real shot. No one else in authority had ever talked to me like that. No one else had seemed to give a damn about my future life as an adult—but *he* did, and it meant a lot to me."

These quiet talks turned Steve around; he began to "really shape up" and became expert at fashioning the Christmas wreaths sold each holiday season to help finance the school's activities. He also worked skillfully with wood and metal in the school shop. As a result, Steve was elected to the Boys' Council and was able to complete the ninth grade before his release in April of 1946, having served an 18-month term. During the year and a half McQueen was in Chino, his stepfather had died, and his mother had moved to New York. She now arranged a reunion with her son, sending him enough money for the trip East.

Those final months profoundly affected young McQueen; he had proven to himself that he *could* function in a society he had previously rejected. The world began to make some sense to him. At 16, he was on a new road, and though it would take many twists and turns it would eventually lead him to the summit of his own personal mountain, to yet-undreamed-of heights. At the Boys Republic, Steve had acquired the single-most valuable tool for future survival: a sense of self-worth.

3. . .

The Roving Years

A hot, dusty afternoon at Indian Dunes, the popular motorcycle circuit near Los Angeles. A lull between races. McQueen, his face sweat streaked, grimed from an earlier event, dressed in his racing leathers, talking about his beginnings as an actor.

"I didn't just *jump* into acting. I mean, in my teens, I never even *thought* about it. More than five years passed between the time I stepped out of the New York bus station at 16 and my first audition as a would-be actor in 1951."

He scrubbed his chin with a brown fist. "Hell of a lot happened to me in those five years. Man, I was really into *life* in those days. There was a big world out there just waiting for me to dig into it—to eat it up. And I was hungry. I wanted the full course with all the trimmings."

McQueen's reunion with his mother was brief and bitter. They quarreled. ("For one thing, I didn't dig the new dude she was with.") The boy heatedly declared that he did not need her or anyone else to "wet-nurse" him in New York. He was used to street action. He would survive.

Steve recalled his mother's warning. "This is a rough city," she told him, "and you're just a kid. You won't last a week on your own." And she made it clear that if he left she wouldn't be taking him back. "I won't be *coming* back," Steve replied. "I've got my plans."

But he had no plans. No job experience. No money. McQueen remembered walking the Manhattan streets in a daze, directionless and uncertain. He ended up in a Greenwich Village bar. "I met these two guys there," McQueen related.

> I was underage, so they stood me for drinks. Ford and Tinker—two working seamen. They told me how great it was, shipping out for new places. Got me hopped up on the idea of going to sea. Next thing I remember is shippin' out of Yonkers on board the S.S. *Alpha*.

They helped young McQueen obtain seaman's papers, adding two years to his age. Deckhands were in short supply, so no questions were asked. ("Ford and Tinker probably got a kickback for bringing me aboard.")

The *Alpha*, a rusted Greek tanker, was bound for the West Indies to pick up a cargo of molasses. "That ol' tub was in really *sad* shape," Steve recalled. "Caught fire not long out of harbor and damn near sank—but we managed to put the fire out and head on down to Cuba."

McQueen quickly discovered that life at sea was anything but romantic. Scrubbing decks under a hot sun was sweaty, exhausting work. ("They also had me tossing garbage—but the cook forgot to warn me never to empty a bucket into the wind. After that first garbage detail, I smelled so bad that nobody in the crew would come within a hundred feet of me!")

By the time the *Alpha* docked in the Dominican Republic, Steve had had enough. He jumped ship in Santo Domingo, hiring out as a carpenter's assistant to earn enough for a passage back to the States.

His next stop was Port Arthur, Texas, where he took on the

most unusual occupation of his crowded young life. "If you read my studio bio, it says that I worked in a hotel there as a waiter," McQueen said. "The truth is, I was towel boy in a brothel—and, man, those ladies all treated me real, real fine. I didn't know much about sex before then, but talk about your overnight education!"

Next, he moved from Port Arthur into the oilfields of Waco and Corpus Christi, signing as a "grunt" laborer on the rigs. "One night a carnival passed through town," McQueen recalled,

> and I got a sudden itch to see what carny life was like. Worked a booth, selling cheesy pen-and-pencil sets. The boss thought I was selling 'em for 25 cents a set, but I was charging a buck and pocketing the profit. That boss was a real crook, who scammed from the public, so I scammed from him. When he got wise, I split.

Young McQueen's moral values were highly questionable at this stage of his life, and he admitted that if he had "just turned the wrong corner I could easily have become a hood. The world didn't seem to be a very friendly place. I learned early not to trust anybody. I was a drifter, bumming around, taking on any job that looked like fun. I was out for adventure."

He found it in Canada when he joined the crew at a lumber camp in Ontario as a "hijacker"—sawing off the topmost branches from trees prior to their being cut down. Wearing hob-nailed boots, McQueen would climb the swaying trunk, clinging to a perch high above the ground, sawing away at branches until he'd cleared the top area. It was dangerous work, which McQueen found exhilarating—but two horrifying near-falls convinced him that logging was not an ideal profession. ("I took off and headed down for the Carolinas to check out the Southern belles.")

He spent his seventeenth birthday with a new girl he had met in Myrtle Beach, South Carolina. ("Her name was Sue Ann. She had big green eyes.") A Marine recruitment poster in front of the town post office inspired Steve with a sudden desire to become a Leatherneck. In April of 1947 he enlisted, becoming a tank driver in the Second Division of the Fleet Marine Force.

Just 12 months had passed since he left New York—truly an incredible year for a 16-year-old boy; from Cuban seas to Texas oil fields, from traveling carnivals to the forests of Canada. The Missouri farmboy had become a crew-cut Marine, yet he was still far from maturity. "I still had a lot of kinks to get out," he recalled. "I didn't really have it together in the service, and my record was not what you'd call outstanding. In fact, over my three-year hitch I was busted from PFC back to private about seven times—plus spending some mean days in lockup for a little AWOL side trip I took."

He had stretched a weekend pass into two full weeks to visit his South Carolina girlfriend. When the shore patrol finally caught up with him, McQueen resisted with his fists and was thrown into the brig for 21 days on bread and water. Another 20 days were added to the sentence when he continued to play the camp rebel (a role, ironically, that he would later play to perfection in films). "That session in the brig didn't really tame me down much," Steve admitted. "But it got one message across to me loud and clear. When you're in the Marines, Uncle Sam calls the shots. What you *don't* do is go running off to see your chick."

Steve's fascination with mechanical objects found full expression in the service.

> I'd often wondered if the engine on a tank could be speed-converted. This seemed like a fine time to find out. Me and some buddies got on it, porting and milling the heads, reworking the timing and carburetion. We figured on having the fastest tank in the Division. What we got was plenty of skinned knuckles and a blown engine. At least I found out whether or not you can soup up a tank. You *can't*.

While a Marine, Steve made friends and enemies in equal measure. He spoke about one "real creep" who enjoyed provoking him.

> His name was Joey, and he was always with this tough-looking buddy of his. Real big dude. These two were liked *glued* together, and I knew I couldn't handle both of 'em at once. So I played it smart. I hid inside the

head until Joey came in alone to take a piss. I said, "Hello, pal," and when he turned around with his fly unzipped, I punched him in the chops. After that he never wised off around me anymore. I'd made my point.

One of the things McQueen constantly complained about was "the limited chow. I never got enough to eat and it was starting to drive me nuts." When the Division was moved to Labrador in Canada for cold-water amphibious exercises, the situation got worse when standard food rations were cut to simulate battle conditions. "I was getting desperate," Steve recalled.

Used to sit and daydream about eating! Then I got my shot. I was sent over alone one afternoon to unload a food shipment for the officers' mess. I drove my Amtrac* down to the boat and heisted a full case of food for myself. Turned out it contained beans—but that was okay because beans are *filling*.

There was a basic problem. All of the cans were cold. Steve decided that the best way to heat them was to have a buddy rev up the Amtrac's engine while McQueen, wearing gloves, held several of the cans over the hot exhaust. "I held 'em there for maybe four or five minutes.

But I'd forgotten to *open* the cans—and suddenly there was this terrific explosion. Knocked me back about three feet and just blew beans all over the friggin' camp—on tents, jeeps, radar equipment, *everywhere*. For about a week after that, I'd go by an officer and salute him and I'd see a bean stuck on his helmet.

Not all of McQueen's service experiences were acts of rebellion. On one dramatic occasion during the Labrador exercises, a large transport ship struck a sandbank, pitching tanks and crews into the sea. Trapped inside the submerged tanks, several men drowned; others struggled to the surface, but were unable to remain afloat for more than a few seconds in the

---

*An amphibious personnel carrier with tractor treads.

freezing Arctic waters. Amphibious craft were launched. Aboard one of these vessels, McQueen acted with courage and dispatch; he was personally responsible for the rescue of five Marines, pulling them to safety just moments before the freezing waters would have claimed their lives.

Beyond this action, Steve declared that the highest honor he gained in the service was to be posted as part of the Honor Guard protecting President Harry Truman's yacht.

"All in all, despite my problems, I liked being in the Marines," Steve admitted. "They gave me a discipline I could live with. By the time I got out I was able to cope with things on a more realistic level. Sure, I was still pretty wild—but I'd had a lot of the rough edges knocked off."

Steve McQueen was honorably discharged at Camp Lejeune, North Carolina, in April of 1950. He had enlisted in the Marines as a boy; now, three years later, he was leaving the service as a man.

With his mustering-out pay in his hip pocket, Steve headed back to Myrtle Beach and Sue Ann. "She was real glad to see me again," he said.

> Sue Ann was 19, a year younger than me, with an accent that made her sound like Scarlett O'Hara. She was part of a rich Southern family—and it was great getting all slicked up, going over to her big fancy house for dinner, meeting her friends, taking her to dances. . . . It was like I was part of a special world I'd only *heard* about before. I just fell into it the way you fall into a dream.

But when his service money ran out and Sue Ann's father offered him a job, expecting Steve to marry his daughter, McQueen "backed off fast." The dream ended abruptly, and McQueen did not like the reality he was facing. "I split out for Washington, D.C., and never saw Sue Ann again," he said. "Got a job as a taxi mechanic, and drove a cab around Washington part time—but New York seemed to be where the real action was, and that's where I headed."

At 20, back in Manhattan, Steve resumed his gypsy existence, drifting from job to job, quitting when the work bored him, living a life devoid of ambition or purpose. He rented a $19-a-month apartment, a cramped, cold-water walkup in

Greenwich Village. The area fascinated him with its bizarre local color and kinetic atmosphere. As he remarked: "Things happened in the Village. Good things. Bad things. But never dull things. People expected you to be a little off-center when you lived there. The chicks were wilder and the pace was faster. I dug it."

Steve did a half hour of weight-lifting each morning with a stolen "No Parking" sign ("I couldn't afford barbells!")— and his job history was equally off center. He carried radiators out of condemned buildings, delivered television sets for a repair shop, trimmed leather for a sandalmaker, worked as a bag loader for the Post Office, recapped tires in a Manhattan garage, and collected bets for a local bookie. "Hell, I even tried to be a boxer," admitted McQueen.

> But I was too skinny. After getting knocked flat on my duff I gave it a quick pass. Then I tried selling pottery in a big downtown department store. Lasted exactly *one* day. I was out scammin' for bread, and I'd try anything with a buck attached to it. Even accepted a gig in a smelly little cellar on Third Avenue, putting together artificial flowers. Then it was door-to-door selling, but I felt like a shark going into these poor family homes and talking the lady of the house into a set of encyclopedias. So I chucked that routine.

Broke and jobless again, he was in a Village drugstore, idly examining a shower nozzle, when a clerk walked over to ask if he was returning it for a refund. "Uh, yeah . . . that's right," Steve replied. "This one's defective. I'd like my money back." And McQueen sauntered happily out of the drugstore with a five-dollar bill in his pocket. ("I ate for two days on that fiver and began using the same gimmick in other stores. It almost always worked.")

Steve also earned survival money from poker (having perfected his card-playing skills as a Marine), winning as much as $200 a week. "But I was in with a rough crowd, and when they started rolling drunks, the cops ended up nailing most of the bunch. By then, I was long gone."

It was winter in New York, a particularly bitter one, and McQueen was determined to find some sun. With a new buddy, he thumbed his way to Miami. "We got a job there as beachboys at one of the big Florida resort hotels," he related. "Pay wasn't much, but the fringe benefits were terrific!" These included access to a variety of bikini-clad young ladies who found Steve's penetrating blue eyes, blond hair, and crinkly smile the perfect combination to enliven a lazy, sun-warm afternoon. ("I learned a lot about aggressive women in Miami.")

With the winter season over, McQueen was "back on the prod" in New York, having acquired the Village nickname of "Desperado." The name, he recalled, originated with a cook who had befriended him at an Italian restaurant in Manhattan.

> I'd show up at the back door, looking awful, all scruffed, needing a shave and ol' Sal the cook would yell out, "Come in, Desperado!" He'd pull me inside the kitchen and fix me a big plate of veal and spaghetti, which was a blast. I mean, I never ate better! And Sal trusted me. He'd lay some bills on me till I could hook a job and pay him back . . . a really great little guy.

Having turned 21, McQueen felt it was time to begin thinking about a career. He knew that he could not continue his present haphazard life; it was leading him nowhere. But as an ex-Marine, Steve was eligible for an education.

> I started going to night school on the GI thing, working days as a bartender. But I wasn't so keen on book learning. Didn't know what the hell I wanted to do with my life. Finally decided to take up tile laying because I'd heard it paid $3.50 an hour, and that sounded like a lot of bread at the time. I had this crazy idea about going to Spain, where there's a *lot* of tile, and studying over there—but this chick I was with, who was trying to break into show business, had an idea that sounded even crazier: She told me I ought to become an actor.

Steve was amused. Actors, he told her, looked like Clark Gable; he had the face of a monkey, and *no* acting talent. What did she see in him? "You're handsome in a *different* kind of way," she declared. "For one thing, you've got *marvelous* eyes! And a great smile. As for talent, you've conned your way around the world. You're a natural. Just give yourself a chance."

But where would he start?

"Right here, at the Neighborhood Playhouse. Sanford Meisner runs the school. Talk to him and see if he'll take you on. He's a really *good* teacher."

Intrigued at the idea, but far from convinced it would pay off, Steve phoned Meisner, who agreed to an interview. "I walked over to his office, tellin' myself the odds were maybe a hundred to one against my having any kind of favorable impact on Meisner. I figured he'd take one look and shoo me out the door. But I was wrong."

That pivotal meeting, in the fall of 1951, set the future course of Steve McQueen's life. "He struck me as an original," Meisner recalled, "both tough and childlike—as if he'd been through the wars of life but had managed to preserve a certain basic innocence. I accepted him at once."

McQueen enrolled at the Playhouse on the GI Bill but was dubious about actors and acting; it seemed "a silly game, a waste of time and energy." His voice teacher, Carol Veazie, commented on her early experiences with McQueen:

> His whole attitude was "Well, so show me." He was awfully short-tempered, and he'd cut classes. Just not show. When he *did* show up he'd often fall asleep. Yet, when Steve chose to put himself into a scene or a character he was absolutely *compelling*. I kept pushing him because I knew the talent was there, beneath the surface. One day I made him listen to his voice on tape. He didn't like what he heard. "I can do a helluva lot better," he told me—and that was the turning point.

From that day on, Steve McQueen really started trying.

4. . .

Broadway—and Neile Adams

As an actor, Steve McQueen never considered himself a major talent. He felt that his range was limited; he tended to downgrade his ability when he talked to interviewers, playing directly against his image as a superstar: "There are a lot of roles I could never do," he'd tell them. "I don't have great flexibility, great range or scope. But there's something about my shaggy-dog eyes that makes people think I'm a deep character."

Actually, as Steve proved in such diverse and demanding films as *Papillon*, *The Sand Pebbles*, and *Love with the Proper Stranger*, he was capable of genuine depth and sensitivity. Physically, in front of a camera, McQueen projected a primal force, gliding across the screen with a jungle cat's easy grace, seemingly in command of every situation. And like all of the great stars, from Tracy to Gable to Bogart to Redford, he made film acting look easy. But for him, it never was.

He'd shake his head and tell me: "Man, I sweat blood every time I step in front of that lens. I don't really *like* to act. At the beginning, back in '51, I had to force myself to stick with it. I was uncomfortable. Real uncomfortable."

A lot about acting bothered him in those beginning days. "There were the dance classes," he recalled.

We had to wear a leotard—which I found damned embarrassing. Felt like a clown in those funky tights. But dancing gives you muscle coordination, teaches you how to move, how to use your body, how to make it do what you want it to do. I also kept in shape by working out at the gym next to the Playhouse, so it wasn't all that rough for me. I determined not to be a goof-off. Once I set my mind to something, I work hard at it.

Indeed he did. One of Steve's fellow students remembered that "he was a one-man powerhouse. When we had to come in with, say, five improvisations as a class assignment, Steve would show up with ten. I never saw anyone so gung-ho to succeed."

McQueen soon found that he could not survive without additional income, and he determined to hold down a full-time job and still attend his classes at the Playhouse. He did it by driving a truck at night, beginning at seven each evening:

I'd drive all night, then show up for class in the morning. This went on for six months, with me grabbing an hour of sleep when or where I could. This routine almost wiped me out, but it was worth it—because at the end of six months I'd learned enough to snag an acting scholarship at the Hagen-Berghof Drama School.

His passion for motorcycle racing began that year. From his truck driving wages, Steve purchased his first racing machine, a used K-Model Harley. He hopped-up the engine immediately. "Almost killed myself riding that baby," he admitted.

I was into a drag race on the West Side Highway with another dude—and I came roaring down this exit ramp doing close to a hundred. I looked back to see where the other guy was and saw he'd overshot. When I looked around again I realized that all the traffic had come to a dead stop ahead of me at the bottom of the ramp. Well . . . I got as far back on the bike as I could—weight's the important thing—and I hit the brakes. It was hairy, and I was coming right at this big Lincoln stopped there. Laying rubber all the way, I skidded up and barely tapped his back bumper with my front wheel. It was *that* close.

Satisfied that he could handle the Harley at racing speeds, McQueen began competing in cycle runs each weekend at Long Island City. Prize money for these events averaged about $50, and Steve usually won "a couple of races per weekend, meaning I took home 100 bucks. That, and my poker money, kept me going without having to drive a truck each night."

Actress Susan Oliver, who was also attending classes at the Playhouse, recalled the young McQueen of this period:

He was already something of a local character, roaring around the Village on his Harley with his shirt off. . . . Steve had a casual, cool, don't-give-a-damn attitude that a lot of women found very attractive. I rode with him a few times on the back of his cycle. . . . One thing I remember is how *hungry* he always was. He'd eat with a slab of pie in one hand and a sandwich in the other, as if each meal was the last. Intense. That's what Steve was—very intense. Even in the Village, people noticed him. And I think he liked the attention.

Early in 1952, just before leaving the Playhouse to pursue his scholarship, Steve made his professional acting debut in a Jewish repertory company stage production on Second Avenue. "I just had *three* words of dialogue," he recalled. "I'd come on, looking grim, and say 'Nothing will help,' in Yiddish. I did that for four nights. After the fourth night they canned me. I figured it was my lousy Yiddish."

Winters in New York continued to depress Steve. It was freezing again in the city when he announced he was "taking a little time off." He recalled describing the warm, sun-drenched Florida beaches with his new drinking buddy, an ex-Marine named Red, at a favorite Village hangout, the White Horse Tavern.

"You make it sound like heaven," Red told him.

"It is, man, it is," said McQueen. "Hey—you ever do any diving?"

"A little. You?"

"Nope—but I've been meaning to. We could go on down to Miami, rent us a boat, and take off from there. How about it?"

Red nodded. "You're on!"

McQueen later described his reaction to diving: "It was like a whole new world down there. . . . The colors were incredibly vivid. We saw all kinds of fish—including some sharks. We kept clear of those babies, but carried spearguns just in case."

With each dive, Steve ventured deeper—growing careless in his fascination with the multicolored forms of sea life. Red filled in the story:

> Steve got real hung up on gettin' a close look at one particular fish, and he followed it all the way to the bottom. Which was a big mistake. At that depth, the water pressure and your interior body pressure don't match. He was lucky he didn't get the bends comin' back up, but he *did* puncture his left eardrum.

It was the same ear in which Steve had suffered a mastoid infection as a boy, and his hearing was now permanently affected. He had paid a severe price for his brief vacation from acting school.

That summer, in Fayetteville, New York, McQueen joined a small theater company formed by Paul Crabtree. Steve had been selected to fill a minor role opposite star Margaret O'-Brien, in *Peg O' My Heart*. "I was real nervous, and forgot some of my lines," he said. "I remember one of the other actors comin' to me after the curtain went down and saying, very slowly and seriously, 'I want you to know that your performance was just embarrassing.' That kinda took the wind out of my sails."

But McQueen kept improving, spurred by a stubborn desire

to master this difficult new craft. He claimed to have learned a great deal from watching the pros. "Like when I worked in Rochester with Ethel Waters in *Member of the Wedding*. She knew how to reach an audience, make them *care* about what she was doing up there every minute on that stage. And I just soaked it in."

Steve next accepted an invitation to join the national road company of *Time Out for Ginger*, starring Melvyn Douglas. During one of their nightly stopovers, in Columbus, Ohio, he purchased his first sports car, a spoke-wheeled, high-fendered MG-TC roadster, mustering the down payment from poker winnings. "I put down $450 of my winnings on this classy little British sports job," he recalled.

> The full price was $750, so I told the guy to hang onto the car, and I'd send him the rest of the bread from the various cities we were due to play along the road. Which I did. The MG was finally delivered to me by the time we reached Chicago. I was broke, having just made the final payment, so I asked for a raise. They said no, and I was out of the play.

Steve borrowed enough gas money to get him back to New York, driving the little MG there from Chicago. But the expenses of owning a British sports machine in Manhattan overwhelmed him ("Axles and spokes kept breaking!") and he was soon forced to sell the car.

Gradually, McQueen was making progress as an actor. He was now able to find occasional work in television. In late March of 1955, three days after his twenty-fifth birthday, he scored a solid dramatic success with "The Chivington Raid" on TV's *Philco-Goodyear Playhouse*.

But his major triumph during this period came when he auditioned for the legendary Actors Studio, run by Lee Strasberg, the man responsible for the Method school of acting. Only five actors were chosen by Strasberg that year from 2,000 applicants—and young McQueen was one of the five.

This was a monumental breakthrough, giving Steve the credentials to keep moving forward into larger, more important roles.

But money again became a problem, and between classes

during his tenure of study at the Actors Studio (which extended into 1956), McQueen worked the Manhattan docks, unloading freight from cargo ships along the Hudson. His foreman, a big, hard-muscled Irishman, began making acid remarks about actors who "play at a real man's work."

McQueen ignored these jibes because he needed the job, but eventually his patience ran out. "I work as hard as any man on the crew, and you *know* it," he said coldly.

"I figure you for a goddam fairy," snarled the big Irishman. "Actors are all fairies!"

"And I figure you for a sod-stupid, fat-necked sonuvabitch," said McQueen.

When the enraged foreman attacked Steve with a cargo hook, he knocked the big man down. At that point McQueen walked off the job. ("I would have been fired anyhow. It was all over for me at the docks.")

He had become a member of the Actors Equity Association when he signed for a 1956 production of *Two Fingers of Pride,* in Maine, with Gary Merrill as star. "Steve took the part of my younger brother in that play," Merrill recalled.

> Show people were already beginning to talk about him, about his talent. The word was getting around. All you had to do was look into those brooding, electric-blue eyes of his to know he was going to make it big someday. But, back then, *he* didn't believe it. He still had a lot of self-doubts.

These doubts intensified late that summer when Steve replaced star Ben Gazzara who was leaving the Broadway production of *A Hatful of Rain.* "I knew I didn't have Ben's technical facility," McQueen explained.

> I had this one big scene where the character, who's a dope addict, gets delirious—and it really spooked me. I mean, each night, doing that scene I got more and more depressed. Got so I couldn't eat, and I began losing weight. I felt lousy. There was so much about acting I still didn't know.

The play's director, Frank Corsaro, remembered Steve as "an eager kid, shy and offbeat. . . . He seemed so naive that we called him 'Cornflake.' But the critics responded to him."

When Steve garnered solid, critical acclaim for the Gazzara role, it gave him a sudden jolt of confidence. He had reached a vital turning point. "For the first time in my life I suddenly had real *pride* in something, a feeling of purpose, of acceptance by other people. That's why I kept on acting—because it was the only thing that gave me self-respect." Steve's appetite returned, and he began "putting away a lot of spaghetti at Downey's every night after the show, to gain back the weight I'd lost."

Downey's was quite popular with the Broadway theater crowd, and Steve was eating there at a table near the door one evening when actress Neile Adams walked in with her date. McQueen vividly recalled that moment.

> I looked up, and here was this absolute knockout, with smooth tan skin and neat dancer's legs in a pair of super-tight toreador pants and with a big, white-toothed smile on her face, laughing up at this guy she was with. I got so shook watching her go by that I dropped a whole forkful of spaghetti in my lap.

Determined to meet her, Steve walked over to their table and introduced himself ("I knew the guy she was with, and used that as an excuse to join them."). Neile later admitted that she was intrigued by McQueen's direct approach—and when she discovered that he was a fellow actor she agreed to a date with him. ("I asked her out when this other guy took off for the men's room.")

Neile's father, Joseph Adams, was British; her mother, Carmen Salvador, was Spanish. She had been born in Manila, in the Philippines, "and, like Steve, I never knew my father. My parents were divorced when I was still a baby."

At the age of nine, when the Japanese invaded the Philippines, she worked for guerrilla forces, smuggling messages through enemy lines—until she was arrested and placed in a concentration camp. She spent a year and a half there under brutally severe conditions. At war's end, Neile moved with her mother to New York, where she attended a girls' boarding school in Connecticut.

At 18, she saw *The King and I* on Broadway and determined to become a professional dancer. The talent was there, and

Neile won a scholarship with Katherine Dunham. Her petite, dark-haired beauty, combined with a natural grace and a sweet singing voice, gained her a part in *Kismet*. Within two years she'd been picked to star in the Broadway production of *Pajama Game*, had received excellent notices, and gained the attention of major producers. At the time she met Steve, she was already on her way to stardom.

Neile expected McQueen to phone her for that first date. Instead, he appeared abruptly at the stage door as she was entering the theater the following night. "I'll be back to pick you up after the show," he told her.

Neile recalled their evening.

> It was insane. He showed up on this motorcycle, a big grin on his face, gesturing for me to climb up behind him. I'd never been on a cycle in my life and asked him what I should do. "Just put your arms around me and hang on!" We took off in a roar, with me clinging to his waist like a frightened monkey. I'd never met anyone like him. He was an absolute wild man.

Neile faced solid opposition in her new relationship. "My mother didn't like Steve, and neither did my producer or my manager." Even her agent, Hillard Elkins, cautioned Neile against getting involved. "The McQueen kid is going nowhere. Believe me, he'll never make it as an actor. And he's *nuts!* You're on the way up—and what you *don't* need right now is this kook in your life." Neile didn't agree. She had watched Steve onstage and responded to his talent and the raw power of his personality.

In looking back on their early days together, she admitted that his offbeat approach attracted her. "Sure, he was wild, but he could also be very charming and sweet when he wanted to be. So I continued seeing him. Steve would pick me up at my apartment and we'd roar off on his cycle for picnics across the Hudson or rides through the hills."

McQueen claimed that he was "showing her a new way of life. No getting all dressed up, no makeup, no phony parties... Just long weekend rides together in the country. Sometimes with my buddies and their dates. Other times just the two of us, Neile and me, alone on a fast bike."

They would talk about the problems of childhood, about how it felt to grow up without knowing your father. "We had that in common," Neile said. "It gave us a special bond."

Emotionally, however, McQueen was difficult to reach.

"He seemed to have only one purpose in mind—sexual conquest," she declared. "He was used to women giving in to him, and was real upset when I didn't immediately hop into bed."

"At first," admitted McQueen,

> all I wanted was to make it with Neile. She was a real good-looking chick, and I couldn't see any other reason for going with her. But things kept getting deeper between the two of us. She showed me a long scar on her leg where a piece of shrapnel had ripped into it during war. . . . She'd taken her lumps in life, as I had, and that meant something.

Despite their closeness, Steve shied away from a long-term commitment. "Whenever we'd discuss our future," Neile said,

> Steve would tell me he wasn't the marrying kind. He'd point his finger, looking dark and mean, and tell me, "I live for myself. I answer to nobody!" He was all knotted up inside. Love and hope had no reality to him. Steve didn't believe in love because no one had ever loved him, and he didn't believe in hope because no one had ever given him any. Hope was a trick people used to soften you up, and he wanted to stay tough. He was sure that life was dog-eat-dog.
>
> Steve had never trusted any woman before I came along, but, slowly, he began to trust me. That's how it started, and it just kept building.

The intensity of their relationship surprised McQueen; he had not expected to become so deeply involved.

Film director Robert Wise, who was visiting New York, saw Neile perform in *Pajama Game*. Greatly impressed, he asked if she'd be willing to fly to California for a screen test. "I said yes, that of course I was willing—and I quit the show in October of 1956, the same month that Steve's *Hatful of Rain* closed down." She told McQueen that he could come with her, that they could be together in Hollywood. He could surely find TV or film work there.

"Nope," McQueen replied. "Me an' a couple of buddies are headin' for Cuba. Just to see what's shakin' down there. Won't stay long. I'll keep in touch." In truth, he wanted to spend some time away from Neile to "get things straight in my head." McQueen described the trip.

> I had my 650 BSA cycle, and my buddies each had their rigs, a one-lung Norton Manx and a 500 BMW, and we all headed down to Key West and took the TMT ferry across to Havana. Castro and Batista were shootin' at each other about then, and things were a little tense. I tried to sell a guy some cigarettes and got thrown in a Cuban jail on a charge of pushing American contraband. I wired Neile for the money to get sprung, but she was hacked at me for leavin' her and said no. Ended up having to sell my crash helmet and some parts off the BSA to bail myself out of there and get back to New York.

Neile had by then also returned to Manhattan from Hollywood. She was awaiting the verdict on her screen test when Steve arrived back in town. "I received a telegram from Wise," she recalled, "asking me to report to MGM; he'd liked the test and had decided to cast me in his new film *This Could Be the Night*. I asked Steve, '*Now* will you come to California with me?' But he wouldn't."

"You go on ahead," he told her. "I still need time to think things over."

Hurt and angry, certain that their relationship had ended, Neile made the trip alone. "I rented a room in Culver City, close to MGM," she remembered. "Three days later the phone rang—and it was Steve calling from New York, telling me he was coming out to marry me. Would that be okay? I took a deep breath and said yes."

McQueen admitted that his decision, on that November morning in 1956, had "come on real sudden. It was when I woke up alone in that cold city. Without Neile, nothing seemed worth a damn."

But finances were a problem.

"I didn't have the price of a flight to California, so I had to pawn my gold pocket watch—the one my Uncle Claude had given me," said McQueen. "I loved that ol' watch, but I loved Neile more."

Stepping off the plane in Los Angeles, in a suit, borrowed from a friend ("You don't get married in jeans and a T-shirt."), Steve happily embraced his bride-to-be, telling her that they were going to be married at the old Mission San Juan Capistrano.

"I read all about it," he said, grinning. "How the swallows fly back there each year. Romantic, huh?"

"But what about a wedding ring?"

"I picked one up for forty bucks," Steve recalled telling her. "No diamonds, but it'll get the job done."

In a rented Ford Thunderbird, with McQueen at the wheel, they headed south from Los Angeles for San Juan Capistrano. When they arrived, excited and impatient, the nun in charge of the Mission church told them that a ceremony was quite impossible. They would have to arrange it through the local priest, and special permissions would be required.

McQueen was furious. "Then, dammit, we'll go live in *sin!*" he snarled, rushing Neile outside to the car.

"Where are we going, Steve?"

"Let's just split outa here," he snapped. "To hell with the swallows!" And he slammed the T-Bird back onto the highway in a shower of gravel.

Neile was in shock. "Steve scared me," she admitted. "He was driving like a madman. I kind of huddled down in the seat and closed my eyes." A pair of red lights flared behind them as two cycle patrolmen roared up to the Thunderbird.

"Okay, mister, what's the big hurry?"

"We've been tryin' to get married," said McQueen. "A hardass nun back there in Capistrano told us no dice and I guess I got kinda bent outa shape over it." Steve softened his tone, flashed a disarming grin at the two officers. "C'mon fellas— is it a crime to want to get married?"

"Nice T-Bird," noted one of the lawmen. "Yours?"

"Rented," said McQueen. "A bike's my speed."

This led to a discussion of technical details relating to police cycles vs. street cycles. Steve knew he had won them over. "Listen," said the second officer, "I know a Lutheran minister in San Clemente. Maybe he'll open his church for you and perform the service. Want me to call him?"

"Sure do!" said Steve.

Escorted by the police, McQueen happily motored along the coast to a small white Lutheran church in San Clemente. He and Neile were married there, with the two patrolmen standing by as witnesses. "It was kind of far out," admitted McQueen. "Here we were getting hitched with those two big cops standing right behind us with their belted pistols an' all. Felt like a shotgun wedding!"

Their honeymoon in Mexico was cut short by Neile's having to report to MGM for her role in *This Could Be the Night*. But the film provided McQueen with an unexpected bonus: Robert Wise was casting his next production, *Somebody Up There Likes Me*, the life story of boxer Rocky Graziano, and gave Steve a walk-on with star Paul Newman as (in Steve's words) "a hardcase pal of his. If you blinked twice in that one you missed me," Steve said. "But at least I'd notched a feature credit, which gave me a toe in the door."

The McQueens returned to New York, where Neile was a guest on Pat Boone's television show. For Neile, the stay was brief; her next job took her to the Tropicana in Las Vegas, Nevada, as a $1500-a-week singer and dancer.

"Steve would fly in from New York to spend every other weekend with me," she said. "He made it clear that he wanted me back in New York, but I had a firm contract at the club and we needed the money. We had some roaring fights over the situation."

Steve's second screen assignment was more substantial; he was chosen for the role of a young lawyer in Allied Artists' *Never Love a Stranger*, from Harold Robbins' novel, starring John Drew Barrymore. "That turkey wasn't released for two years," McQueen recalled, "and the only notice I got was from one critic who said my face looked like a Botticelli angel had been crossed with a chimp."

Early in 1957 McQueen won favorable attention from several critics for his work as a young killer in the *Studio One* production of "The Defender" (pilot show for the popular 1961–1965 TV series). But despite a few other television roles that year, Steve felt his career had "bogged down." As a result, he grew more tense and edgy with each passing month. "Our marriage almost split apart that year, in '57, over an auto accident," Neile related.

> Steve bought a used Corvette one weekend and taught me the basics of driving, more or less. Then he flew back to New York the following Monday, leaving me alone with this powerful sports car. I'd never driven before in my life, and I was petrified. I really didn't know how to handle that Corvette.

She proceeded to spin it out, slamming into two other parked vehicles. No injury to Neile, but a great deal of injury to the three cars.

"Steve blew his top when I told him about the accident. Began yelling at me over the phone. I yelled right back at him. For two weeks after that he didn't phone. But then he cooled down and wrote me a very sweet note."

In describing her marriage to McQueen, Neile admitted it was "anything but dull. Steve was never what you'd call, in any sense of the term, an 'ordinary' husband."

One writer who interviewed the couple during this period summed up their relationship: "Neile frequently had to treat Steve as you would a child, humor him, soothe him. . . . He was changeable and moody, at one moment savagely frustrated or impatient or angry, the next moment gentle, protective, loving. She never quite knew where she stood with him."

McQueen's marriage to Neile Adams would endure for more than 15 years, into 1972. When it began he was a screen unknown; when it ended he was a world success.

In large part, the character responsible for initiating that success was a bounty hunter named Josh Randall.

5. . .

Riding for Candyland

We'd often talk about the television character Steve portrayed so effectively on *Wanted—Dead or Alive*.

"Josh was real to me," Steve would declare. "I felt that I *knew* him. Lived inside his skin for years. You do a character that long and you begin to *be* that character. It's like *I* was living in the Old West, chasing bad guys. I'd look in the mirror and see Randall. For a while there I thought I'd never be anybody else! Man, that series seemed to go on forever."

By the beginning of 1958 Steve McQueen had both feet planted firmly on the ladder of success.

Neile was still at her job in Las Vegas when Steve flew to Missouri for *The Great St. Louis Bank Robbery*, a low-budget action film based on a real holdup. He played a campus football hero gone wrong who drives a getaway car for the bank gang.

Concerning *The Great St. Louis Bank Robbery,* McQueen recalled: "The only *great* thing about this one was the title. Most of the gang gets wiped out while I surrender to the cops. Nothing really worked in the film, but it *was* another screen credit. And each credit helps get you the next one. You're young and you're hungry and you grab what comes along."

Steve celebrated his twenty-eighth birthday in March 1958, maintaining that his "best present" had come to him the previous month: the news, from Neile, that she was quitting her job at the Tropicana. "The tension got to be too much for me," she admitted. "Steve hated the idea of our being separated, living in different cities. So, that February, I finally gave in and quit."

In New York, McQueen was obtaining television assignments but was dissatisfied with many of his roles.

> I usually played a killer or a delinquent, and I did a lot of snarling. Producers would tell me I had "mean" eyes. That's when I began to sweat over being pegged as a heavy. Once they hang that label on you, it can knock out your chances for a lot of other stuff. So I began looking for something to improve my image—and what I got was *The Blob.*

In this hastily produced, grade-B science fiction melodrama, Steve was cast as a teenager doing battle with what one critic called "a lethal lump of interplanetary plum preserves." Another film reviewer described the outer space menace as "a crawling roomful of Jello that eats you instead of the other way around."

The Blob cost $150,000 to make and grossed over 30 times that amount. Although he was the star of the film, Steve received a flat fee of just $3,000. "The main acting challenge in this one consisted of running around, bug-eyed, and shouting, 'Hey, everybody, look out for the Blob!' I wasn't too thrilled when people would tell me what a fine job I'd done in it."

Disgusted with Hollywood, Steve returned to New York, intending to resume his stage career. But no substantial offer came his way. ("Doing off-Broadway stuff can be artistically satisfying—but you also starve your ass!") Venting his frustration, he spent the better part of an afternoon bombarding Central Park with cherry bombs, until a police officer intervened. ("I had to do some fast talking to keep him from hauling me off to jail. I told him that my favorite brother had just been run over by a train, and that I'd gone temporarily insane with grief.")

That same week Steve got a phone call from Sy Marsh, a Hollywood agent. "I can nail down a guest shot for you on *Wells Fargo,*" he told McQueen. "Three days' work for 400 bucks."

"Well . . . I could use the 400."

"Great. Then I'll set it up."

Back in California, Steve appeared in the *Wells Fargo* segment, "Bill Longley," telecast that February—but found that he had no taste for westerns. "That's the last of these cockamamie cowboy shows for me," he told Neile.

To shore up the family funds, Neile had accepted a starring role in *At the Grand,* a Civic Light Opera production staged at the Los Angeles Philharmonic.

Steve felt that his luck might improve with a new agent, and he signed with Abe Lastfogel, who headed the powerful William Morris Agency. A few days later he received an urgent phone call. "Come see me, kid," Abe told him. "I think I got something hot."

McQueen recalled the scene at Lastfogel's office. The agent was beaming. "I just talked to Vince Fennelly. He's been looking for a special guy to play a bounty hunter in *Trackdown,* the show he's doing for CBS. It's a one-shot, but he thinks he can tie down a whole new series if he can find the right actor. I told him all about you, and he's interested. *Very* interested."

"Well, I'm not."

"Huh?"

"No more Old West crap for me, Abe. No damn ten-gallon hats. No guns. No horses!"

"But this is a golden opportunity! I can't believe you're serious."

"Look, I'm no damn six-foot cowboy! All cowboys on TV have to be six feet tall. Does Fennelly know I'm only five ten?"

"I swear to you, that's no problem. C'mon, Steve, what can you lose by *talking* to the guy?"

They talked, and Fennelly found, in McQueen, the missing element he had been searching for: vulnerability. "I didn't want another John Wayne," Fennelly explained, when he was asked why he had picked McQueen.

A bounty hunter, by nature, is a sort of underdog. Everybody's against him—lawmen, bandits, townfolk. They don't like what he does for a living—hunting down fugitives and being paid a bounty for either capturing or killing them. So if he's some big, aggressive football type your audience will turn against him. I needed a kind of "little guy" who looks tough enough to get the job done, but with a kind of boyish appeal behind the toughness. He had to be *vulnerable,* so the audience would root for him against the bad guys. McQueen was just what I had in mind. I knew he was my man the minute he walked through the door.

When the McQueen *Trackdown* episode was aired for CBS network executives they liked what they saw and ordered the series. Steve would be paid $750 a week to star as Josh Randall in *Wanted—Dead or Alive,* out of Four Star Productions. "I was a little mixed up in my feelings at that point," admitted McQueen.

I wasn't sure I wanted to do a weekly series and get caught up in that factory routine. I asked myself how many TV stars ever make it big in feature films. I thought maybe I was stepping into a bear trap, but I went ahead and signed the contract. I was in no position to turn it down.

The half-hour show was launched on September 6, 1958, and McQueen's offbeat qualities attracted audiences from the opening episode.

On the set, however, and in the offices of Four Star, Steve's quirky personality was something less than appealing. "Frankly, he was a royal pain in the ass," declared one of the show's early directors. "*Nothing* would suit him. He didn't like the hat we gave him, or the saddle, or even the horse. I've been in this game a while, and I've personally never known an actor who fired his horse!"

McQueen had done just that. Despite his personal aversion

to horses, he knew that he needed a tough, spirited mount. Dubious about his ability to ride, the studio had provided an animal who was, according to McQueen, "so slow they had to wheel him into a scene on roller skates." Steve "fired" the tired beast after six episodes and sought out a rancher-friend in the area who raised quarter horses. "I found this black, with white stocking feet, which I liked," said McQueen. "He'd just been broken in and still had plenty of fire. I climbed on his back and he bucked me right off. That did it. I took him."

The horse, whose name was Ringo, did not enjoy working in television; the lights, cables, sets, and crew all annoyed him. "The first week he kicked out five set lights," Steve related.

> He also bit the other horses and broke my big toe by stomping on it. Ol' Ringo and me, we fought each other. He'd reach his head back to bite me and I'd lean forward and punch him on the nose. This kind of thing went on for months, but I refused to replace him. I liked his style. He had nerve and wouldn't back down to anybody.

Another equally important item, in McQueen's opinion, was the gun he would use in the series. He didn't want an ordinary sixgun; he felt that Randall should carry a unique weapon, one that an audience would respond to and remember. Steve described the final choice:

> We took a Model 92 Winchester lever-action rifle and turned it into a belt gun by sawing off most of the barrel and fitting it with a special stock. This gave us the power and accuracy of a rifle with the mobility and easy handling of a revolver. And it *looked* fierce!

In each episode McQueen wore this special weapon holstered on his hip, or slung over one shoulder. But the gun had a lot more kick than McQueen had expected.

> We tried full-power blanks, and the first time I fired that thing it blew the hat off the cameraman's head and knocked all of the pages out of the script girl's hands. In the Old West, they call a gun a "hog's leg," but we dubbed this one a "Mare's Laig," because she kicked harder than a

hog. In order to reduce the recoil, we switched to quarter-power blanks.

After hours of practice, Steve learned to swivel-spin the gun smoothly up from his hip and cock it one-handed in a single, fluid move. The Mare's Laig became one of the show's most popular features, and Steve always carried it with him on personal appearance tours.

Ed Adamson, the show's producer, got along well with McQueen. "I found out how to deal with him," said Adamson.

> Steve was very sensitive about his lack of education—and just as long as we handed him scripts with short sentences and short words in the dialogue he was a pussycat—but when some director refused to shorten a speech for Steve he could turn into a real mean son of a bitch, and could be hell to work with.

Wanted was a solid hit and provided McQueen with a steady income for the first time in his acting career. Out of his new earnings he bought two sports cars, a black 1600-cc Porsche roadster (the Super Speedster model) and a sleek green magnesium-bodied XK-SS British racing Jaguar. "The Jag was unique," said Steve.

> It was a direct development of the D-Type that won Le Mans four times. Due to a fire, the factory turned out only 15 of the cars. I re-engineered the combustion chambers and the cams, worked over the oil sump and radiator, and bushed the front end. I loved that ol' Jag. Trouble was, I drove it too fast.

Indeed he did. McQueen collected so many speeding tickets that his driver's license was suspended. Twice.

Steve recalled the day, early in 1959, when he and Neile were in the Jag on their way to Phoenix, Arizona, Steve let it "hang out past a hundred." The road was smooth, and the torpedo-shaped sports car roared over it at 110 . . . 115 . . . 120. Suddenly, a pair of red lights blinked behind them.

"Shit!" exclaimed Steve, looking back at the approaching

patrol car. "Another ticket and they'll take away my license permanently."

"But what can you do?" asked Neile, then six months pregnant with their first child.

"Leave it to me," he said, braking the dark green Jaguar as the patrol car pulled up to them. McQueen jumped out, ran back to the two officers.

"Listen!" he said, a desperate note in his voice. "You gotta help us! My wife's in labor. She's about to deliver, an' every second counts!"

"Sure, we understand," the driver told him. "Just follow us, buddy." And, under full siren, they led Steve to the nearest hospital. A nurse rushed out to help Neile inside.

"Will your wife be okay?" the anxious driver asked Steve.

"Oh, definitely—thanks to you guys."

The two officers shook hands with McQueen, then drove away down the highway. As soon as their car was out of sight Steve rushed after the nurse. "False alarm!" he told her, taking his wife's arm. "Everything's cool." He grinned. "We just made a little mistake, okay?" The nurse looked stunned as Steve hustled his angry-looking wife back to their Jag.

"Neile was pissed," admitted Steve. "She didn't speak to me for the rest of the day. But, by God, it worked. I *didn't* get the ticket!"

McQueen was becoming interested in the local racing events sponsored by the California Sports Car Club, but his XK was too rare a machine to risk in competition. The 1600 Super Porsche, however, was ideal. He took the black car up to Mulholland Drive, a long stretch of twisting asphalt roadway in the hills above Hollywood, and began to "shake it down." "There were about six of us with sports cars that used to go up there at night," Steve recalled.

> After ten o'clock the road was deserted, and we'd stage our own private races. We had switches fixed under the dash that turned off the lights on our license plates. That was in case you had to outrun the cops, so they couldn't get your license number during the chase. I was young an' stupid which is what you have to be to pull that kind of thing. But I *did* learn something about fast driving.

Steve entered his first sports car event at Santa Barbara, California, in late May of 1959.

> They ran it at the airport—and there was a real mix of cars, big and small, in my race. I had no idea where I'd finish. I remember storming off the line like mad when the flag fell, passing a gaggle of Porsches and Triumphs—until after about four laps there I was, leading everybody! That shook me. I was skidding around the circuit between cars, going as deep into the turns as possible before braking, on the ragged edge all the way, and I thought, "Man, what are you *doing* out here?" But I hung on and won. After that I was hooked.

Neile did not share her husband's elation with sports car competition; she was about to give birth to their first child, and Steve had promised he would stop racing when the baby arrived. "Steve was absolutely *certain* we'd have a son," Neile said.

> He hadn't ever considered the idea that it might be a girl. It had taken me over two years to get pregnant, and when I finally did I began to worry about not having a son for Steve. And, of course, that's exactly what happened. . . . In June of 1959 I had Terri Leslie—and Steve went into total shock. He became angry, as though I had personally betrayed him by not giving him a boy.
>
> Naturally, he got over it and learned to love Terri a great deal. But when I asked him to keep his promise and stop racing, he said that he couldn't.

Steve continued to win with his Porsche at California's Del Mar and Willow Springs road circuits, proving that his first victory at Santa Barbara was justified. "Racing gave me a fresh identity," he said. "I was no longer just an actor, I was a guy who raced. And it was real important to me—to have this separate identity."

Being a father made McQueen more edgy than ever. He began to have trouble sleeping at night. "A city crew put up a big new street light which shined right into our bedroom in Hollywood," Neile related. "Steve phoned the city and asked them to move the light. When they refused, he took a .22 target pistol and shot it out. He was never very patient about things like that."

McQueen's agent had insisted on a clause in Steve's Four Star contract that would allow him to act in feature films as well as television, so long as these roles did not interfere with the production schedule of *Wanted*. In 1959, therefore, during a lull in the series, McQueen accepted the part of Bill Ringa in a war adventure, *Never So Few*. The star was Frank Sinatra, and Steve's supporting role had originally been written for Sinatra's friend Sammy Davis, Jr. When the two members of the "Rat Pack" (as the Sinatra clan was then known) had a temporary falling-out, a replacement was needed. John Sturges, who had directed *Bad Day at Black Rock* and *Gunfight at the OK Corral*, chose McQueen. "I'd been watching him on television," Sturges said, "and he had the bounce and vitality I was looking for."

Based on a novel by Tom Chamales, *Never So Few* dramatized the battle between a rag-tag group of guerrillas and a vastly larger contingent of Japanese troops in Burma during the Second World War. Sinatra played the American leader of the guerrilla band; McQueen was his wise-cracking supply sergeant, who could be counted on to come up with everything from elephants to ammunition.

Steve was well aware of Sinatra's reputation for "one-upsmanship" on a set and had determined to remain aloof; he was there to do a job, collect his salary, and get back to his series. Sinatra had other ideas. As McQueen told it:

> One afternoon on location, between camera setups, I was sitting there reading my script, being very businesslike, and Frank crept up behind me and slipped a lighted firecracker in one of the loops of my gunbelt. When that thing went off I jumped about three feet straight up. Which naturally delighted Frank.
>
> So I grabbed one of the Tommy guns we were using in the film and jammed in a full clip—fifty rounds. Sinatra was walking away, laughing it up with his buddies, when I yelled at him, "Hey, Frank!" He turned around and I let him have it, zap-zap-zap-zap, the whole clip.

At close range, the paper wadding from blanks can be painful. Steve's action sent a shockwave through the crew.

> The whole set just went dead still. Everybody was watching Frank to see what he'd do. He had a real bad temper and I guess they all figured we were gonna end in a punchout. I wasn't sure myself, as we stared at each other. Then he just started laughing, and it was all over. After that, we got along fine. In fact, we tossed firecrackers at each other all through the picture. Off-camera, that is. I'd done the right thing. Once you back down to a guy like Sinatra, he never respects you.

By the close of *Never So Few*, McQueen had become friends with the actor he had replaced, Sammy Davis, Jr. They discovered a mutual passion for gun tricks and fast draws. Davis was then known as one of the industry's fast guns, and could draw, spin, and quick-fire a Colt with amazing speed. Determined to beat him, Steve began practicing rigorously, and when he felt he was ready, he challenged Davis to a draw-and-shoot contest.

"Most of Sammy's pals, who knew how fast he was, figured I didn't have a chance of beating him," Steve recalled. "I took all their side bets. The prize was a neat nickel-plated memorial Colt .45 Peacemaker—a real show gun. Well, I guess all that practice paid off, 'cuz I walked away with the Peacemaker."

Although *Never So Few* was blasted by critics, Steve's performance was rated as "lively." Yet the film did little to strengthen McQueen's motion picture potential; he was still considered a television personality who would probably never strike gold as a major film star.

And the exhausting day-to-day chores as Josh Randall were now draining his energy. "You just don't have any idea what a rough grind it is, doing a TV series," McQueen said. "I had to be up at 5:00, to the studio by 6:30. . . . Then I worked all day on the set and usually didn't get home till 9 at night. Sometimes, under deadline pressure, we'd film a whole episode in a single day!"

Also, McQueen was growing more and more unhappy with the show itself.

They were trying to turn Josh Randall into a superman. I wanted to play him for real—as a guy trying to do a dangerous, unglamorous job with a minimum of fuss. But the Four Star honchos kept trying to turn him into a jaw-busting, sure-shot hero. I had some bad times with them over this.

McQueen's major confrontation occurred during a scene that called for Randall to knock out three husky badmen who had ordered him to leave town. In the midst of the scene, Steve turned on the director: "This is crap! Where I come from if three tough dudes tell you to leave town you *leave*. Maybe I'd sneak back later and take 'em on one at a time, but not all three at once. Never!"

"Just stick to the script," the director told him.

Steve looped his hat atop the director's head and handed him his gun. "Here, man, *you* play the role."

And he walked off the set.

Producer Dick Powell, then heading Four Star Productions, invited McQueen to his office for a personal talk. Steve recalled the confrontation.

"I hear you've booked three airline tickets," Powell said. "For Australia."

"That's right," McQueen nodded. "For me an' my ol' lady an' my kid. Going there to look over the land. I may become a sheep rancher."

"But you've got a contract with *us*, Steve."

"So go ahead and sue me. I'm through making an ass of myself doin' those dumb hero scripts."

Powell hesitated, meeting Steve's level gaze. "Tell me what *you'd* do with the show if you had the power to change it."

"You want the whole scam?"

"I do."

McQueen eased a battered notebook from his hip pocket. He had been jotting down ideas for the series, and he read these aloud to Powell. A compromise was reached. If McQueen would return to the show immediately, Powell would see to it that he had a major say-so in the creative and production ends.

Years later, in recalling the power he exerted on *Wanted*, McQueen admitted that he may have pushed too hard in certain areas.

One mistake I made was forgetting about the dignity of my directors. I'd get into a scene, and I'd suddenly be tellin' the other actors how to play it. Then I'd have to go over and apologize to the director. But one thing was for sure, I *understood* the character of Josh Randall. I played him for real, and audiences *appreciated* that sense of reality. The show's ratings confirmed it. So I was on the right track.

Steve began putting his television earnings to work for him. He purchased 50 acres of land near Big Sur in Northern California; he became a copartner in a garage catering to high-performance cars, and he invested in a number of other properties, from health food restaurants to a Christmas stocking factory.

Sports car racing continued as a prime expense. He had by now abandoned his Porsche in favor of a much faster machine, a sleek, ground-hugging Lotus Le Mans Mark XI. "In that Lotus, I started to become really competitive," he said. "I was smoother, quicker around the turns, more relaxed. I was beginning to find out what speed was all about."

McQueen entered the Santa Barbara (California) races Labor Day weekend in 1959. He engaged in a stubborn wheel-to-wheel battle with Lotus ace Frank Monise in another Mark XI, winding up Saturday's event just a split second behind him, "about six inches off Frank's tailpipe!"

In Sunday's main event, still chasing Monise, Steve over-extended himself while charging into a hairpin turn. "I spun and killed the engine, which cost me the race. I was embarrassed about that, but I was still learning. Each time you compete you learn more."

"By 1960 *Wanted—Dead or Alive* was into its third year, and McQueen's annual earnings had climbed to over $100,000. At 30, he had become an extremely valuable property in the television marketplace.

Neile had mixed feelings about having given up her career to become Mrs. Steve McQueen.

Steve never wanted his women to have outside careers. He had a very rigid, old-fashioned view of what a wife should be . . . the cooking, the cleaning, the caring for her man. I even cut his hair! And now that I was a mother as well as a wife it became impossible for me to think about getting back into show business. It would have meant the end of our marriage.

For "kicks," and to ease some of his wife's obvious frustration, Steve agreed to make a series of television appearances with Neile that year. They teamed on an Alfred Hitchcock segment and accepted guest shots on the Bob Hope and Perry Como shows.

Director John Sturges had become a drinking pal, and Steve recalled that over beers in his studio dressing room Sturges talked about his latest film project, an American version of Japanese director Akira Kurosawa's *Seven Samurai*.

"And I want *you* in it."

"C'mon now, Johnny, I could never play a samurai. All that slant-eyed makeup and trick sword stuff. . . . They'd hoot me off the screen."

Sturges grinned broadly. "You've got it wrong. I'm not doing a *remake*. I'm taking the basic plot and doing it as an American western. You'll play one of seven gunslingers hired to protect this little Mexican village from a horde of rampaging bandits."

"Well . . ."

The director leaned forward to snap his finger against the brim of Steve's sweat-stained Stetson. "Hell, you won't even have to change your hat!"

In the film, which Sturges called *The Magnificent Seven*, it *did* appear that McQueen never bothered to change his hat; his was by far the most weathered headpiece worn by any of the actors.

Yul Brynner, costumed entirely in black, was the star and leader of the Seven. McQueen played Vin (receiving $65,000 for his services); other featured players included James Coburn, Charles Bronson, and Robert Vaughn—all, like McQueen, at the edge of stardom. The bandit chief was portrayed by veteran Eli Wallach. Backed by this superb cast, Sturges achieved an epic quality with his fluid direction and swift sense of pace.

McQueen's performance was solid; terse, tough, and moody. It was most certainly his best cinema role to date—although he did not get along with Brynner. "I was a threat to him," said Steve.

I knew something about horses by then, and quite a lot about guns. Brynner didn't, and it made him nervous. Word got around that we didn't much care for each other.

I remember we were well into production when he walked up behind me after a scene and grabbed me by one shoulder. "Now, listen," he says, scowling at me. "There's a story in the paper about us having a feud. I'm an established star, and I don't feud with supporting actors. I want you to call the paper and tell them the story is completely false!" He was *ordering* me to phone that newspaper, so I told him what he could do with his orders. He was a real uptight dude.

The Magnificent Seven was a hit, and Steve won more than his share of critical praise, with one reviewer predicting: "If he can ever get sprung from television, McQueen's going to be a *big* star."

Of course, Steve had the same idea—to "get sprung" from his demanding role as Josh Randall. By the end of March 1961, he had obtained his freedom: *Wanted—Dead or Alive* was finally canceled.

McQueen was then the father of *two* children. A boy, Chadwick Steven, had been born December 28, 1960. (Neile jokingly commented: "If I'd had another girl I think he would have shot me! He absolutely *beamed* when he was told that he had a son.") To house their expanded family, the McQueens purchased a new home on Solar Drive in the Nichols Canyon area of Los Angeles. (The street name would later be used for Steve's own Solar Productions.)

Fatherhood had not mellowed McQueen, as demonstrated by a well-publicized incident that season. A neighbor, Edmund W. George, complained about Steve's street driving and about his unleashed dog. "I walked over to his place to sort things out," Steve related. "But he got sore and shoved me, so I had to slug him. Somebody called the cops, and our little fracas made the papers."

A reporter used this occasion to question Steve about losing the television series. Was McQueen angry about the network's decision to drop the show?

Hell, no! I was delighted. That series was sheer murder on me. Still, I'm very grateful to ol' Josh Randall. I'll always owe him for giving me a running start in this business. Right now I've got a real chance to grab that big brass ring, and, man, you better believe I'm ready to do some grabbin'. I got me a house on a hill, an ol' lady who digs me, two healthy kids, and plenty of fruit and nuts on the table. The lean days are over—and the ride from here on leads straight to Candyland!

McQUEEN

A 1950s portrait, when McQueen was breaking into films with a bit
role in *Somebody Up There Likes Me* (1956). (MGM)

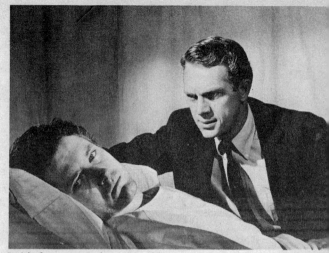

In his first supporting role, with star John Drew Barrymore, playing an intense young lawyer in *Never Love a Stranger* (1958). (Allied Artists)

Starring in a film he hated, *The Blob* (1958), as a teenager fighting a jellied menace from outer space. (Allied Artists)

An early McQueen role, as bad guy George Fowler, with two gangster confederates in *The Great St. Louis Bank Robbery* (1959). (United Artists)

As television's Josh Randall in the series that gave McQueen his start, *Wanted—Dead or Alive* (1959).

Socializing with Neile, in the early days of their marriage. (Unite Press International Photo)

Jungle hopping in *Never So Few* (1959). (MGM)

At Santa Barbara, California, gunning off the line in his Lotus Mark XI for the Labor Day races in 1959. (William F. Nolan)

During a break from his TV series *Wanted—Dead or Alive*, in August 1960, McQueen tinkers with the engine of his classic XK-SS Jaguar. (Note his "Mare's Laig" belt weapon.) (Wide World Photos)

As Vin, a fast gun for hire in *The Magnificent Seven* (1960), with moody star Yul Brynner. Their feud made the papers. (United Artists)

Mugging for the camera as a wacky Navy man in *The Honeymoon Machine* (1961). McQueen hated his performance in this film. (MGM)

As doomed pilot Buzz Rickson in *The War Lover* (1962), with Robert Wagner. (Columbia)

During the 1962 holiday season, McQueen helps promote sales of Christmas wreaths made by youths at the Chino Boys Republic.

A spill at the barbed wire, from *The Great Escape* (1963), the film that made McQueen a major star. (United Artists)

A superb comedy performance as Sergeant Eustis Clay, in *Soldier in the Rain* (1963), with star Jackie Gleason. (Allied Artists)

With Neile at the 1964 Academy Award Oscar show. (Note bandaged left hand—from a bike crackup.) (Wide World Photos)

Doing a wheelie for the camera. (William F. Nolan)

Dancing the Watusi with Luci Baines Johnson, the President's daughter, at a Citizens for Johnson rally in Beverly Hills (1964). (Wide World Photos)

As a member of the American cycle team in East Germany during the International 6-Day Trials in 1964. (William F. Nolan)

Strumming his guitar for *Baby, The Rain Must Fall* (1965), McQueen belts out a song. (Columbia)

With Lee Remick in *Baby, the Rain Must Fall*. (Columbia)

High-stakes poker against veteran card shark Edward G. Robinson in *The Cincinnati Kid* (1965)—as costars Ann-Margret and Karl Malden watch the action. (MGM)

As sailor Jake Holman in *The Sand Pebbles*— a performance that earned McQueen an Academy Award nomination for Best Actor of 1966. (Courtesy of Twentieth Century-Fox. Copyright © 1966 Twentieth Century-Fox Film Corp. All Rights Reserved.)

On location for *The Sand Pebbles* in 1966, McQueen and costar Candice Bergen escape the sun between scenes under a wishing elephant in Lin's Garden at Pan Chiao. (United Press International Photo)

McQueen becomes the 153rd star to inscribe his name in wet cement in the forecourt of Hollywood's Chinese Theater in March of 1967. (United Press International Photo)

McQueen and costar Faye Dunaway engage in some lip nibbling for the camera in *The Thomas Crown Affair* (1968). (United Artists)

McQueen's best-dressed role, as dapper playboy-crook Thomas Crown. (United Artists)

McQueen takes Dunaway for a fast ride in his super-charged Crown dune buggy. (United Artists)

6. . .

Breakthrough

I once asked Steve why stardom was so important to him.

"Stardom equals financial success, and financial success equals security," he said. "I've spent too much of my life feeling insecure. I still have nightmares about being poor, of everything I own just vanishing away. Stardom means that *can't* happen. But there's more to it. It's a way of carving a place in the world. I had a lousy education, and I'm not into books. I can't write, or paint, or compose music. Hell, you can throw a rock out the window and hit a guy who knows more about music than I do! What I *can* do is act. So I want to take what I can do as far as I can take it. And that means *all* the way."

Despite his television popularity, Steve had not yet achieved genuine stardom. His film work, spread over five years, had given him some solid credits, but he'd never carried a picture on his own; he had done his best work in backup roles. Now he was looking for a film that would properly showcase him as a star.

When Frank Sinatra refused the lead in *Pocketful of Miracles* director Frank Capra wanted McQueen, but United Artists felt that he was not "bankable," and turned thumbs down. In frustration, Steve signed with MGM to star in a thinly scripted comedy, *The Honeymoon Machine*, based on Lorenzo Semple's play, *The Golden Fleecing*. McQueen was cast as crewcut Naval Lieutenant Fergie Howard who programs a missile computer system to beat the roulette wheel at a gambling casino in Venice, Italy. The highly improbable plot revolved around a last-minute avoidance of World War III, with the Russians believing that the computer signals McQueen was transmitting indicated plans for a global attack by the United States.

Steve's work in this film was strained and unsubtle, as he attempted to bolster awkward material with zany humor; he mugged, smirked, and grinned throughout the picture, overplaying almost every scene. At an MGM executive preview, Steve walked out of the private projection room shortly after the screening began, unable to endure his self-conscious performance. "I decided to go after something gutty for my next one," he said, "so I signed up to play a real mean son of a bitch."

He switched from MGM to Paramount for *Hell Is for Heroes,* a grim war drama of trench fighting against the Nazis, set in France near the end of World War II.

The film was originally to be directed by Robert Pirosh, but script problems resulted in the director's withdrawal, and Don Siegel took over with a new screenplay. The final script was tough and bitter, as McQueen etched the role of Reese, a loner who revels in bloody fighting, has no friends, causes trouble for his squad, and is ultimately killed in a solo attack on a German hill position.

Steve shared star billing with Bobby Darin, the ex-teen singing idol. Attempting a serious dramatic role, Darin was tense and nervous on the set. He clashed violently with McQueen over several script points. "Look, Bobby," a fellow actor told him. "Just forget McQueen and do your job. That guy enjoys making trouble. He's used to fighting for what he wants. In many ways, he's his own worst enemy." Darin slowly shook his head. "Not while *I'm* alive he isn't."

Director Don Siegel also clashed with McQueen early in the production.

> He walked around with the attitude that the burden of preserving the integrity of the picture was on *his* shoulders, and all the rest of us were company men ready to sell out to the studio bosses. One day when we were sitting together on the set, I told him that his attitude bored me, that I was as interested in the picture being good as he was, and that when this fact sunk through his thick head we would get along. I could see he was angry. I knew he was capable of violence, and I knew he could whip me. But I decided that if he stood up and came for me, I would hit him first as hard as I could and hope for the best. Fortunately, for me, he didn't stand up. Eventually, we grew to like each other.

Siegel described a particularly difficult scene:

> We came to an important emotional sequence in which McQueen was supposed to turn away from this disastrous attack and walk toward the camera, beginning to cry. We tried it, but Steve couldn't bring up any tears. So we tried onions, but that didn't work either. Then I got an idea. I told Steve to go through it once more, and I had the shot set up so that for a moment, as he walked, he'd be out of camera range. In that moment I stepped up to him and slapped Steve as hard as I could, hoping that the sudden sting would make his eyes water. But when we looked at the dailies later there was still no trace of tears, so we just said the hell with it and dropped the scene.

The brass at Paramount were concerned about the film's mounting cost. Siegel was told to stop all location shooting and wrap up the rest of the scenes on a studio sound stage. Backed by McQueen, he refused. The studio sent a grim delegation of executives to the location to seize the cameras. McQueen faced them. He picked up a stick, walked to the cameras, and drew a circle around them in the dirt. Then he turned back to the executives. "Anybody steps over that line . . . he gets the shit kicked out of him!"

The location filming continued.

Hell Is for Heroes brought Steve McQueen more solid critical attention but did nothing to advance his career. "I'd made eight films up to then and only *one*, the John Sturges western, was any damn good. I just wasn't making the right connections in the States—so I decided to try doing a film in Europe."

At a salary of $75,000, he signed for another costarring role (with Robert Wagner) in Columbia's *The War Lover*, to be produced entirely in England.

Again, the plot (based on a novel by John Hersey) was set in World War II, and again Steve played a loner who enjoys the dangers of battle—this time as a headstrong pilot, Buzz Rickson, who betrays his best friend over a woman and dies by plunging his crippled Flying Fortress into the side of a mountain. "This guy Rickson is a complex character," McQueen told reporters during an interview in London.

> He's selfish and selfless. He has the respect of a crew that pretty generally hates him. But Rickson is one hell of a flyer . . . can make a B-17 stand on its tail and dance. His love of war makes him incapable of love for other human beings.

Steve had his own ideas about how Rickson would react to the woman in this film (Shirley Anne Field), and it took four days of shooting to get his love scenes "just right."

Beyond the challenge of this new role, McQueen was attracted to England as the hub of international racing. Because *The War Lover* would be shot entirely on British soil, he'd have an opportunity to drive on many of the famed British racing circuits such as Aintree, Oulton Park, and Brands Hatch. But Columbia executives took a dim view of his plans.

Steve received legal warning from studio lawyers that if he seriously injured himself racing—and production had to be shut down on the film—he would be sued for its cost (close to $3,000,000). Steve ignored the warning.

He had now renewed his friendship with Stirling Moss, Britain's legendary racing champion. Moss had first met Steve in 1959, in California, and their mutual love of fast cars forged an instant bond between them.

"He impressed me as a fellow who believed in action," said

Moss. "He was very keen to learn everything he could about high-speed motor racing. He'd listen carefully, take advice, and was a quick learner."

Moss helped Steve find the fastest way around each circuit by driving just ahead and signaling with two fingers if the turn required second gear, three fingers for third gear, and so on.

It was at the Brands Hatch circuit in Sussex that Steve got into serious trouble. "I was running on a wet track with this Mini-Cooper when a brake locked. This threw my car sideways as I was coming out of a fast turn, and I knew I couldn't hold the road. Not in the wet."

A British sports writer graphically described Steve's performance under stress:

> As he hurtled downhill, off the road, McQueen did a superb job of propelling the Cooper between a series of poles and metal signs that could have demolished it. He controlled his slide until the final instant, looped, and slammed the car at an angle into a dirt embankment. The Cooper snapped around like a top, whirling and bouncing, but miraculously did not turn over.

Steve had split his lower lip in the impact, and required several stitches to close the wound. He worried about what the studio would do if he delayed production: "I had close-ups due the following Monday, but Phil Leacock, the director, saved the day by letting me do all my scenes wearing an oxygen mask in the cockpit."

Through his association with Moss, Steve contacted John Cooper, head of the British Motor Corporation's racing team, and purchased a Formula Jr. Cooper. He had this fast British racing machine shipped to California, with the idea of running the Cooper on the West Coast following his return to the States.

During his stay at the sedate, ultra-conservative Savoy Hotel in London, McQueen drew some unfavorable attention from the press for his "outrageous conduct." As he told the story:

> I had a few racing pals up to my rooms, and we were scrambling eggs over a hot plate—which the management frowns on—when a curtain caught fire. Well, I quick-hopped into the hall to grab a fire extinguisher and ran smack into two dignified old English ladies. I was

barefoot, in my shorts, with no shirt on—and they let out a yell and reported to the manager that a naked man was running amok in the hallway. I tried to explain, but they kicked me out of the hotel.

McQueen wound up his British stay in a four-story town house in Chester Square, owned by diplomat Lord Russell, "where I managed to avoid setting anything on fire."

Early in 1962, with *The War Lover* completed, Steve returned to California and immediately entered the Four Aces Moose Run, a cross-country motorcycle race.

I'd been doing some cycle riding on the dirt, but I was still new at the game. Had a bit of a problem early in the race. Some of the riders resented the fact that I was an actor. They didn't trust my motives for being there— so they blocked me at the start. Still, I did okay, finishing third in the Open Novice class.

Steve was learning dirt-cycle technique from Bud Ekins and Don Mitchell, experts whose many trophies testified to their knowledge of rough-country competition. (Ekins soon became one of Steve's closest friends.)

In that same month (March 1962), McQueen competed at Sebring, Florida, with Stirling Moss as a team member of the British Motor Corporation (BMC) under John Cooper. Sebring was a major international event, and Steve's performance there was proof of his ability to handle fast machinery.

"In the twelve-hour Sebring main, I codrove a Le Mans Healey for Cooper," he said. "After seven hours we were leading our class and headed for a trophy, but engine problems forced us out. Still, I think I did okay."

Designer Donald Healey felt that Steve had done much better than "okay." He was impressed with McQueen's performance. "It was exceptional. As a driver, he could really get somewhere if he'd devote himself to it."

A month after Sebring (having taken delivery of his Formula Jr. Cooper from England) McQueen swept the field at California's Del Mar track, winning both days. Later, running the Cooper at Santa Barbara, Steve again won both events. Flushed with success, he told his buddies that he was thinking seriously of competing professionally. For McQueen, racing had become "a kind of fever. It just *burned* inside me."

He faced a major career crisis. Should he continue to act, or should he accept an offer from John Cooper and BMC to race in Europe?

> They gave me a weekend to make up my mind. I spent two full days in a sweat, trying to decide whether I wanted to go into pro racing, earning my money on the track, or whether I wanted to continue being an actor. It was a very tough decision for me to reach because, right then, I didn't know if I was an actor who raced or a racer who acted. But I had Neile and our two children to consider, and *that* made the difference. I turned down the BMC offer. But I came *very* close to chucking my film career. I hadn't done anything really important or outstanding on the screen, and I was tired of waiting for the "big picture," the one that would hopefully break me through. If I'd been single I think I would have gone into full-time competition.

McQueen's decision to remain in films was extremely fortunate, since his "big picture," *The Great Escape,* was about to be produced. For this film, director John Sturges offered Steve the part of a cocky, rebellious prisoner of war named Virgil Hilts, known as "The Cooler King."

McQueen recalled Sturges' explanation of the nickname: "Hilts keeps trying to break out of this POW camp, and the Germans keep dragging him back and throwing him into the cooler. But they can't break his spirit. He just keeps trying."

"I dunno, Johnny...I mean, Jeez, I just *did* two World War II flicks and they both died in the stretch."

"This one's a guaranteed winner," Sturges assured him. "It's a *real* story, based on a book by a guy named Paul Brickhill, about these 75 RAF prisoners who tunnel out of a Nazi maximum-security camp, and how the Germans recapture 'em and execute 50 of the poor bastards. I've got a sweet script on it and I'm using some of the gang from *Seven*—Charlie Bronson and Jim Coburn. Be like old home week for you, Steve."

"Where you shooting it?"

"In Germany—Bavaria. The whole picture."

"Okay, Johnny, I owe you one. The only good film I ever made was *Seven*—so count me in."

And they shook hands on the deal.

The Great Escape was another Sturges "team" picture, but without a central starring role. James Garner (who was to become a racing pal of Steve's) had been signed, as had David McCallum and Richard Attenborough; Coburn, Bronson, and McQueen filled out the main cast.

The screenplay was based on Brickhill's true account of an escape attempt from the heavily guarded *Stalag Luft Norden*. Rated as the greatest POW breakout in World War II, the search and recapture had involved some 5 million Nazis. Certain fictional elements were added, but the film basically followed Brickhill's book.

McQueen recalled being responsible for a major story change, which proved to be the most talked-about sequence in the film. Going over the script with Sturges, he had paused at a section in which Hilts boards a train in his escape attempt.

"I've got an idea that'll put a lot more juice into this," Steve said.

"Let's hear it."

"We forget the train bit. We have Hilts rig a trip wire across a road. This Nazi cycle rider hits the wire and goes down. Hilts rushes out, grabs his bike, and takes off cross-country, with the Germans riding his tail. He finally comes to this big barbed wire border fence where it looks like he's trapped for sure. But he revs up the bike and *jumps* the whole fence, cycle and all! How's that sound?"

It sounded fine to Sturges, and this sequence was written into the shooting script.

On May 30, 1962, McQueen left the States for Munich, West Germany, to join the *Escape* cast. He would be paid $100,000—and allowed to do his own cycle riding.

Interiors for the picture were shot at studios in Munich, but all of the outdoor location shooting was done at a specially constructed camp (which simulated a Nazi prison compound) built by technicians just outside the city. "Bud Ekins went along as our chief stunt rider," said Steve.

> We had four bikes for this film. I was running a TT Special 650 Triumph. We painted it olive drab and put

on a luggage rack and an old seat to make it look like a wartime BMW. We couldn't use a real BMW, not at the speeds we were running, since those old babies were rigid-frame jobs, and couldn't take the punishment.

Local reaction to McQueen, Ekins, and the other riders amused Steve. "The first time we tried out the bikes at full chat the Bavarians just gaped, open-mouthed. They didn't believe that a bike could *go* that fast over this kind of uphill-downhill terrain."

In the filmed chase Steve roars through the Rhine River countryside, hotly pursued by Nazi cyclists. McQueen enjoyed this action so much that he also doubled for his pursuers, wearing a German helmet and uniform, with Ekins bouncing along beside him in the sidecar. ("They intercut these scenes— and there I am on the screen, me chasing me!")

The most dangerous stunt in the picture involved the 60-foot cycle jump over a high barbed wire fence. "If I'd gone on my melon trying that stunt we couldn't have finished the picture," Steve said, "so it was done by Bud Ekins, who doubled for me. I always felt a little uptight about it—especially since the studio PR boys played things up big about how I did all my own riding in this film."

"The jump wasn't *quite* as dangerous as it looked," said Ekins.

They removed a section of the barbed wire, the section I was jumping the bike over, and substituted string— with dozens of rubber bands tied to it for the barbs. In the film it looked just like the real fence. Steve always gave me credit for the jump. In fact, on television, when Johnny Carson congratulated him for doing it, Steve corrected him, "It wasn't me. That was Bud Ekins." The studio got a little upset over his admitting that to a nationwide audience, but Steve never tried to hide the truth about what he did or didn't do in his films.

In 1963, prior to the summer release of *The Great Escape,* Steve was in New York to begin filming *Love with the Proper Stranger* for director Robert Mulligan. He portrayed an Italian trumpet player, Rocky Papasano, described by a critic as "a bed-hopping charmer who is shaken when one of his passing conquests, Angie (Natalie Wood), runs him to ground and announces her pregnancy."

The tough and tender love story (much of it shot on Brooklyn streets) dealt with Rocky's attempt to help Angie obtain an abortion. At the last moment, shocked by the crude woman who is about to perform the (then-illegal) abortion, he refuses to allow Angie to go through with it and ends up marrying her.

This was, by far, Steve's most romantically appealing role. He exuded a cool, controlled sexuality, combining solid masculinity with humor and gentleness. Females across the nation responded enthusiastically, elevating him to the status of instant sex idol.

At 33, with the blockbuster release of *The Great Escape*, McQueen had suddenly become, in industry terms, "white hot." For *Escape*, he captured the top award as Best Actor at the Moscow Film Festival, and *Newsweek* called him "brilliant . . . deserving of an Academy Award" for *Love with the Proper Stranger*; *Life* featured him on their cover.

It had taken him 11 years to achieve international stardom, but he was unprepared for the flood of "offers and deals that came rushing in. It was scary, the way everybody began hitting on me. Man, they were like comin' out of the woodwork!"

In partial self-defense, he formed Solar Productions. With his own company, Steve felt that he would have "some artistic control, some leverage." As he stated his goals:

> I want to know everything I can about this business. I make notes, I watch the cutter run film through the machine, watch where he cuts, how and why. I ask questions, study camera technique, direction, sound . . . and I'm also learning about the distribution end. Solar will have a meaning. It won't be just a title for a tax write-off. It will be an *active* production company, and I'll be in on every phase.

He had taken another important step forward; he was no longer simply an actor for hire, he was Steve McQueen, producer.

7...

From Cinema
to Cycles

April 1970. I had an appointment at Solar Productions. When I got there, McQueen had not yet arrived. His delay gave me a chance to wander through the suite of offices that occupied an entire upper floor in a building on Ventura Boulevard in Studio City, California. I recall being amazed at how *functional* it all seemed. No frills. No stained-glass windows, no gaudy chrome-and-cork offices with Picasso prints on the walls. This was a working company, designed to get a job done.

McQueen's conference room held many of his racing trophies (I counted more than 20), and the art department down the hall featured large poster-sized drawings and paintings of Steve on a cycle for his planned (but unfilmed) production, *Yucatan.*

When McQueen arrived we walked into his office. Comfortable, but unpretentious. He was

61

not there to impress visitors; he was there to work. I asked him if he took any particular satisfaction in running his own company.

"Mostly, it's a hassle," he told me. "Being head honcho means I'm responsible for the final yes or no—which is like playing Monopoly with *real* money! A wrong decision can cost millions. [He was about to make one, with Solar's participation in *Le Mans*.] But here I have the clout I need in this game. I can set my own deals and not end up doing some piece of studio shit because I've got no other choice. In this place, I *make* my choices. When I'm right, we all go to the party. When I'm wrong, I hang for it. Like ol' Harry Truman said, 'The buck stops here.' And *that's* what being head honcho really means."

McQueen disliked magazine interviews, but he now agreed to talk to writer Tedd Thomey, provided that certain restrictions were clearly understood.

"I'd been warned by his PR man, Dave Foster, to use discretion in all of my questions about McQueen's personal life," Thomey said. "I was told that if I said the wrong thing I'd be tossed out on my ear. McQueen had done just that to a nosy sports writer in London when the questioning had become too personal. I promised Foster that I'd behave." Thomey recalled their talk:

We met at his home in Palm Springs. McQueen looked like a bum when he came out to shake my hand. His hair was a dirty tobacco-brown, and looked as if it had been trimmed with a dull Bowie knife. He hadn't shaved, and a rough beard-stubble covered his chin and cheeks. He didn't talk so much as mumble, and his eyes flashed mean and hostile. I got the impression of a nervous, easily irritated juvenile delinquent who had never grown up.

They spoke mainly of Steve's racing.
"He was okay when we stuck to that subject," said Thomey.

"But the only 'personal' thing I got out of him was when I asked about his family, about why he risked their future as well as his own by continuing to race." Thomey quoted McQueen's reply.

> You can't suppress aggression. If you do, it pops up in bad ways. Well, me, I'm naturally an aggressive guy, and I've *got* to have a release. I don't booze much, and I don't run around with wild women or shoot craps at Vegas for high stakes. I get the edge off by racing. And racing is worth all the risk and the hassle because it keeps me human.

After completing his final scenes for *Love with the Proper Stranger*, Steve flew back to California to enter the 1963 Greenhorn Enduro. This top cycle event attracted 300 of the nation's toughest riders for a 500-mile "bash" over a wheel-bending, back-snapping course laid out across the southern Mojave Desert. The competitors ran over sand trails, dirt roads, through old mining towns, up slopes studded with boulders and cactus, along stretches of dry, desolate country, on through rugged mountains and valleys into the Rand Range of hills, over land heavily potholed with abandoned mine shafts dating back to Gold Rush days. The race involved an overnight stop, during which the riders slept as their pit crews replaced nuts and bolts, changed tires, cleaned air filters, and tightened spokes on badly battered cycles.

Steve survived the first day's run, sliding and slipping and gunning his cycle along the route. But on the second day, just 20 miles from the finish, leading his class, he blew a cylinder. ("I pulled the spark plug and just limped the rest of the way to the line on one cylinder. It was a tough break.")

McQueen claimed that he had earned his spurs in bike racing by "showing them how thick my mud is." He needed to prove he had the nerve and courage to stick with the fastest riders. "These guys have a strict code," said McQueen.

> You don't lie about the sport. And you don't cheat at it. You play it straight. I broke a shoulder and I broke an arm in two places *and* I had four stitches in my head, all before these people accepted me for real. Finally I

convinced them I wasn't out there for publicity or for laughs. I was out there to win.

He talked about the damage that cycle racing inflicts on a rider's hands: "They get cut up plenty, and gloves don't help much, fighting the bike bars the way you have to do. You're doing maybe seventy, really honkin' on, and you see a big ditch comin' at you. Well, you tense up and grab those bars and try to hang tight. You hit holes that'll bend the bars right down."

Competing out of District 37, within the jurisdiction of the American Motorcycle Association (the most competitive district in the United States for beginning riders), McQueen won enough points to move up to amateur (from novice) in just one year. "Out of some 5,000 new riders every year," one racing veteran admitted, "only one rider in ten moves up in class that fast. McQueen was outstanding, no question of that."

Things were getting crowded in Nichols Canyon. With Neile, their two children, a Malemute dog, and a rapidly expanding stable of cars and cycles—including a new Berlinetta 12-cylinder Ferrari (a gift from Neile), his Cooper, the XK Jaguar, a Cobra, a British Land Rover, and a massive Lincoln town car—Steve and Neile felt that it was time for a move to larger quarters.

That summer they found exactly the place they wanted in Brentwood, an exclusive suburb of Los Angeles.

"We drove through this big electric gate and started around a mountain with a rock wall on one side and all these trees," related Steve. "Finally we came to the top, and drove under a stone archway into this medieval Spanish courtyard—and my eyes were popping."

A combination of ranch-style, Mediterranean, and modern, the two-story mansion sat high atop Brentwood's Oakmont Drive, with a clear view of the Pacific Ocean in the distance. Among its special features were a marble fireplace, an Olympic-sized swimming pool, a den the size of a tennis court, an outdoor playhouse for the children, and a custom pool table in the sunken living room. The price was $250,000 plus" (more than $2 million in 1983 dollars). "It was a lot of bread for me at the time," McQueen recalled. "But Neile really wanted it, so I said okay."

No matter how involved he was with the present, Steve never forgot his past. During the first year of their marriage, he had taken Neile back to Missouri, to his Uncle Claude's farm in Slater, to show her "how it was, when I was a kid." Now, in 1963, he returned to the Boys Republic at Chino to lend his personal support to this school for wayward boys and to establish the Steve McQueen Scholarship.

"I dig you guys," he declared, sitting on the bed in his old room at Chino, surrounded by teenagers who could barely conceal their awe at seeing this genuine movie star in their midst. "I was a hardnosed tough guy—just like most of you—but I shaped up, and this place helped set me straight."

One of the counselors at Chino described McQueen's effect on the youngsters:

> They really appreciate seeing him. They listen and they relate to him. He doesn't preach, just tells them the truth, that he was headed wrong, until he broke the pattern. They figure since *he* did it maybe they can, too. Steve's visits here are extremely valuable. He's a real inspiration to the boys.

McQueen made one more film that year, *Soldier in the Rain*, a comedy costarring Jackie Gleason. It was the first of many films in which Solar Productions was directly involved, and Steve had chosen this project in the hope that a lighter role might balance his usually grim screen persona.

"I hadn't done any comedy since *The Honeymoon Machine*," he said. "Felt it was time to do something different. But the picture just didn't come together. I really don't know why, because all the right elements were there."

On paper, the project promised success. Ralph Nelson was an accomplished director; the script was faithful to William Goldman's excellent novel; Gleason was in top form as grouchy-but-lovable Master Sergeant Maxwell Slaughter; Tuesday Weld was bright and appealing in a role that allowed full use of her considerable talents. But an injection of heavy drama undermined the film's comic aspects, and *Soldier in the Rain* failed to generate box-office dollars. Still, McQueen came off quite well in his best comedic performance, clearly demonstrating his versatility.

One of the scenes called for him to wrestle a stunt man through a latticework partition in a savagely staged bar brawl. In the melee, fighting the stunt man, Steve was smashed flat across a pool table. "That guy knocked me dingy. I was just out of it for a while," he admitted. "Still, I'd a lot rather do this kind of action stuff than the heavy emotional scenes. For those, you have to turn yourself inside out, empty all your emotional pockets."

At the studio gym, between sequences, Steve punched bags, hefted 130-pound weights, and did endless sit-ups on a tilt board to strengthen his stomach muscles. He proudly reported to a friend that a stunt man had complimented him on the toughness of his body. "Told me he'd never met another actor who worked out the way I do."

McQueen's constant fascination with machines surfaced during the production. There were several golfing sequences in the picture, and Steve modified the motorized cart Paramount provided, gleefully bragging to Gleason (who hated speed), "Man, I bet this is the first time you've ever seen a golf cart burn rubber!"

Gleason found McQueen easy to work with, declaring: "Steve put all he had into the role, being well aware that comedy is a very serious business."

In an industry starved for colorful new stars, McQueen was *news*. His name on the cover of a magazine meant guaranteed sales. He had become, in the media-hype words of one writer, "a man's man and a woman's dream." Reporters and journalists scrambled to interview him, and their printed impressions of the badboy-turned-superstar verged on the ludicrous. *Newsweek* described him as "a blue-eyed Pan with disarrayed blond hair . . . a prototype American. With his wide ears and open face, he looks like a young Dwight Eisenhower after sophomore year at San Quentin."

Life summed him up as "an oddball, who combines the cockiness of Cagney with the glower of Bogart . . . He talks the lingo of the rough world that spawned him—a world of hipsters, racing car drivers, beachboys, drifters and carnival barkers." *McCall's* wrote of "this cocky young newcomer with the case-hardened face, the seen-everything eyes, the hipster vocabulary and the mania for speed."

Steve attempted to project a more mature image to interviewer Edwin Miller.

I'm not some dipped-out speed freak. I take this business seriously. And I depend on *myself*. I had to learn to look out for myself when I was a kid. I had no one to talk to, I was all alone. It taught me to be self-reliant.

I just finished a crash course in business administration to learn how to negotiate contracts. If you don't stay on top of things, you can lose out. I call my agent at two or three o'clock in the morning to ask a question about something. I make notes, memorize them, and the next day I'm ready to negotiate. I'm a good businessman.

Steve's distrust of strangers was intensified by his experiences in Hollywood. He was shocked and depressed by what he termed "personal hypocrisy."

It's hard to take. Some guy you've never met starts up and brings his whole soul into it, I mean he really *bares his soul*—and you just gotta believe him because he's way out there, way out, telling you things you figure he wouldn't tell God. Then, later, it turns out the guy is a total son of a bitch and it makes you feel terrible. You feel sick inside.

McQueen was aloof toward his neighbors for this reason. "I didn't want 'em nosin' around. Just because some dude lives next to you, that doesn't qualify him as a friend. But, there were exceptions . . . such as Jim Garner."

James Garner's house was directly down the hill, and the two actors liked one another. "We hit it off from the start," said McQueen. "We had a lot in common . . . both of us liked fast machinery for one thing. And we had some laughs."

Garner's sense of humor, however, was put to the test by a puckish McQueen.

I could see that Jim was very neat around his place. Grass always cut. Flowers trimmed. No papers in the yard—that sort of thing. So, just to piss him, I started lobbing empty beer cans down the hill into his driveway. At first, he just couldn't figure out where in hell they were comin' from. He'd have the drive all spic 'n' span when he left the house, then get home to find all these empty cans. Took him a long time to figure out it was me . . . we had ourselves some chuckles over how pissed he got.

By January 1964, Steve was in Bay City, Texas, on location for *Baby, the Rain Must Fall,* a cinema version of Horton Foote's Broadway play, *The Traveling Lady.* In this downbeat drama, McQueen portrayed a problem-ridden guitarist/singer, an ex-convict named Henry Thomas who cannot adjust to a wife and child. Actress Lee Remick played McQueen's wife. Their outdoor location scenes in Texas took a full month to complete.

Again, as in *Soldier in the Rain,* Steve was injured in a realistic bar fight, described by one set witness as "a savage knockdown, in which tables, chairs and pitchers of beer were flying. And, man, McQueen was really into it!" Director Robert Mulligan, applying an ice pack to Steve's cut eye, added his personal estimation of the actor's drive. "He's not afraid to *use* himself when he acts. Steve has what I call a kind of daring theatricality."

"Hell, what I've *got* is a black eye!" grinned McQueen.

During lunch breaks Steve ate with the grips, carpenters, and electricians, claiming that a meal on the set was preferable to the executive dining room used by the other stars. "They never let you relax in there," he said. "People are always comin' on to me about properties or tryin' to sell me something or talk me into a deal—when all I want to do is *eat.*"

Repeating the poor box-office reception of his previous film, *Baby, the Rain Must Fall* proved to be another disappointment. Critic Joanna Campbell offered a reason: "The picture lacked a unity of mood and style. McQueen's sketch of the inadequate, violent, almost subnormal Henry Thomas was skillful in the extreme, but it was not the kind of characterization that his growing legion of fans are keen to see."

Anxious to escape the frustrations of acting, Steve embarked on a full schedule of cycle events, taking home five trophies during that 1964 season against rough competition. In most of these, he competed on a modified Triumph prepared by his friend Bud Ekins (out of Ekins' shop in Sherman Oaks). "Bud is one of the top bike racers in the game," McQueen declared.

He's also a serious businessman. People tend to think of cyclists as leather-jacket nuts. Sure, we wear leather when we ride, but that's because the desert can rip you up bad if you take a spill in ordinary street clothes.

Bud's family and mine are very close; we all get along fine together. We stuff everybody into a pickup, tie down the bikes in back, and take off for a race in the high desert. I tell you, there's nothin' like bein' out there with the puckerbushes and cactus and warm sand.

But at racing speed, McQueen's desert could be as deadly as it was beautiful. "When you race cycles, you take spills, 'cuz you're out there twisting the tiger's tail. Man, I've been thrown into the air so often I can peg the soft landing spots. I just kind of wiggle my ass in the right direction and head for one!"

Steve blandly recounted a "double-race afternoon" at Hi Vista when he competed in the Pacific West Coast Championship Scrambles: "There was this big pile-up in the fourth lap, and in avoiding the tangle I hit a tree, split my mouth open, and knocked some teeth loose. But I was okay. I got back into it and won. Then I entered a second event that same afternoon, ran it with my face all puffed and bandaged, and won that race, too!"

The fast cycles obsessed McQueen that year, and he turned down several film offers to keep active in the sport. Neile recalled: "Steve was desperate to prove he wasn't just a local racer, that he could compete with the best. That September he got his chance in the Six-Days—the Kentucky Derby of motorcycle races."

McQueen had been accepted as part of the American team for the International Six-Day Trials in East Germany, the year's peak prestige event for professional cycle riders, including the best from England, East Germany, Sweden, the USSR, Czechoslovakia, Poland, Finland, Scotland, Austria, and the Netherlands.

Neile would remain in California with their children until the race was over and then join Steve in Frankfurt. McQueen took off for London, where the team picked up their racing cycles. ("My bike was a 650-cc Triumph, running knobby tires with a few extra goodies installed.") The other four Americans with Steve that year were Bud and Dave Ekins, Cliff Coleman, and John Steen. They met the British team (who ranked as prime competition) and a quick friendship developed among the riders.

The International Six-Days was first run in Great Britain in 1913, and attracted a scattering of riders. By 1964 there were 226 entrants set to race more than 1,200 miles (in 200-mile daily stages) through woods, up mountains, along rock-strewn trails, and choppy cart paths—fighting time as well as terrain.

The goal for each competitor was a gold medal, awarded to those riders able to finish the entire run with no marks lost on time. (Silver and bronze medals were also awarded to riders losing only minimal points along the route.) The reward for the winning team was the privilege of hosting the following year's race. East Germany, whose team had won the trial in 1963, was the current host.

As one participant outlined the rules: "Each rider has to maintain an average which depends on his cycle's engine capacity. The rider follows arrows which mark out the course, getting his route card stamped along the way to prove that he has not taken a short cut. Keeping an eye on the clock and his mileage-counter, he must adjust his speed to hit the time clock on the right minute. His time through each section is stamped on a card, and if he loses too many points for being late into a check area his record is spoiled and his medal is gone."

In England the five Americans obtained a van, had an American flag painted on the side, loaded in their racing bikes and tools, and headed for Germany. "We drove all night," said McQueen,

> and then got hung up for four hours at the border. The delay had something to do with their interest in Western money. Anyhow, we finally made it across to Erfurt and into our dormitories. And, I can tell you it was kind of *weird*, being there behind the Iron Curtain, with everybody watching us.
>
> The night before the race they had this parade of nations in a big hall the size of a football stadium. The guys from each team marched for their country. I stood up there, holding the American flag, right between the Russians and the East Germans, and it was a great moment for me. I was proud to be there. For breakfast, in the mess hall, they gave us each a strip of cold eel, some

awful kind of gelatine, a piece of green tomato, and a cup of coffee black enough to dye your socks in. This was what some Russian scientist decided we should eat to be at maximum health for the race. Can you feature having eel for breakfast?

Each rider was assigned a competition number, firmly affixed to his machine: McQueen's was 278. Bud Ekins' was 250. ("The heavy bikes started last and rated larger numbers," McQueen explained.) On the starting line in East Germany, wearing his striped crash helmet, black leather jacket and heavy-duty boots, gloved hands poised on the throttle, racing goggles masking his eyes, Steve McQueen was a long way from Hollywood. There would be no favored attention given him here; he was simply one rider in a vast field. Here, in ranked rows, were the Czech team's CA 250s, the Russian Jawas, the MZ machines of East Germany, BSAs from Great Britain, the Husqvarnas of Sweden, the KTMs of Austria and the American team Triumphs—each cycle ridden by a top world talent.

McQueen carried some basic tools in his back pocket, since the rules required that each rider repair his machine only with the tools he carried en route. Steve recorded his memories of the event in graphic detail.

Near the end of the second day we were tied with England for first team position—and we were actually leading overall on bonus points. At this stage I was definitely lined up for a gold medal. Part of the last section for the day led over an open road through the forest. I was running alongside the British champ, John Gills, a marvelous racer, staying close to him, and we were moving along at full chat in the rain.

We could figure where the road would go by watching the way the trees lined up. But we got fooled, because at one point the trees marched straight ahead while the road *turned*. We came booming into this section, a full turkey leg, at about eighty—and I began sliding for traction. Went off the road and parted company with my bike. I saw marks where other riders had got themselves into this same kind of trouble. My cheek was cut from the goggles, but nothing was broken. I looked over my bike. The tail pipe was smashed. I flipped a tool out of my back pocket and bent the pipe back into usable shape.

I was in a real sweat because if you're three minutes late into a checkpoint you lose your chance for a gold medal. But I was okay, because I made it to the next checkpoint in time.

But on the third day the prospect of an American team victory dissolved as Bud Ekins clipped a stone bridge at speed and broke his leg. And by dusk of this same day, with rain still miring the roads and turning the circuit into shifting mud, McQueen's racing luck ran out: "I broke a chain on a steep hill climb, repaired the chain, but within a half mile another link snapped. After I'd fixed the chain again I was running four to five minutes late. I knew that I had to make up the lost time by the next checkpoint, so I really began riding hard."

McQueen kept increasing speed, blasting his powerful 650 Triumph through the rain-gray German countryside, mud and rocks spraying back from his sliding wheels; he was "riding the edge," using all of his skill to regain the lost minutes.

Then, on the brow of a slope lined with spectators, along the narrow lip of a pine-thick ravine, this guy on another bike cut right across the course. He didn't hear me or see me, he just blundered out into my path. When he looked up and saw me bearing down on him, he hit the panic button. I was planning to squeak by on the left and was cranking it on, figuring he'd leave me room to get past. But he panicked, cut left at the last split second, and side-swiped me. My Triumph sailed over the side of the ravine, buzzed off into space, and I unloaded in midair. The bike slammed into some small pine trees, while I bounced around a few times, ending up against a rock. My face was gashed, my kneecaps were torn up, but I'd survived.

My bike hadn't. The front wheel was badly dented, the tire was shot, and the forks were bent clear back to the chassis. I knew my run was over. That spill had cost me the race.

The remaining Americans finished the full six days. Dave Ekins and Cliff Coleman won gold medals and John Steen took home a silver medal. "We were a battered-looking lot," summed up McQueen.

> Bud's leg busted...Steen with five stitches in his chin...Dave all black-and-blue from having unloaded on pavement doing about 80, and me with my cut knees and all. Still, our team had come away with three medals for the U.S. And even though I was plenty disappointed at not being able to finish, I'd proved that I was capable of holding my own against world-class riders, and that was my *real* satisfaction.

8. . .

A Death in the Family—and a Triumph in Taiwan

We were talking quietly in a corner booth at a small steak house on Ventura Boulevard when Steve suddenly raised a silencing hand.

"Listen!" he said, canting his head, favoring his good right ear.

I heard what he was hearing: the sound of a cycle running through the gears.

Steve looked at me, a faint smile on his lips. "I've never been in a restaurant where I didn't perk up when a good bike goes by. A Husqvarna 405 at 12,000 revs... that's *music!*" His eyes seemed fixed to a distant point. "I'm really into rough-country riding. I mean, I love the ground, the *earth;* I don't love asphalt. On a bike you're dealing with natural environment... you learn to *read* the terrain. In the open desert, if I see a rabbit tear off I can chase after him. If I spot some Indian petroglyphs on the rocks I can stop to look 'em over. No hurry. No pressure. I just sit out there, alone, maybe for an hour or so, looking, feeling the earth around me... with a 360-degree view. Nobody to bother me."

He hesitated for a long moment as the vision of open desert receded from his eyes. Then he grinned sheepishly at me. "Now... what were we talkin' about?"

Neile joined Steve in Europe after the Six-Day Trials, meeting him at the airport in Frankfurt. Following a weekend tour of the historic German city, they took a train to Paris, renting a penthouse suite at the Crillon. "This was Steve's first real vacation," Neile related.

> Since I'd left both of the kids back in California, it was a kind of a second honeymoon for us. The French are fanatic movie buffs and Steve was so well known we couldn't set foot on the street before he was swamped by fans. So he wore a false mustache and beard when we went out to dinner! We attended the opening of one of his films, and I posed for the cover of *Elle,* the French fashion magazine, wearing a Lanvin gown. We really enjoyed ourselves.

Beyond Paris, they drove through Belgium, France, and Spain, stopping at small inns, enjoying the peace and solitude. "We got lost on a side road for a while," Neile said. "But it was fun to be lost, fun to be free and alone, just the two of us. We *needed* this time together."

By January of 1965, after a year's layoff from acting, Steve was (in his words) "back in harness." He had signed for the title role in MGM's *The Cincinnati Kid*. The screenplay was based on Richard Jessup's novel, and concerned a tough young master of stud poker and his attempt to defeat the game's reigning champion, brilliantly portrayed by Edward G. Robinson.

Robinson appreciated the irony of the situation, realizing that below the surface of the film itself, a *real* conflict would be staged between a young star and a seasoned veteran. "Once, back at the start of my career, I had *been* another McQueen,"

Robinson said. "I'd played the same kind of parts, cocky and tough, ready to take on the old timers and beat them at their own game. I identified strongly with McQueen, and I had a lot of respect for his talent."

The respect was mutual; Steve knew that he faced a real acting challenge against Robinson and was tense and nervous at the outset of shooting. "I'd been away from the camera for a year," he said, "and the depth I was trying for in this role just wasn't coming for me. For the first three days on the set I felt like I'd never acted before in my life! Then things got better. I loosened up and began to get my juice back."

Most of the film was set in New Orleans, and Steve saw to it that the script included at least one fast-action sequence, wherein the Kid is trapped by toughs and must fight his way clear by smashing through a window. Running from his pursuers, he escapes by jumping across railroad tracks just in front of an onrushing train. As he did with nearly all of his screen stunts, McQueen insisted on tackling this one himself.

"I had to run across thirty-five sets of tracks for this scene," recalled Steve. "I talked with the engineer of the *Sunset Limited* and asked him how many yards he needed to stop the thing, and he assured me he couldn't possibly stop it in the required area, so I was aware of the setup and used my own timing."

The sequence was successful—with McQueen leaping across the final set of tracks just as the train thunders past him, inches away from his back. "Doin' this kind of stunt is plain nuts," remarked one of the crew on hand for the scene. "I wouldn't try it for *any* amount of money—but you could tell that McQueen got a real charge out of the thing. Hell, I think he woulda done it for *free!*"

Sam Peckinpah was the director MGM originally chose for *The Cincinnati Kid*, but at the last minute the studio replaced him with Norman Jewison, who firmly guided McQueen and Robinson through superb performances. The poker table scenes fairly crackled with the drama of high-stakes play, challenger vs. champ, youth against veteran. These scenes were orchestrated by Jewison for maximum tension, and his direction of the film's romantic interludes (involving McQueen with Tuesday Weld and Ann-Margret) proved equally powerful.

During the prerelease screening at MGM, McQueen squirmed uneasily as he watched the big-screen action.

"I get suicidal when I have to watch my films," he said. "When I see myself up there, 24 feet high on that screen, I'm into a cold sweat. Each time I think, 'Man, this thing's gonna bomb at the box office!' In this case, I was wrong." Indeed he was. *The Cincinnati Kid* was an international hit, with *Time* commenting on the "bristling good show by McQueen and Robinson."

That summer, with dubbing on the film completed, Steve once again joined forces with John Sturges on a projected auto racing film to be called *Day of the Champion*. The plot dealt with a crash-prone Formula One Grand Prix driver who becomes world champion "despite severe psychological problems."

The film was to be shot in Europe during the 1966 Grand Prix season, and McQueen (insured for $2 million) was to star. Warners agreed to finance the project, but McQueen and Sturges invested $25,000 of their own money in preproduction costs. Part of this sum involved mounting a camera on a full-race vehicle to obtain dramatic high-speed race footage at Riverside. ("We had to *show* Warners just how exciting such a film could be.")

With a script by award-winner Edward Anhalt, Sturges and McQueen left for Europe that summer to scout drivers and locations. Stirling Moss (now retired after a near-fatal crash in 1962) was to be production consultant, and he joined them overseas at the end of May for the Grand Prix of Monaco in Monte Carlo.*

Steve also attended the French Grand Prix in June and the German Grand Prix in August, arranging exclusive contracts to film both events the following season as background for *Day of the Champion*.

McQueen was actively competing with director John Frankenheimer for 1966 European race sites. Backed by MGM, Frankenheimer was preparing his own racing film, *Grand Prix,* to star Steve's pal James Garner. Eight million dollars of MGM's

---

*McQueen also hired Scotsman Jackie Stewart, who had finished third that year in the Monte Carlo event. It was Stewart who told McQueen of his (McQueen's) Scottish ancestors. "He told me they have a whole bunch of McQueen castles over there," Steve recalled.

money were committed to this Cinerama production. Since both films featured American driver/heroes who became world champions the studio rivalry was intense.

"We wanted to beat MGM to the punch," said Sturges.

> But Frankenheimer had a head start, and Steve had two films to make before he could do *Champion,* so we finally had to abandon our picture. Steve was real unhappy about it, because he'd been looking forward to dicing around European circuits in those hot Grand Prix cars.

The first of McQueen's next two films dealt with a character played by Alan Ladd in *The Carpetbaggers* named Max Sand, known as Nevada Smith. Solar Productions would have a major hand in making *Nevada Smith,* with Steve in the title role (his first western since *The Magnificent Seven*).

In the story, Sand is portrayed as the bitter young son of an American Indian mother and a white father who rides in blood pursuit of the men who murder his parents. The part called for action with fist, gun, and knife. In the course of the film Sand is captured and sent into the swamps as a prisoner on a chain-gang. He escapes to seek his final vengeance. It was a rugged, demanding role for McQueen, and few actors were as physically qualified.

Scenic backgrounds for *Nevada Smith* were spectacular and authentic. The action began at Mammoth in Northern California, near Banner Peak and Mount Ritter, then moved to Baton Rouge, Louisiana, for a series of day-and-night sequences in the wilderness bayous of the Atchafalaya Basin and at the prison compound at Fort Vincent. Alone and under pressure in his exhausting role, McQueen phoned Neile and demanded that she join him on location. She said that she had to remain with the children. Bring them along, he told her. No, not to such a dangerous area. Neile recalled their argument:

> Whenever we were away from each other for any period of time we fought like crazy on the phone. Real marathons. Neither of us would hang up until the argument was settled. As a result, our phone bills were ridiculous! Well, this time Steve was really uptight; he'd been wading through dirty water, coping with leeches, spiders,

and swamp snakes. He demanded to know why I wasn't there with him, to give him the support he needed. Why should I be living in luxury in Brentwood having tea with my girlfriends while he fought those swamps? I gave in and told him I was packing that night.

Thus, Neile was on the set (a longboat) when Steve waded up to his armpits in the slime of Two O'Clock Bayou. But he was smiling. His "old lady" was with him, which made it okay.

The day after the McQueens returned to Hollywood, an alarming telephone call sent them hurrying to San Francisco. Steve's mother was critically ill at the Mount Zion Hospital. At 55, she had suffered a massive brain hemorrhage.

When the McQueens arrived Steve was informed that his mother had lapsed into a deep coma. Her survival was extremely doubtful. McQueen told the doctor he would wait there in the hope that she might revive. Through the long hours of the night, Steve and Neile maintained their vigil, but the situation was hopeless. On the following day, October 15, 1965, Julia Crawford McQueen died without regaining consciousness.

While he was making arrangements to have the body shipped to Los Angeles for burial at Forest Lawn Memorial Park, his mother's friends told Steve how diligently she had saved all of his news stories and how much she had valued the photos of her grandchildren. Once or twice a year, Steve had mailed her the most recent shots of Chad and Terri (usually without a note). He had not spoken to her, by telephone or in person, for many months. "He did send her enough money for her to buy a new Volkswagen," one of his mother's San Francisco friends recalled. "She just *adored* that little car... ran it up and down the hills... told anyone who'd listen that her son bought it for her."

During the burial, Steve made no attempt to hide his tears. He had been denied the final opportunity to tell his mother he was sorry that things had never been right between them; he wanted to tell her that he had forgiven her for the pain, but there had been no chance. He had waited too long. The shock of her death would fade, but the guilt would not.

McQueen resumed his career. Within a month he was en route to Taiwan to tackle the most ambitious film of his life, the spectacular, monumental production of Richard McKenna's novel *The Sand Pebbles*.

On November 22, 1965, the film shooting officially began on the island of Taiwan (formerly known as Formosa). Two square miles of Taiwan's Keelung Harbor were carefully rebuilt by studio technicians to pass for Shanghai as it had looked in the 1920s. The studio also put $250,000 into building a replica of the *San Pablo*, a fully functioning, 150-foot steel-hulled naval gunboat, complete with an antique steam engine weighing 41,000 lbs. Because of such painstaking attention to period details, plus star salaries and delays caused by bad weather, the original budget of $8 million would eventually total $12 million, making it, in Hollywood terms, a "blockbuster." (McQueen was paid $650,000 for his services.)

The Sand Pebbles cast McQueen in the central role of Jake Holman, a moody, tough-minded sailor serving as chief engineer on this U.S. gunboat cruising China's Yangtze River. The boat's mission was to protect the lives of American missionaries.

A loner, misunderstood and denounced by his crewmates, Holman's job is to keep the gunboat's cranky steam engine operating. He meets a young schoolteacher (Candice Bergen) at one of the port missions and, despite himself, comes to love her. He finally decides to leave the Navy and work with her in the war-torn Chinese heartland. Too late. Nationalist troops attack the mission. In a rearguard action, Holman sacrifices his life to allow the woman he loves and the other Americans to escape via the waiting gunboat.

The picture's background was authentic, involving young revolutionaries who, in 1926, forged a Chinese Republic from a feudal state.

The producer/director of *The Sand Pebbles* was an old friend, Robert Wise. Responsible for McQueen's first screen appearance, he recalled this fact between scenes in Taiwan.

> After I gave Steve that walk-on in *Somebody Up There Likes Me* I never dreamed I'd be working with him here in the Orient as the star of a multimillion-dollar production. But the truth is, he's a perfect choice for the part of Jake Holman. I've never seen an actor work with mechanical things the way he does. He learned every-

thing about operating that ship's engine, just as Holman did in the script. Jake Holman is a very strong individual who doesn't bend under pressure, a guy desperately determined to maintain his own personal identity and pride. Very much like Steve."

Costar Richard Crenna, who portrayed the ship's captain, was mystified by McQueen. "When I first talked to him, his jargon was so odd it was like conversing with a Zulu warrior," said Crenna. "Eventually we got along okay, but I found him to be extremely cautious about friendship, about allowing people to enter his life. You had to sustain the relationship on *his* terms."

Another member of the crew, who kept a diary of the filming, wrote about McQueen: "You can't peg him. He wants desperately to be memorable as an actor—but in his private life you get the impression that he is trying to speed up time, to get into the next hour without quite living out the present one."

Shocked by the number of homeless, underfed young girls wandering the Taiwanese streets, McQueen and Robert Wise each contributed $12,500 to a local missionary priest, Father Edward Wojnaik, enabling him to buy land on which to build a home for impoverished young women. Again, as with past charities, McQueen wanted no publicity regarding his contribution.

To keep his body in peak physical shape, he had five crates of gym equipment imported from California and set up his own workout area aboard the *San Pablo,* bolting a full-sized boxer's body bag to the ceiling, then installing weights, pulleys, and barbells.

Completing a scene in which he defends a mission as a kind of one-man army—using several large weapons, including a Browning automatic rifle—McQueen impressed Wise with his weapons expertise.

Steve's zest for guns was genuine. In California, he kept a firearms collection in his den—a working assortment of some two dozen handguns, dueling pistols, and rifles. A prize item in the collection was his $700 Italian Beretta shotgun. Asked why he had gathered such a store of weapons, he declared: "I'm fascinated by the machinery of guns and gunmaking. A prize handgun is a work of art, just as much as the engine in a Grand Prix Ferrari."

Neile, who had turned down a costarring film role with Marlon Brando to accompany Steve to the Orient, was able to put her dancing ability to good use in Taiwan. While the two McQueen children attended school at the naval base, she volunteered to entertain Chinese troops garrisoned on the island of Quemoy, off the coast of the People's Republic of China. Flown in by helicopter, she danced for a cheering mass of servicemen in the KDC auditorium, 600 feet underground. "I had a fine time," she said, "and they had a fine time, and it all played beautifully. Dancing is never work for me; it's as natural as breathing."

Steve's passion for speed was frustrated on this island location. One morning, while Neile was still in Quemoy, he rented a touring car with a driver who knew the island and took off for a run over the narrow Taiwanese roads (mostly dirt and ambling cow paths). "I'll take over," he told the driver. And he roared away at speed. Steve's excursion was cut short by the local police, who waved the car to a halt and blamed McQueen's guide for allowing the American to exceed speed limits.

"I'm the one to blame," Steve admitted.

They sputtered and fumed, unable to decide on a course of action. Did the wild American intend to go on speeding in this mad fashion, or would he agree to slow down? Steve responded by removing a small bicycle from the trunk of the touring car. He climbed aboard, and pedaled all the way back to the hotel— at a top speed of eight miles an hour.

When the McQueens left for the Orient, they expected to finish the location work in two months. But as the cast and crew struggled against language barriers, tropical insects, disease, political turmoil, and monsoon rains, the two months stretched to four. Much of the shooting depended on the tides of Taiwan, and they proved to be totally unpredictable; also, the lack of potable water was a severe problem. Steve and Neile were both affected by the bad water, and McQueen suffered a weight loss because of an illness.*

---

*Taiwan also had some special hazards. The McQueens had been warned a snake called the bamboo viper was common in the area.

The McQueens moved from their cramped little house in the rice fields outside Taipei to Hong Kong for the last two weeks of shooting.

After almost seven grueling months, *The Sand Pebbles* finally wound up, and by May 1966, Steve and Neile were back in Hollywood. He claimed it was

> the roughest film I ever made. I had my skull twisted a couple of times, got sick, inhaled tear gas, worked myself dingy and ended up exhausted. Believe me, whatever sins I'm guilty of, I *paid* for 'em making this picture. I just hope something decent comes out of it.

What came out of it, for Steve McQueen, was an Academy Award nomination and the greatest critical acclaim of his career.

At 36, he had reached the top of the ladder.

Their bite was fatal. "The people use *geese* to deal with the snakes," Steve related. "So we bought our own goose to protect the house we rented. His name was 'Ha Ha' and he did a damned good job while we were over there."

9. . .

Among the Boston Bluebloods

McQueen talking, sprawled on a deep sofa in the living room of his house in Palm Springs, wearing strap sandals, bleached white cutoffs, and a knitted burgundy Italian T-shirt. Tanned and relaxed. In a contemplative mood. Subject: his children.

"I want them to grow up without any of the hate that damn near consumed me as a kid. I don't try to run their lives, but I do try to show them the right way around the course, you know what I mean?"

He got up, opened a can of beer, settled down again. "My kids have gotta learn that we all have a choice as to who and what we finally become. I'm against drugs. Speed kills, and I don't mean the kind that comes out of an engine! Who needs to blow his mind with that kind of stuff? Life itself is a trip. Secret is, don't let yourself get bored, find things to stay excited about.

"Chad likes to mess around on a bike, same

as me. He's a savvy kid. He'll make out okay. Terri's a lot like her mother, real smart. Earned second-highest marks at her school. She'll do fine. I'm proud of 'em both."

He was silent, head down, for several seconds. And then, looking up with serious eyes, he said, "They know their old man loves 'em. And that's more than *I* ever knew!"

After his long ordeal on *The Sand Pebbles*, Steve bundled his family into their camper and took off for "the wild country, where nobody can get at you, where your agent can't phone you and producers can't send you scripts and where the birds and the squirrels and the rabbits don't give a damn about your being a movie star."

The wild country included Montana and Canada, where the McQueens camped under the stars near clear-running creeks in shaded green forests. Neile described the outing:

> We saw bears and possum—and all kinds of deer. We fished, discovered waterfalls and hidden lakes, and woke each morning in our sleeping bags under a clean blue sky. It was a great way to get back in tune with nature again after those endless monsoon months in the Orient.

For Steve, the trip was marred by a shooting incident: "I was never much for hunting, but we needed some meat so I tracked a buck and shot it . . . in the heart. I can still see it, the look on its face and the bleating noise it made. I asked myself, 'Why in hell did you *do* that?' I was sick inside."

"Steve never liked to see things suffer—not even insects," said journalist Ernest Havemann who spent a weekend at the McQueen home in 1964. The writer was having breakfast with the family, and he recalled that McQueen was upset.

> He looked around the table, at the two kids and at Neile, and he said, "Somebody in this family crushed a grass-hopper last night, only they didn't *kill* it. That thing was still twitching in the trashcan this morning. It was in pain. Next time, make sure it's dead, okay?" McQueen

wasn't kidding. He was really upset about that grass-hopper.

Steve's disappointment at not being able to make *Day of the Champion* was somewhat lessened that summer when he was invited to road-test an exotic variety of fast sports cars at California's Riverside Raceway for the Time/Life organization. The resulting article in *Sports Illustrated* was so well received that the editors of *Popular Science* asked Steve to test a group of off-road racing cycles. McQueen agreed to take six fast bikes out to a desert scrambles course and "twist the tiger's tail" for *PS* readers. He selected a BSA 650-cc Hornet, a four-stroke 750-cc TT Norton-Metisse, a 650-cc Triumph Bonne-ville, a Honda 450, a Montesa La Cross, and a Greeves-Chal-lenger 250-cc two-stroke.

The six-mile scrambles course embraced sand washes, rocks, washboard dips, and high-speed jumps. "Cow-trailing with a top close to 70 was possible over the faster portions," he said. "So the bikes got a really good workout." Of the six, Steve naturally favored the 650-cc Triumph Bonneville, the type of machine he had competed on many times in the past.

He discussed his own hybrid, a competition cycle he had set up with the help of Bud and Dave Ekins: "We used a 650-cc Triumph four-stroke in a special light Rickman-Metisse frame. We cut down weight by eliminating the conventional oil tank. The power was like supersonic!"

While Steve was busily testing cars and cycles that summer, Neile (encouraged by the reception accorded her dancing in the Orient) starred in a stock revival of *Pajama Game*. "I'd done the show so many times on Broadway," she said, "that it was a kind of homecoming for me." The two McQueen children enjoyed watching their mother sing and dance on stage, but by the second week of the engagement Steve began to miss her at home. He got "a little uptight"—and Neile once again put away her dancing shoes.

A close family friend explained Steve's attitude:

> He feels that with Neile at his side he can cope, he can face what he considers to be a basically hostile world. He is innately distrustful, overly sensitive to real or imag-ined slights. Strangers bug him. He hates glad-handers.

However—and this is an important part of his nature—he's genuinely concerned with the underdog, with people who have not been given a fair shake by society. He identifies with them, tries to help them.

At three-month intervals, carefully avoiding publicity, McQueen would load up the family panel truck with food, blankets, and medical supplies and head for the desolate Four Corners area (where Arizona, New Mexico, Colorado, and Utah intersect) to deliver these supplies to impoverished Navajo Indians.

He was also deeply committed to land preservation, and narrated a conservation film that season, *The Coming of the Roads*.

Steve's successful work with youngsters at the Boys Republic at Chino led to his being appointed a board member of the Advisory Council of the Youth Studies Center at the University of Southern California. McQueen took special pride in the fact that he was the only actor thus honored, but admitted that he felt "kinda jumpy" about having to attend his first board meeting. "I'd never set foot on a college campus," he said. "But here I was, a mug with a ninth-grade education, rappin' with all these tweedy professor types. It was a little spooky, but they seemed to dig me."

The world premiere of *The Sand Pebbles* was scheduled for December 1966 in New York. Before leaving on the trip East, the McQueens hosted a lavish catered party in their Brentwood home. Steve's superstar pals James Garner and Paul Newman knocked elbows with Bud Ekins and other racing buddies. The party was a success, and Steve enjoyed himself, though he drank very little.

"Gotta keep my head straight," he recalled telling Newman. "I'm due early to finish readin' a new batch of scripts they just laid on me. Guess how many shitty scripts I've looked at in the last three months?"

"You tell me."

"One hundred and two! These scripts—they just keep comin' . . . more every day."

Newman mock-punched McQueen's shoulder. "Hey, pal, the time to worry is when they *stop* coming!"

The Sand Pebbles was a major hit, and solidified McQueen's superstar status. He received the *Photoplay* Gold Medal Award that year, and was cited by the Foreign Press Association as "World Film Favorite." And Japan's theater owners declared him to be "the most popular foreign star" for the second year running.

But Steve's most important honor was his Academy Award nomination as Best Actor of 1966. His distinguished rivals for the Oscar that year were Paul Scofield (*A Man for All Seasons*), Richard Burton (*Who's Afraid of Virginia Woolf?*), Michael Caine (*Alfie*), and Alan Arkin (*The Russians Are Coming, The Russians Are Coming!*).

Scofield won, but McQueen's nomination proved his worth as a serious actor. *Los Angeles Times* critic Charles Champlin paid McQueen high praise for his work in *Pebbles*.

> He lost to Paul Scofield, whose portrayal of Sir Thomas More was undeniably majestic. But Scofield had in a sense rehearsed the role and explored the character in hundreds of stage performances. McQueen, amid the strains of a difficult location, had created Jake Holman as if by bolts of lightning in small, vivid pieces.

"I bitched a lot about making *Pebbles*," Steve told reporters. "But I'll be lucky if I ever find another role that good." Then he grinned. "Neile claims I wouldn't have been fit to live with if I'd carted home that gold Oscar. She's glad I lost!"

Having attended university meetings with the Youth Council, McQueen was now a bit more comfortable in a college environment. Therefore, in January of 1967, he accepted an invitation from critic/teacher Arthur Knight to address a USC cinema class. McQueen agreed to take along journalist Frank Conroy, who was preparing a major profile of him for *Esquire*. Earlier that day, Conroy had been shooting pool with the actor's children in their Brentwood home and was impressed with their skills. At six, Chad was already a veteran—and Terri was equally adept.

"At least they learned at home," McQueen told him with a grin. "Me, I learned to handle a stick in a seedy Indianapolis poolhall, playin' when I should have been in school."

Steve was obviously proud of his two offspring. "They're still too small to handle a regular stick, so I had some special ones made up for 'em. Chad likes to make trick shots with the cue behind his back, and Terri's no slouch either. Then again, I wouldn't rank 'em with Minnesota Fats!"

During the USC session, held at a theater on the Fox lot, McQueen was at ease with the eager students. As Conroy observed: "On stage, he created an image for that audience, the sense of contained power, of a *presence*. . . . He got right into the groove, charming them, making them laugh, experiencing what he termed 'good vibes' from those kids."

Juggling questions from the students, Steve was asked how he picked one property over another from a sea of scripts. "I look for characters and situations that feel right to me," he told them. "Even then, when I've got something that seems to fit, it's a hell of a lot of work. Every script is an enemy to conquer. I put a chunk of myself into each role."

The film that Steve finally chose to follow *The Sand Pebbles* was a fast-paced crime caper, portraying what he called "a rich dude who decides to goose the establishment." The title was *The Thomas Crown Affair,* and locations were set for Boston and Cape Cod.

That same month the *Saturday Evening Post* printed a feature profile on McQueen, "A Loser Makes It Big." The writer, Trevor Armbrister, described Steve as

> a shrewd nonconformist who knows exactly what he wants and doesn't mind going outside established channels to get it. He is impatient, impulsive and not at all humble. He is also honest and without guile . . . and fiercely loyal to his friends.

Armbrister quoted his subject: "I've played a lot of losers, but now I'm through with that. It took me a long time to realize that I wasn't a loser myself."

In March 1967 Steve McQueen pressed his footprints into wet concrete in the forecourt of Grauman's Chinese Theater in Hollywood, becoming the 153rd star to do so. He appreciated the unique honor but admitted that "all the hoopla bugged me. I mean, you can't say no to something like this, but the whole scene is like a circus act with you as the performing elephant."

When the time came to leave for location on *Thomas Crown,* Steve was once again eager to escape the pressures of Hollywood. "Man, I couldn't wait to finally shake loose and head for Boston," he said. "By the time I got Neile and the kids all packed and on the way I was half out of my tree. I mean, when I got that call for location I just *ran!*"

In *The Thomas Crown Affair* McQueen portrayed a self-made Boston millionaire, bored by his own success, who enlivens his jaded life by planning the "perfect" robbery. Working unseen, as the head of a hand-picked group of professionals, he masterminds a $2.5 million bank heist—and soon finds himself in a battle of wits with a brilliant female insurance investigator (played by Faye Dunaway, fresh from her starring role in *Bonnie and Clyde*). She is determined to tie him into the crime. Their clash of wills and eventual romantic entanglement sparked the plot of this sardonic antiestablishment film.

When McQueen signed to star as the dapper, polo-playing aristocrat, there were those who doubted his ability to be convincing as a suave intellectual. "I was advised not to do it," said Steve.

> They told me it would be like trying to make a silk purse out of a sow's ear. But I said, wait a minute, this dude wants to show he can beat the establishment at its own game. He's essentially a rebel, like me. Sure, a high-society rebel, but he's *my* kind of cat. It was just his outer fur that was different—so I got me some fur.

McQueen was measured for custom tuxedos and $400 suits. He replaced his scuffed loafers with handcrafted Italian shoes. A selection of contoured silk shirts and Boston ties completed the "outer fur." No one was more pleased with the dapper new McQueen than his wife. ("Neile said I looked like a gentleman for the first time in my life.")

"Tommy Crown wears a Phi Beta Kappa key across his vest," said Steve. "I needed one. I finally borrowed our set designer's key. Now all I had to do was climb behind the wheel of Crown's big Rolls and I was home."

In truth, it wasn't quite that simple. First, Steve had to learn to play polo. "For me, polo was kinda stepping out of my bag—and it took me three full weeks to hack it," he said. "I'd get up extra early, drive out to the polo field, and spend a couple of hours there each morning before shooting started.

Then, after we wrapped the last scene of the day, I'd go back and practice till dark."

Although he'd done a good deal of riding in the *Wanted* TV series and in the westerns he'd made, McQueen had never sat an English saddle. "I was used to a western saddle," he admitted.

> The first time the horse stopped quick I was right up on his neck hanging onto his ears. He was a lot smarter than I was. He knew the game and I didn't. He'd go left— and I'd go right, flat on my butt. A polo pony is guided by knee pressure, leaving your arms free to swing the mallet. I finally got the hang of it and began having fun batting down that field. But lemme tellya—I got blisters over my blisters learning to stick in that saddle.

The polo sequences were shot at the elite Myopia Hunt Club near Hamilton, Massachusetts, and Steve enjoyed riding against what he called "social heavies, with their blueblood running back three hundred years."

McQueen also had to learn to fly a glider. The script called for skydiving, but McQueen and director Norman Jewison substituted gliding since it seemed more in keeping with Crown's character. Sky gliding, for a Boston blueblood, was a more socially acceptable pastime.

"With no motor in those things you pretty well go where the wind takes you," Steve said. "Pinpoint landings are tricky. Our crew had all the camera equipment set up in this field I was supposed to land in. Well, some wind grabbed me and I missed the field entirely, ending up in a potato patch. Nothing broken. Only my pride was damaged."

Several action scenes involved a souped-up, high-speed dune buggy Steve had helped design. When this machine was shipped to the sand dunes at Cape Cod for location shots, McQueen was somewhat dubious about its potential.

> We'd used a shortened VW [Volkswagen] chassis and a fiberglass body shell into which we'd stuffed a hairy Corvair turbo-charged 180-hp job with four two-barrel down-draft carbs. It *looked* great, and it was all right once you got it locked into the lip of a 190-foot sand

bowl. You could drift the lip at eighty, smooth as anything, just kind of piddling the wheel to keep her in line. Or you could get the front end straight up in the air and just squirt along on the rear wheels for a while. But with all the torque you felt like someone was gripping the skin of your face and pulling it back around your ears! And no roll bar. If you turned over you just flopped out into the sand and bounced around a little.

McQueen claimed that his costar Faye Dunaway deserved a Purple Heart for riding with him in the buggy.

We had these two fat Indy-type tires on the back, which made the thing understeer something fierce. We did one big jump for the camera right off the edge of a high dune and it was wild—with the rear wheels clappin' each other in the air. I looked over and Faye was all bug-eyed; the back of the floorboard was scratched raw from her heels diggin' in.

For one filmed sequence near the ocean, Jewison wanted Steve to gun the orange dune buggy straight for the water and then, at the last second, spin the machine at the edge of the surf. "It'll make a great shot," Jewison said.

With Faye braced beside him, McQueen roared over the packed sand and aimed for the ocean, engine howling. So far, so good. Now it was time to spin the buggy. "I wrestled with the wheel and nothing happened," recalled McQueen.

The thing just *wouldn't* turn. Then the throttle jammed— and we were heading right for the ocean at a terrific rate of speed. Well, on film, all you could see was this orange bug disappearing into the water. Faye came out of it soaked and smiling. Some trooper! They had to take the whole engine apart to get the salt water out.

Faye Dunaway was impressed with McQueen's willingness to do things other stars wouldn't dare try. "He's a risk taker," she stated. "And that cutting edge of his comes across on film."

In one of their many scenes together Steve and Faye played a brilliant, classically correct chess game. (Move by move, it was based on an actual game played by experts Zeissl and Walthoffen in Vienna in 1899.) The sequence was highly erotic as Jewison staged it, a "love game," with chess as a sexual battleground. In the words of one critic, "McQueen and Dunaway steamed up the screen."

Another talked-about scene involved complex use of the camera during a kiss between the two stars.

"I was supposed to kind of *nibble* on Faye," McQueen explained. "Then she nibbled back—with the camera under us and over us and circling us, creating this sexy mood. That kiss took *eight hours* to shoot, with a break for lunch. Our lips were sore for a week."

There were family problems to solve while Steve was making *Crown*. The McQueens had rented a house for the summer in an upper-middle-class suburb of Boston, with the idea that a "real home" would give their two children a sense of proportion and that they would feel less uprooted. "However," reported Neile,

> it didn't work out too well. Terri made friends with some children old enough to know who Steve was, and our quiet was suddenly shattered. All of the neighorhood kids began to descend on Steve for autographs whenever he came home. This caused a real hubbub, and for the first time our children began to think of their father as someone special. And that made *them* start to feel and act special, which was wrong. We didn't want them to lose their sense of emotional balance. It's so easy to spoil a Hollywood child. That summer in Boston frightened me; it showed me how difficult it is to raise children normally when their father is a public idol.

As Tommy Crown, Steve was every inch the gentleman. Not since *Love with the Proper Stranger* had McQueen been presented so romantically onscreen; he was suave and elegant, with a devil's glint in his eye, and women flocked to see him. The "Belles of Memphis," a group of Southern college women, chose McQueen as "the sexiest man in America," and he was now a romantic idol to millions of females around the world. His image as a national sex symbol was greatly intensified by this sleekly produced film.

Jake Holman, the sweaty, crewcut sailor from *The Sand Pebbles*, had given way to Thomas Crown, the dapper Boston blueblood. It was a remarkable transformation, and few actors in Hollywood could have pulled it off with such polished ease.

The Thomas Crown Affair was proof that Steve McQueen's range as an actor far exceeded his own modest estimate.

10. . .

Motorized Madness

In talking to industry people about McQueen, I often heard him described as a "loner," a man without close friends, to whom only his wife and children really mattered. These opinions were based on the fact that he had few friends within the film industry itself and thus seemed far more reclusive than he actually was.

Steve's business partner, Bob Relyea, said that McQueen "had the greatest need to be liked of any guy I've ever known...but it was a one-way street. He wanted people to like him, but he figured that he didn't need to like *them*."

Steve and I talked about friends and friendship one afternoon at a garage in North Hollywood, and McQueen nodded when I brought up his image as a loner.

"Yeah, that's how a lotta people see me. Ol' Steve the hermit." He grinned. "And I can't deny I like to keep away from that whole phony Beverly

Hills crowd and those hippy-dippy, finger-poppin' parties.... I just don't dig their scene. It's not for me. They go for how much bread you make, how hot your last picture was, how you rate with the studios... all that kind of crap. I have friends— the *right* kind, ones you can count on in the nitty-gritty. They work hard, and they don't compromise. Maybe they run a garage like this one, or race bikes, or own a little shop of some kind. One of my pals, Elmer Valentine, owns the Whisky a Go Go on the Sunset Strip. We're starting our own Spanish restaurant there.... The point is, these people are genuine and they dig you for what you are as a human being. Sure, some of my friends work inside the industry, like Bob Relyea and Jack Reddish, who are with me at Solar— and old Johnny Sturges—but the people I'm tight with are all the people I can *trust*. They keep my head straight. When I act like an ass, they call me one! They really *nail* me."

He paused, thinking, then smiled.

"Something funny?"

"I was just remembering how some bike pals of mine got on me about a photo layout I did. For a women's magazine. They'd posed me next to these skinny models, an' had me wearin' a lot of fashion stuff, like neck chains and gold wrist bands.... When my buddies saw the magazine they laughed like monkeys: 'Hey, McQueen, we think you're just *darling* in those bracelets!' Man, they sure got on my case about that layout. It was phony, and they knew it, and I knew it, and they weren't *about* to let me get away with that kind of stuff."

He paused again, growing serious. "Guys like that, when it gets down to the short stroke, they'll give blood, they'll put their *life* on the line for you... same as you will for them. You don't find many like that... but when you *do*, you hang tight with 'em because you know you've got the real thing."

Following his role as a millionaire criminal in *The Thomas Crown Affair,* McQueen switched to the opposite side of the law for *Bullitt*—from crook to cop. He played a tough, rebellious San Francisco police detective, Lieutenant Frank Bullitt, investigating the death of a Mafia mobster.

This new project, destined to become one of McQueen's biggest hits, was financed by Warner Brothers but was entirely the responsibility of Solar Productions. In prior film deals, on pictures such as *Soldier in the Rain, Nevada Smith,* and *The Sand Pebbles,* McQueen's production company had functioned in the background. With *Bullitt,* Solar moved up front to take full control of production.

Steve brought in Robert Relyea as executive producer, Jack Reddish as production manager, and saw to it that Britisher Peter Yates was hired as director.

"I liked what Yates did with a car chase in *Robbery* which he directed in England," said Steve. "We'd written a pretty hairy car chase into *Bullitt* and I figured him for the guy to handle it. So we brought Yates over for his first American film."

Regally beautiful Jacqueline Bisset was signed as Frank Bullitt's love interest (a part more decorative than substantial), and Steve hired one of his old buddies from *The Magnificent Seven,* Robert Vaughn, as the detective's corrupt political enemy. Given a strong, gutsy role, Vaughn delivered what many critics consider the best performance of his career.

The screen story was loosely based on a Robert Pike novel, *Mute Witness,* but McQueen was never satisfied with the script and made many alterations throughout the filming. The resulting screen version was complex to the point of outright confusion, but Yates and McQueen kept the action moving so swiftly that audiences didn't seem to care if the final story made sense. As one bemused critic summed it up:

> Halfway into the picture, I was totally mystified as to who had done what to whom, and why. Mafia men were appearing and disappearing so fast that Frank Bullitt himself obviously didn't know what the hell was going on. But by the time our flint-eyed, indestructible hero was bouncing his car over the hills in hot pursuit of some bad guys, and 707s were nearly running over him on

airport runways, I gave up on the logic of it all and just sat there enjoying the film on a purely visceral level. In this case, the word "thriller" is not studio hyperbole, it is an understatement. *Bullitt* is a film to *experience*, not to analyze.

McQueen was dubious about accepting this detective's role.

I'd never expected to play a cop. As a kid, running the streets, I'd been hassled a lot by the police and I'd always figured that they were on one side of the fence with me on the other. I never felt easy around cops. But here in 'Frisco, I saw the other side of police work, and it was a real eye-opener.

In preparation for his role, Steve rode in a squad car with two San Francisco detectives and found them to be "straight, honest guys, with a mean job to do. They really won my respect."

A major action sequence was filmed on a cold, windy night at the city airport. Bullitt has tracked his man there and sprints after him across the dark runway, directly into the takeoff path of a giant 707. He barely escapes death by dropping flat to the rough tarmac just under the wing of the moving jetliner as it blasts over him.

Yates wanted to use a stunt man for this dangerous run, but McQueen refused.

"I'm not going to let you do this one, Steve!"

"Sure you are," snapped McQueen. "Hell, Pete, it's no worse than that train stunt I did in *Cincinnati Kid*. Just a matter of timing, of knowing when to get my butt down. Believe me, I can do it."

The director sighed, "Well . . . we shall find out, won't we?" And he raised a hand to the pilot of the waiting 707.

A moment of suspense—then the "roll 'em" order was given and the big plane began to move. As it gathered speed, Steve sprinted directly toward it from the opposite side of the runway. The fanjet engines sent out a deafening blast of sound as McQueen ducked expertly under the moving wing, slamming himself to the runway, belly-down, just in time to escape the 240-degree surge of heat from the jet pods.

"The vibration tweaked my neck a little," he said afterward. "When you hit the deck you've got to open your mouth and hold your ears. It blew me around some but I'm okay." He turned to the director. "How'd it look, Pete? Was it realistic?" A shaken Yates assured him that it looked *very* realistic.

Alarmed by McQueen's risk-taking, Warner executives threatened to cancel the car chase entirely, unless it could be staged "under properly controlled conditions" on the Warner lot. Yates and McQueen flatly rejected the idea; they felt that authenticity was at stake. Skidding around a phony studio street and bouncing off rubber-padded curbs just wouldn't get the job done.

"We wanted a gut-buster. Something to make an audience yell," said McQueen. "That meant we had to do it on location right in the city. You can't *fake* those steep San Francisco hills. I told Warners that we'd kill the whole goddamn picture if they forced us to fake the car chase."

The studio capitulated, but they made it clear that the insurance risk was enormous, and that a suit would be leveled against Solar if any deaths or serious injuries resulted.

"One of the advantages of being your own producer," declared McQueen, "is that you can get things done the *right* way. Film audiences are tougher to fool these days. They want reality, the genuine stuff. And you can't get that by shooting on some back lot." Steve made detailed preparations:

> I huddled with chassis designer Max Balchowsky and we worked out some modifications for the two cars involved in the action: a new 390 GT Mustang, which we figured a cop like Bullitt could afford to own, and a 440 Magnum Dodge Charger for the bad guys to drive.

Balchowsky was to prepare these cars for the incredible beating they'd take as they were banged down, up, and around San Francisco's steep hills. Suspension systems were heavily beefed. On the Mustang, Koni shock absorbers and heavy-duty coil springs were used. The Charger's torsion bars were shortened and NASCAR springs added on the rear, as well as special Bonneville shocks. Both cars were fitted with disc brakes and wrap-around interior roll bars.

"I wanted Bill Hickman in the Dodge," said McQueen.

"Bill's an old stunt pro and I knew we could depend on him—so he drove the Dodge Charger in our film, playing the baddie, while I chased him, as Bullitt, in the Mustang."

San Francisco officials took a dim view of the proposed auto chase through the streets of their city. "We got tossed out of the mayor's office the first time we tried to get his okay," admitted Steve. "They figured we were out to make the cops look bad."

On a second visit, McQueen carefully explained that the film was not, in any manner, antipolice; the car chase would be brief and simply handled.

"So they agreed to block off some streets for us, but they didn't realize just *what* we would be doing with those cars! Even we didn't know how wild it was gonna get!"

Locations included several of the steepest hills within the city and incorporated a very fast waterfront run and a full-throttle chase along a freeway, climaxed by a spectacular spin-out and explosive crash.

"I had this explosion written into the end of the chase," said McQueen. "The Dodge shoots off the highway right into this filling station and *blam!* the whole thing blows sky-high!"

Several top stunt actors were employed to ensure realism, but since McQueen was boss, he planned to do all of his own stunt driving. "Neile would have raised hell if she'd known what I was up to," McQueen admitted. "I just didn't tell her about this chase stuff. She was down in Los Angeles with the kids, and I figured what she didn't know wouldn't upset her."

Although only two cars were seen, there were actually *four* cars in *Bullitt*, since a back-up model was provided for each machine. These "doubles" were also competition-prepared. If one car was vitally damaged, the back-up model could fill in for the cameras until the original was repaired. (As it turned out, these doubles were *very* necessary.)

Preparations for the chase moved into their final phase on the morning Steve received a special delivery letter from Warner Brothers' Ken Hyman. It specified that until the film's completion McQueen was forbidden to ride his motorcycle to and from the set. The studio would provide safe transportation. An agreement form was enclosed for his signature.

"Instead of signing the form I scrawled something obscene across it and mailed it back," Steve related. "Nobody, at this point, had the legal right to keep me off my bike. Actually, when you think about it, the whole thing was incredibly stupid." He referred to the irony of being asked not to ride a cycle to a location where he was to risk his neck flinging a race-prepared Mustang through city streets at speeds in excess of 100 mph.

Practice runs were not possible, and no one in the company knew quite what to expect in the way of problems during that first morning in downtown San Francisco. The side streets had been roped off by police, equipped with walkie-talkies, and several stunt drivers had lined up ahead of the normal street traffic, keeping a four-way intersection clear for the slam-bang run.

Veteran camera operator Bill Fraker would film most of the hazardous action from a special flat-bed camera car, a V-8 Chevy. Cameras were mounted on the nose of Steve's car to capture the stomach-wrenching, heart-in-the-mouth moments when the black Mustang would soar over the cliff-steep brow of a hill, bottom with a rending metallic crunch, then roar straight down in tire-smoking pursuit of Hickman's fleeing Dodge.

"Okay, roll 'em!" shouted Yates—and with a guttural roar of exhaust Hickman cannoned down the hill in the Dodge, McQueen hard after him in the Mustang. Trailing them both, driven with equal vigor, was the V-8 Chevy, Fraker grinding away with his camera.

A reporter described the scene:

> Suddenly, here's the Charger, the Mustang and the Chevy, all careening through the intersection at top speed, making a tremendous racket, burning rubber and screaming away up the next hill and out of sight. Pedestrians were left open-mouthed, in a state of shock!

Usually a single run at a location was the rule, since the thundering parade of machinery drew crowds, making subsequent runs extremely risky. "Sometimes we'd go twice," said Steve,

> but most of the time we'd have to grab our footage on the first shot. We couldn't keep an eye on everybody, couldn't hold 'em all out of range. Also, the realism was

spoiled if there were too many people around. It had to look ordinary, with the normal number of pedestrians on the streets.

Stopping the cars after such desperate sprints was a problem in itself, as McQueen related. "I'd panic brake from eighty or ninety and the back end would start chattering, and those Firestone F-100 radials would be jumpin' and smokin'. It took a while to get things under control."

McQueen found that even his extensive track experience had not prepared him for this unique style of driving.

There was this one scene where I was supposed to swing fast around a narrow side street and clip a parked car, then speed away. But when I reached the corner I overcooked it completely and smashed right *into* the parked car, just wrote it off entirely and bounced into another one next to it. We got a bit more realism than we'd bargained for.

Bill Hickman also had his problems. On a fast run, halfway down the hill, the Dodge Charger's brake pedal suddenly snapped dead to the floor. Hickman threw the car into a tire-shrieking broadside, barely making the corner at the bottom of the hill and narrowly missing the assembled police and production crew. "One of our cameras got wiped out when Bill slid into it," said McQueen, "and we left that piece of footage in the final print. The Dodge comes boiling round, slides right toward the screen and everything suddenly goes red. That was our camera blowing up!"

Eight cameras recorded the action. Two were mounted inside the cars, both 35-mm units, using 200-ft. magazines and painted black so they could not be detected.

The punishment each car suffered went far beyond what even McQueen had envisioned as the dead-flat intersections at the bottom of each hill took their toll. "I'd hit the intersection," Steve recalled, "and I'd hear this loud 'thwack bang' noise inside the car. I'd pull over, get out, and sure enough the oil sump would be cracked wide open with all the oil gone. We'd clean up the street, bolt on another sump, pour in fresh oil and take off again."

Both cars had to be checked after each run, since a broken spindle or a loose wheel could be fatal. And each night the crew would gather around a blackboard with a stack of city maps to plot the following day's action. Then, early the next morning, McQueen would receive his wake-up call at the hotel and be told where the crew wanted him to appear for shooting. "One morning I didn't get my call and overslept," said McQueen.

> When I woke up I didn't know what the hell was happening. I phoned around, found out where the crew was shooting and rode my bike over there—only to see ol' Bud Ekins coming down the hill in *my* Mustang, wearing *my* jacket and sunglasses. I rushed over to Pete Yates and Bob Relyea and began yelling bloody murder. They told me, very gently, to shut up and sit down because I wasn't *about* to do any more hill jumps for these final runs. Which is when I found out the full story.

A family friend of the McQueens had innocently described Steve's daredevil driving to Neile back in Los Angeles. She immediately phoned Relyea, begging him to keep her car-happy husband out of the Mustang for the final steep Chestnut Street hill jumps. Relyea had agreed and called in Bud Ekins to substitute for Steve. Informed of Neile's worried state of mind, McQueen backed down and allowed his old bike buddy to complete the dangerous hill sequences.

Ekins described the action: "I'd hit the intersection at sixty, bottom, then take off for a thirty-foot jump. The landing was critical because I knew that if a wheel dug in and the car started flipping it would have barrel-rolled all the way to the bottom."

By the completion of the hill jumps, both cars needed extensive repairs. On the Mustang, the door handles came adrift and both front shocks were broken, as was the steering armature on the right side. As Ekins got out of the car after the final shot, the entire door fell off. "It was like one of those old Keystone Kop comedies," Steve said. "Pieces just kept falling off the cars, and we'd kind of stick 'em back on for the next shot."

Neile did not know about the waterfront and high-speed freeway segments. No promises had been made to her about keeping Steve out of this action. Thus, Ekins went back to his cycles and McQueen again took over the Mustang.

"These highway runs were just as wild as the hill stuff," said Steve. "Here was Bill Fraker hangin' out of that stripped-down Chevy, sittin' on a chair with his camera stuck out there at 114 miles per hour right down the city street about six feet away from me while I drove flat out with cement standards whippin' past."

Local police had blocked off this section of freeway, and all of the "traffic" in these scenes consisted of company vehicles handled by stunt drivers. The action called for Hickman to graze the side of a truck, bounce into a guard rail, and then engage McQueen in a savage car-bashing contest—during which the two machines, roaring along side by side at over 100 mph, would bang into one another, each trying to force the other off the road.

Peter Yates was responsible for much footage; he rode in the rear seat of the Mustang, using a hand-held camera.

McQueen admired his director's nerve. "Here I was, really belting the Mustang along, but ole Pete was back there yellin' for more speed. Or for me to clout Bill's car harder!"

During this chase sequence, the story called for a frightened motorcycle rider to panic as he sees the two cars bearing down on him; he slides out of control and takes a long skidding fall directly in the Mustang's path. "Bud Ekins was the rider," related Steve.

> When he told us he was planning this stunt I didn't want him to do it. "You're liable to get kissed off and your wife'll never forgive me." But he was stubborn, convinced he could do it okay, so we let him go ahead. Man, I'll tell you, I never saw anything as scary as having him throw that BSA down in front of us. When he unloaded, he must have slid at least seventy-five feet along the blacktop.

Blowing up the gas station was to be the final, fiery climax of the chase. Dummy service pumps were constructed for the Dodge to hit, and nitroglycerine charges were carefully rigged. McQueen's Mustang would appear to force the Dodge into the station, and at the moment of impact an explosives expert would trigger the charges, as car and station erupted into gouts of flame. The timing had to be exact, because once the station blew, retakes were impossible.

"We had Carey Loftin dressed in my jacket driving the Mustang for this sequence," said Steve.

> Loftin's a real veteran. There's almost nothing he can't do. Anyhow, we had him come down the highway, side-towing the Charger. The two cars *looked* as if they were still racing. Then he had to work a quick-release gimmick at just the right second, sending the Dodge across the road into the gas pumps. At which point the nitro blows and we've got our scene.

Things did not go exactly as planned. The Dodge took longer to cross the highway than expected and missed the pumps, smashing directly into the station. But the special effects expert triggered the nitro, and the station blew on schedule. "If you watch the film real close," said McQueen, "you can see the Dodge overshoot the pumps. But it all came out fine."

"That wrapped up our San Francisco car chase," related Peter Yates. "It took us three weeks to get just *twelve minutes* of edited footage on the screen. But it was well worth the trouble and risk. We all realized we'd pulled off something really special."

As a gesture of gratitude, McQueen screened a rough print of *Bullitt* for the chief of police and other San Francisco officials, and made a solid impression on several city detectives after the screening when he demonstrated his skill in a specialized form of Chinese hand combat. (Watching him, one detective declared: "This guy is really *sudden.*")

Because of the film's mounting costs, Warner-7 Arts terminated their agreement with McQueen. By May, costs had climbed past $5 million, and the studio called off its deal on all future Solar productions; McQueen would have to find another parent financing company. "We didn't worry about that," said Steve. "We all knew we had a hit in *Bullitt*. Nobody closely connected with the film ever doubted it would make big money."

Even Neile was pleased, despite her misgivings about Steve's stunt work and high-speed driving. For one thing, as she said, "It was our first 'million-dollar movie.' Steve's salary was twenty percent of the budget, and *Bullitt* cost five million."

Queried by a reporter regarding her husband's future plans, Neile smiled. "It's simple. Steve wants to build an empire."

Bullitt was Steve McQueen's fifth box-office hit in a row, and, at this stage of his life, empire-building seemed not only possible, but probable.

11...

Mississippi Rascal

We talked about Chino, of how it felt to be there and why he kept going back—what compelled him to return.

"You know, I can still feel the *heat* in that laundry...after all these years!" Steve ran the fingers of his right hand slowly over his forehead. "The sweat would almost blind me...and the steam was *murder* in there." He looked up at me with a tight grin. "Every four months I go back. I shoot pool with those guys. I rap with 'em. I eat ice cream with 'em.... Why? Because I owe the place. And you pay your debts. They tell me that I do a lot of good there. And maybe I do. But, lemme tell ya..." He leaned forward, pointing a finger at me. "If I thought, by going back all these times, if I thought I'd helped just *one* kid who was headed the way I was headed—helped him get straight with the world...that would make all the trips okay. Just *one* kid."

I told him that he had undoubtedly helped *many* boys by his visits.

"Yeah...well..." And he shrugged, lighting a cigarette. "You got to give back, you can't just *take*. And at Chino I'm givin' back a little is all. Like with the Indians at Four Corners. Same thing. I'm in a position to help, so I *help*."

His expression darkened; he frowned, eyes growing hard. He turned the cigarette nervously in his fingers.

"Something bothering you?"

"What bothers me is how writers make out that it's all some kind of publicity gig. That I'm there to get my name in the papers. They ask me about Chino, and I tell 'em and they do a number on me. About how I'm *using* the school to promote myself! That's hard to take. I feel like bending some noses when I read stuff like that. I mean, I really get pissed!"

"No problem getting your name in the papers," I said. "You could find easier ways."

"Sure! *Sure* I could—but they don't believe that. They don't want to believe I go back because I can maybe do some good for some poor fucked-up teenage kid."

"You shouldn't let it bother you."

"Lots of things bother me that shouldn't," he said, stubbing out the cigarette. "C'mon, let's go grab some chow. When I get mad I get hungry."

And, in Steve's phrase, we "split out."

Shortly after completing *Bullitt*, McQueen agreed to an interview with *Coronet* magazine writer Katie O'Sullavan at his Brentwood home. She reported:

The McQueen spread is overwhelmingly impressive, from the plaza-like courtyard with its clusters of multicolored geraniums in earthen pots; across the highly polished Spanish tile flooring inside; to the exquisitely molded wrought-iron staircase railing, the magnificent collection of English, Italian, and Spanish antiques, the beautiful paintings on the walls.

She quoted McQueen on one of these.

That painting over there, of the small Mexican girl, that's by Montoya. Neile bought it. She knows very little about art except what she likes, and I know even less. But, that one, that's our favorite.

Living up here, it's like being out in the country, yet we're only minutes from town. I like trees, and we've got all kinds of pines—Jack, Monterey, and Chinese pines—and there's wild life, too—deer, fox, possum. Of course, the kids are always coming home with stray cats and dogs. We've got room for 'em all.

McQueen's final remark echoed a complaint of Neile's regarding his compulsion to help down-on-their-luck strangers: "He just bumps into somebody, finds out they have some kind of problem, and feels *compelled* to try and settle it for them. Steve is a great problem-solver, but I think he carries it to extremes."

The slam-bang street action in *Bullitt* had fired McQueen's desire to resume automotive competition. The event he chose for his return to racing was the Stardust 7-11, a brutal off-road marathon scheduled for a start in Las Vegas, Nevada, in June 1968. "I've lined me up a sweet machine for this one," Steve told the press. "Called the 'Baja Boot.' Chevy powered. Four hundred and fifty horses under the bonnet. Space frame construction. Four-wheel drive. Independent suspension. And *smooth!* I can notch close to a hundred over a sand wash and you better believe that's moving." Bud Ekins had agreed to accompany Steve in the Boot as rider-navigator.

The hazards in the 7-11 were severe enough to paralyze the ordinary motorist, yet no less than 137 entries were there that June to tackle the dusty Amargosa Desert. Sponsored by the National Off-Road Racing Association, the event comprised a sprawling 320-mile loop, stretching down through Nevada along the California border, through hills and washes and dry lakes back to Las Vegas. Competitors were required to run two complete loops to win. The starting point was the Stardust Raceway outside Las Vegas.

When Steve and Bud Ekins rolled the Boot up to the line for their 12:06 start the race was already under way for the smaller vehicles, the first of these having been flagged off at 11 A.M. Neile was there at the line with Bud's wife, Betty Ekins.

As Steve buckled himself into his shoulder harness Neile smiled at him, but there was obvious worry behind the smile. He recalled her warning: "Try not to drive *too* fast!"

"Hey, willya listen to the lady!" Steve snorted. "This is a *race*, remember? Driving fast is what it's all about."

As the flag snapped down, the Boot roared forward with a plume of smoke from its big tires, heading for the first checkpoint.

To reach "Checkpoint Charlie," near Ash Meadows, about 100 miles from Las Vegas, Steve had to rip over roadless washboard desert, run across the buttes to stateline, push on up along the California border over hills strewn with sharp, tire-slashing deposits of lava, bump through boulder-choked washes, and forge two dry lakes filled with treacherous silt.

Arriving at the checkpoint over smooth Nevada highways, Neile and Betty waited through the long day for Steve and Bud to appear, but there was no sign of the red machine.

Disturbing reports reached the checkpoint: a bike rider had unloaded in the rough and broken his wrist; a Jeep was on fire; several machines had overturned, and many more were bogged down or had broken their metal bodies against the rocky terrain.

Had anyone seen the Boot?

"Yeah, I saw it," declared a Jeep driver, wiping his dust-caked face with a damp towel. "I know for certain it passed stateline 'cuz I saw ole Steve 'bout fifteen miles this side of the line goin' like hell's hammers."

Now the sun dropped behind the mountains and the desert darkness closed in. At 9 P.M. official word reached the checkpoint: Steve and Bud were stranded 32 miles out on a high rock dune. A wheel had sheared, but both drivers were safe.

McQueen recalled the incident: "We were really battin' along, feeling good about the car and our chances with it, when we see this big fat wheel rolling along beside us. It's *our* wheel! The axle had popped. Well, that did it. We just sat on our tails in the desert till help came."

In a television appearance that October, Steve was back on a cycle, doing "wheelies" for the Ed Sullivan show, then taking

Ed for a ride in a special McQueen-designed buggy.

The TV stint was strictly business. McQueen was financially involved with Solar Engineering, a firm he had organized to produce off-road vehicles, equipment, and cycle kits. The buggy on the Sullivan show was equipped by Solar, and Steve revealed that he was also marketing a new safety seat for off-road machines. "This started when a friend of mine flipped his buggy and messed up his neck," McQueen said.

> The seat hadn't supported him. I thought I could design a better one. So I got me a big hunk of clay, and some drawings made, and worked out this seat, then had a rotational mold cast from the clay model and laid a special covering over it. We call it the Baja Bucket and we've been selling it to racing guys. The Bucket has saved more than one life on a flip-over. I'm proud of the results.

As an actor, Steve felt it was time to do "something fresh." He didn't want to follow *Bullitt* with another action-crime thriller, "because that's what people *expect* me to do, and I like to toss 'em a few curves, keep the ball in the air, so to speak. You can get stale, doing the same stuff over and over. It was time for me to *stretch* a little."

Steve had decided to "stretch" by playing Boon Hogganbeck in the film version of William Faulkner's light-hearted novel *The Reivers*, to be filmed on location in the Deep South and directed by an old friend of the McQueens, Mark Rydell.

"After *Soldier in the Rain* I promised myself I'd never tackle another comic role," Steve said. "Yet here I was, hamming and grinning and strutting away down there in Mississippi. It seemed the right thing to do at the time, after *Crown* and *Bullitt*, but I ended up not liking it very damn much."

Indeed, director Rydell found Steve difficult to work with. "That was mainly because he felt uneasy about his role," Rydell said.

> Also, I had a real problem in the scenes with Steve and Rupert Crosse, who was playing his buddy. Doing comedy, McQueen claimed he had to be entirely instinctive—and, sure enough, after just one or two takes he wasn't funny anymore. After that he'd freeze and become

self-conscious. Crosse was just the opposite; he was never at his best until the tenth take! So I solved things by standing in for Steve through the first nine takes on a scene, then bringing him out for the tenth, when Crosse was all warmed up. Worked like a charm!

Cinema Center Corporation bankrolled the venture—even providing McQueen with an executive jet to use as he wished during production.

The period story featured McQueen and Crosse as two "reivers" (turn-of-the-century slang for rascals) who steal a fine new automobile—a 1905 Winton Flyer—for a wild ride from Mississippi into Memphis, Tennessee. Young Lucius (played by Mitch Vogel) goes with them, and the trip becomes a rite of maturity for the boy, as he is introduced to some of the more colorful facts of life by shiftless, fun-loving Boon.

In Memphis, they trade the stolen Winton for a race horse who gallops fast *only* if he is fed sardines. They run this quirky beast at a local horse track and the sequence is a comic highlight in a nostalgic and lighthearted film.

The trip along Southern backroads was filmed in the country around Carrollton, Mississippi, an area that had changed little since the early 1900s.

"One of our big problems concerned the *real* star of the picture," said Steve. "Where, in 1968, do you find a 1905 Winton Flyer in perfect condition—especially one you can ram into mudholes, slam over ditches and drive flat out on rutted roads? The answer is, you don't find a car like that, you *build* it."

McQueen went to the shop of his friend Von Dutch, a specialist in exotic automotive creations. "He provided our Winton," said Steve.

Made it all himself, from the frame up, out of old aluminum furnace sidings and God knows what else. When he showed it to us we all gasped. The thing was just *beautiful*—bright yellow, gleaming with polished brass— a perfect replica of a genuine 1905 Flyer, but with a modern power plant under the hood. We needed some kick on those Southern goat trails.

In the film, McQueen stalls the Winton in a mudhole and attempts to push it out. Always a stickler for realism, Steve was covered in mud, nose to toes, before the scene ended.

The wildly comic Memphis horse race was actually staged at the Walt Disney ranch back in California and provided an exciting climax to *The Reivers*.

Newspaper publicity ads featured a shot of McQueen in a straw cowboy hat, hair full and thick-waved, winking and grinning broadly, chewing on a cornstalk. This photo was accompanied by the words: "You'll LOVE him as Boon!"

Steve was less than delighted with what he called "this cornball ad campaign. I looked like a village idiot in that shot. But you can't control everything!"

It did not approach the phenomenal box-office success of *Bullitt*, but this carefully crafted little comedy was well received by the public, who responded to McQueen's deft, energetic performance. And this time he kept his promise: *The Reivers* was his last comic role.

Steve returned from Mississippi with several Mason jars of Southern moonshine whiskey. ("That stuff was liquid dynamite!") When he heard that a delegation of top Russian editors was touring the United States under State Department auspices, and had expressed a desire to meet American film stars, he invited them to his home, where he had assembled a group of Hollywood celebrities. Steve gleefully handed each Russian a Mason jar of the powerful moonshine and saluted them: "Bottoms up!"

He tipped up his own jar and took a long swig. The Russians, not wishing to offend their host, did likewise. Amid loud coughing and sputtering, the Russians, eyes watering, faces beet red, smiled weakly at McQueen and pronounced the moonshine "a superior American beverage."

That November, in an attempt to ease the marital tension created by his racing, Steve arranged a lavish surprise party for Neile at the Candy Store, a favorite Hollywood discotheque. The occasion was their twelfth wedding anniversary, and dozens of guests crowded into the club to help them celebrate.

During the evening, as they danced together, Neile told Steve that if their marriage was going to continue, he would have to go out more with her "to see other people instead of just your cycle pals." But racing was still the main point of conflict in their relationship, and Neile could not persuade him to abandon the sport.

Invited to London in June 1969 for a tribute by the Royal Academy of Dramatic Arts, Steve used the invitation as an excuse to attend the Le Mans 24-hour race in France with his Solar camera crew. They shot 30,000 feet of "workhorse footage" for a film he planned on the famous international event.

Losing *Day of the Champion* still bothered him and the race at Le Mans offered Steve a chance to realize an old dream. "For some while I'd had the idea of doing a kind of definitive treatment of automotive competition," he told the press. "To put it bluntly, I wanted to make the best damn racing movie ever!"

McQueen realized that obtaining the proper financial backing for such a venture was going to be difficult.

> Which is why I took my camera crew along that year. The footage we brought back would show the excitement, the drama. . . . Then, too, we wanted the officials at Le Mans to trust us. We wanted them to understand that we were pros who knew how to stay out of their way and who respected the sport and the race.

Steve admitted that he had not anticipated the actual tension and excitement of Le Mans until witnessing it. "The emotional buildup is fantastic. When the countdown starts, with the long line of cars poised for their run in front of those jammed grandstands . . . well, you can *feel* the vibes."

Steve closed the deal with CBS/Cinema Center Films to finance the production in conjunction with Solar. The film was scheduled to begin a year later (in June 1970), and *this* time Steve was determined that nothing would stop it; he would not repeat the frustrations of *Day of the Champion*.

But his friends were worried. "What's Neile gonna say when you take off for France to do a racing film?"

McQueen didn't have an answer. "I'll face that little problem when I come to it."

It would be more than a "little problem." It would be the final element that destroyed their marriage.

12. . .

Twisting
the Tiger's Tail

Respect was a word McQueen used often when we talked together. It was absolutely vital to him that he be respected within the industry.

"Actors have a bad handle," he'd say. "And I can dig that. I mean, most of 'em *are* just over-grown kids. They sit around waiting for a call from their agent or some producer. They don't have anything going for them, beyond the talent to act. What did Hitchcock say? That actors should be treated like cattle. That's a *mean* statement. Still, that was his experience. He didn't respect actors, really, he just *used* them."

McQueen was on his knees, in dirt-blackened coveralls, adjusting the innards of a racing cycle as he talked to me that afternoon. He held up a greasy hand. "See that? I get dirt under my nails because I don't just sit around waiting to act, I *do* things. When I raced in Germany, for the U.S. team, I earned *respect*—for something completely beyond acting. And when I produce my own films,

I earn respect for that, too. I'm not cattle. Nobody tells me where to jump. If a director doesn't respect me I won't work with him. If I can't be in on every phase of a film I won't sign up for it. But you have to go after those things, you can't just sit on your ass."

Didn't it have a lot to do with his childhood and young adulthood, when no one took him seriously?

He nodded, eyes intense on his work, vigorously twisting a small hand wrench to tighten a stubborn bolt. "Maybe that's a part of it, but *nobody* takes a young kid very seriously, right? You gotta grow up and become somebody for people to notice you. But getting them to *respect* you is a whole other bag. You gotta work for it, go for it."

"The brass ring?"

"Yeah, but that's the glitter end. You grab the ring and you get big bucks, and success, but I can think of a lot of dudes with money that I don't respect worth a damn."

He got up, tossed the wrench aside, kick-started the cycle's engine. The roar was deafening. Then, smiling, he cut power.

"That's some beast," I said.

"Sure is," he agreed, looking pleased. "This little gal can step out."

He wiped his hands on a towel. "My kids respect me. And that's important." He nodded, speaking softly, as if only to himself: "They respect their old man."

According to his longtime pal Bud Ekins, McQueen was a man driven to win. "Whether it was matching pennies or pitching rocks into the ocean or you name it, Steve was out there to win," Ekins recalled.

It really bugged him when he couldn't beat you, especially in bike racing. We were in a lot of motorcycle races together and he never managed to beat me. Then, about two years after I'd officially retired from racing, I got a phone call from Steve. Wanted me to meet him at Indian Dunes for "a little go-round." Turns out he'd been practicing out there every day, and he figured he was finally ready for me. We climbed on our bikes and had at it—and I was so rusty that Steve just plain beat the socks off me. Afterward, we had a beer together, and Steve was sitting there with this big ear-to-ear grin on his face. I realized that beating me on a bike was just something he *had* to do.

By late summer of 1969, Chad McQueen had demonstrated an obvious talent for cycle riding. The boy had his own dirt bike and he and his father often rode together into the desert around Palm Springs—with Steve proudly declaring, "He's damn good for an eight-year-old. Understands the dynamics of fast riding. Sure, he's been on his melon a couple of times, but he's a game kid and doesn't let a spill or two slow him down. Got a lotta *heart*."

It was Chad who talked his father into taking him to see the newly inaugurated off-road races that August at Ascot Park. The famous oval raceway in central Los Angeles had hosted the best in dirt track events for decades, but Jeeps and dune buggies had now joined the sprint cars and midget racers in what was being hailed as "the birth of a new sport."

Off-road racing had heretofore been conducted over stretches of desert, beach, or backcountry. No one had seriously considered staging it on a closed track until Ascot came into the picture. In many ways, however, the site was ideal. The Jeeps and buggies bumped over an intertwining series of dirt trails as well as a spectacular 25-foot leap from a raised dirt mound, plus two other 6-foot jumps during a single lap.

Steve was impressed with the action, and admitted: "It was as far out as anything I'd seen in racing." When a friend in the pit area offered to let Steve borrow his machine for a try at the course, McQueen gladly accepted. "I had myself a real bash.... It was nothing but great."

Steve figured that ended it. But he was wrong.

The following afternoon Steve got a call from a reporter. "I hear you're running at Ascot next week."

"Not me, man," said McQueen.

"Well, the word is out that you're running, and a lot of people are going to be there to see you go."

Steve pondered the situation.

"I'd never really competed on a dirt track, and I knew I could get bent way out of shape doin' those crazy jumps and all. But I thought, well, the people want to see me, so why not give it a shot."

McQueen readied a 400-horsepower Jeep he owned by changing the plugs, removing the air filter, and putting on dirt tires. "It handled real good in the dirt and was much faster than I figured. I did well enough that first night to want more. In fact, I began competing at Ascot on a fairly regular basis that summer."

A racing journalist who watched McQueen drive a night race described the action.

> The main event is in progress around the big dirt speedway with its seven turns and chassis-bending triple jumps. McQueen, doing 90 in his Chevy Jeep, is fighting it out among the leaders. A cut-down buggy is violently center-punched by a Jeepster and spins into the path of McQueen's hard-charging machine. Panic braking doesn't help; he is into the tangle with the mud-splattered machine ahead of him tumbling end for end, sparks shooting as steel meshes steel. The race is stopped. No one hurt, but several cars out. The event is restarted in a surge of high-torque engines. McQueen guns forward, makes the 25-foot jump, bounces, keeps charging, slides wide on a turn, is slapped by another Jeep, spins and stalls. He starts again in next-to-last position, turns on the steam, and roars up through the pack, passing the third-place runner, then the second-place machine...until he's banging along at full throttle right behind the leader. On the final lap, McQueen can't quite get around him, but takes a very impressive second overall at the flag. Top driving in anybody's league.

How did it feel out there?

"When you get air-mailed over that main jump," said Steve, "it's *weird*. On one stretch of roadway they've got six half-buried telephone poles for you to bounce over. They make your suspension stand up and yell 'ouch!'—but it's that main jump that spooks you."

McQueen's acting career was moving ahead almost as fast as his modified Jeep, and that September he received another major honor, flying to Washington to accept a trophy as 1969's Male Star of the Year from the National Association of Theater Owners, representing 10,000 film houses in the United States. This award reflected the runaway success of *Bullitt*. ("People are going back two and three times," Steve reported, "just to see our crazy race through the streets!")

McQueen maintained his abiding concern with "problem kids." He became very disturbed that fall by a news story reporting that two teenage boys had been sent to an adult prison. A Florida judge had sentenced Donald Douglas, 14, and Richard Copas, 15, to three years' confinement in an adult maximum-security prison. Their crime: breaking and entering with intent to commit a misdemeanor.

"Those kids don't belong in that lousy place!" McQueen told Neile.

He phoned officials in Florida to offer his help and was told there was nothing he could do, that the boys must remain in prison until an appeal could be heard. This could take several months.

Steve phoned Florida's State Health Secretary, James Bax, and declared that he was ready to make himself personally responsible for the two youngsters and that he would get them into the Boys Republic at Chino. Bax told him that the boys were already out of reach in the Lake Butler adult prison.

McQueen refused to quit. He contacted Florida Governor Claude Kirk. "You've *got* to get them out of there," he told Kirk. Steve's plea was effective. A week later he received news from Bax. The governor had broken precedent; he had gone to Lake Butler and removed the boys. "He's put them under his custody until they can be placed in our local juvenile rehabilitation home," said Bax. "Looks like you've won, Steve!"

McQueen was satisfied; he knew the teenagers would be treated fairly now; they would have the same chance that he had at Chino to make good in the adult world.

"Sometimes being a superstar pays off," he told Neile. "As John Doe I couldn't have done a damn thing about those two, no matter how hard I tried. But they *listened* to Steve McQueen."

"When Steve did things like that it brought us much closer," Neile said. "You couldn't help loving a man who cared so much about young people in trouble. But each time things seemed to be getting better between us he'd enter another race, and we were right back where we started—yelling at each other."

This time, in that fall of 1969, the yelling was over McQueen's entry in the Baja 1000, the roughest off-road event of them all. News helicopters were ready to follow the star drivers, and documentary teams would film the action.

They called Mexico's Baja peninsula "the devil's playground" with good reason. With the Pacific Ocean on the west and the Gulf of California on the east, this long finger of desolate land is a hell-spawned area of blazing heat, dust, and rock. The route started at Ensenada, approximately 70 miles south of the international border, and included eight checkpoints* before the finish at La Paz—a total of 832 miles, requiring more than 20 hours of day and night racing among souped-up trucks, cycles, buggies, Jeeps, and an odd assortment of "muscle" cars.

Steve's friendly rival James Garner was driving a race-prepared V-8 Olds Cutlass in the production sedan class—which added spice to the race. An old racing pal, Harold Daigh, was riding with McQueen in the Chevy-powered Boot. (Asked if he was nervous, Daigh snorted, "It could be worse. I could be playing Russian roulette with all the chambers loaded.")

Beginning at 8 A.M., rolling between packed lines of eager spectators, 247 entrants roared off at staggered one-minute intervals from Ensenada on what was the fastest leg of the race (most of the road was paved into Camalu). Brute power counted most over this 90-mile stretch, and McQueen stormed along in fine style.

Tragedy struck early just south of the first checkpoint when a Ford Bronco rolled several times, killing its two drivers; a dune buggy crash injured two other competitors, both of whom were flown to a hospital.

McQueen gunned the Boot into the mountains, sliding around hairpin turns flanked by 500-foot dropoffs. The pavement ended

---

*At Camalu, El Rosario, Rancho Santa Inez, Punta Prieta, El Arco, San Ignacio, La Purisima, and Villa Constitución.

abruptly, and the last miles into Camalu were rugged as Steve bumped over ruts and moon-crater potholes.

"In the fast sections," he said, "it was not unusual for us to get airborne for 50 to 70 feet over road dips. The Boot rides so smooth you can overdo things. Even in bad, choppy sections it'll do 60 or so, and if you slam into a big rock at that speed you can crack an axle or worse."

Machines were dropping out of the race with slashed tires, blown transmissions, cracked blocks, broken steering arms, rock-punctured radiators. Only 97 of the entrants would make it to the finish at La Paz; 150 would not.

The road grew progressively rougher into the second checkpoint. And beyond El Rosario, known as "the last outpost," the race entered the wilds of central Baja.

Card stamped, Steve thundered away for Rancho Santa Inez, 86 miles farther down the rock-ribbed peninsula. The route was now a hellish mixture of sage, huge boulders (which racers call "rim crackers"), boglike silt, and cardén cactus. McQueen blasted through this impassable wilderness, goggles misted with dust, his mouth caked with gritty sand. He was still moving very swiftly, holding a solid overall position among the fastest machines. He could still win. In particular, he wanted to beat Jim Garner, and figured his Boot should out-perform Garner's Olds to La Paz.

But just before the third checkpoint the Boot began to slow down. There was an ominous rasping from the automatic transmission. "Sounds like we've lost a gear," said Daigh.

Steve nodded. "Yeah, we've *had* it."

The broken transmission gear put the Boot out for good. Just 238 miles into the race, they parked the crippled machine at Rancho Santa Inez and took a private jet back to Los Angeles. The overall winner, in 20 hours, 48 minutes, was a Ford Bronco.

Jim Garner earned a well-driven second in class.

By February 1970 Steve was again in entertainment headlines, voted Golden Globe World Film Favorite in a poll conducted in 41 countries by Reuters. His film price had risen to more than $1 million per picture, and scripts were flooding in to him. He turned them all down.

"I'm doing the Le Mans thing next," he told reporters. "We'll start it in France this summer."

"And after Le Mans?"

"One called *Yucatan*," he declared.

To be filmed in Mexico. Way back about nine hundred years ago the Indians used to cover these Mayan chicks with jewels, and the weight would carry them to the bottom of sacred wells. The legend is that all the jewels are still there in those hidden wells, wrapped around these skeletons. Our story will center on a guy who takes his cycle into the Mexican wilds on a personal treasure hunt. Naturally, I'll play the guy on the cycle. . . . I've got to sharpen up for all the driving I'll be doing at Le Mans. Got a neat new machine lined up.

The car was a power-laden 3-liter 908 Porsche Spyder, the full-race model that had come within a hair of winning Le Mans in 1969, when Steve had been a spectator. He'd been mightily impressed with the 908's potential and (through CBS) had arranged to purchase the ex-factory machine for his Solar stable. "Le Mans is a very fast race," Steve explained.

I needed to familiarize myself with a car like the 908 in order to drive there with any kind of authentic feel for the course. In most Hollywood racing movies the star is doubled, but I don't want any doubles for me at Le Mans. If I can't cut it in the 908 then I figure there's no point in making the film.

Realizing that the Porsche would require expert preparation and maintenance, Steve hired ex-Grand Prix star Richie Ginther. One of motor racing's outstanding talents, Ginther had retired from competition driving in 1967. "Rich is a very sharp fellow," Steve said. "He knows Porsches. Raced them for years. With him setting up the 908 I know I'll get full potential out of the car. The rest is up to me."

As a test, McQueen decided to enter the Porsche in a Sports Car Club of America (SCCA) event at Holtville, in Southern California. Steve roared the white, ground-hugging 908 onto the circuit, in February 1970, and swept to a blistering win in the main event, leaving the second-place car almost a full minute behind him.

The victory encouraged Steve to enter the upcoming Riverside (California) road races, a much tougher challenge. "Winning at Riverside requires a lot of horsepower for that mile-

long back straight," Steve said. "You can go as fast there as
your engine and your nerve will take you."

Riverside was a deadly, unforgiving circuit. A severe spin
almost anywhere on the course could have fatal results.

At Steve's request, Neile was there that weekend in the
main grandstand, nervous and frightened. She had watched
him set a new lap record and win Saturday's preliminary event.
McQueen was cool, confident, pleased with the car, but Neile
couldn't relax. She sensed that serious trouble waited for him
in Sunday's main event. And she was right.

"On Sunday, by the seventh lap, I was leading the race,"
McQueen related.

> We were running Le Mans gears because of the long
> straight, which gave us a top speed of 160 in fourth. I'd
> cleared turn nine and had shifted from third into fourth
> again on the pit straight, lining up for turn one, which
> was blind and fairly swift. I was into the turn at about
> 150 when the whole gearbox exploded under me! Neile,
> who witnessed the thing, said she could see black pieces
> of metal sailing high into the air. The fourth gear had
> blown right off the counter shaft and knocked a big hole
> in the crankcase.
>
> I began to slide wildly across the track, from one side
> to the other, using up all the road. It was real nip-and-
> tuck there for a while and I didn't know if I'd come out
> in one piece or not.

Steve finally eased the smoking Porsche to a stop by the
road edge and pulled himself out of the car. "What we need,"
he said to his shaken pit crew as he stripped off helmet and
goggles, "is a new gearbox."

> I made up for Riverside by winning the next race, in
> Phoenix. By then, I was leading all SCCA drivers in
> points for the Class A Sports Car Championship, but I
> didn't stick around to finish the season. I was itching to
> get back on a two-wheeler, so I headed down to Lake
> Elsinore, about 70 miles southeast of Los Angeles, for
> the annual race there.

This was another rugged run. The course began on a winding paved road, zigzagged onto a half mile of dirt, spanned two drainage ditches, ran along more pavement into choppy terrain, alternated between desert trails, sand washes, and graded dirt, narrowed to a single-lane mountain road flanked by a rock wall and a 500-foot plunge, dipped into the town of Elsinore, switched and swerved through the paved city streets as it crossed train tracks into a 180-degree hairpin turn, whipped past the city park into some tricky esses—and finally led back to the winding paved road again. Ten laps of this for 100 miles, with half a thousand riders competing.

An uncontrollable mass of 40,000 spectators crowded this third annual Lake Elsinore Grand Prix. Many were standing or sitting on curbs, inches from the speeding machines. A blown tire, an oil skid, a single mistake—and a roaring cycle would be into the spectators.

For McQueen, hunched over the bars of his agile Motocross Husky, feeding power into the 405-cc engine, Elsinore was another challenge to be met and conquered.

"Yeah, I was hot to trot that day," he related. "I mean, I was *ready!*"

In the 500-cycle field over the rugged 10-mile circuit, Steve took just three laps to work his way forward to run with the leaders, having passed a host of faster competitors. But trouble was waiting in the fourth lap. "It was a stupid thing, *my* fault, actually," admitted McQueen.

> When you're runnin' with the top ten, as I was, you're really honkin' on pretty good an' what happens is that with so many bikes choppin' up the dirt the holes in the course get worse . . . deeper with each lap. I was comin' out of a wash under a bridge with this road dip ahead and I just kinda took one of those big jumps where you're sure you're gonna make it but you don't. And I didn't. My bike nosed into the dip, which was, like, *deep*—and I went ass-over the bars into the crowd. Didn't hurt anybody but me. My left foot was busted in six places.

McQueen righted his cycle, climbed back aboard, and kick-started his dented machine.

I had my juice up, so I took off and ran the last six laps with my broken foot. Which was not so bad on the faster portions, when I could use the seat, but when I had to stand on the pegs through the rougher sections . . . well, that was kinda hard on me. Anyhow, I finished in the top ten, but I messed up my foot doing it.

Ordinarily, such an injury would have been routine for Steve ("When you race bikes, you break bones."), but this time it was serious. He wasn't sure he would be able to qualify for the prime event of his competition career.

In just two weeks he was due to drive the Porsche 908 in Florida's Sebring International Twelve-Hour Endurance Race.

His performance there would earn world headlines.

13...

A Race
to Remember

Rimcrest. Top of the mountain. Just past noon, under a furnace sun.

McQueen. Shirtless, slouched against the fender of his Jeep, talking about the end of his auto racing career.

"That '70 run at Sebring was my last big one," he said. "Except for Le Mans that year, of course, when we did the picture. Sebring and Le Mans are the top sports car events in the world. After those two, there was nowhere for me to go."

He thought for a moment, idly running his hand over the Jeep's fender, as a jockey might stroke the flank of his best horse.

"By then, I'd lost Neile—going as far with racing as I did. Too far, maybe."

He walked away from the Jeep, nervously pacing under the sun, considering his words. He spoke carefully, thoughtfully.

"People ask me if you get scared in a race. I

mean, not *smart* people, they don't ask that. Because, if you have any smarts, you gotta know that *every* competitor gets scared racing. Mostly before the start, when you're all wired up and waiting for that flag to drop, with the whole race there ahead of you—that's when you go dry in the mouth and the heart starts to hammer. Once you're underway and rolling you're too damn *busy* to get scared. You're into the action, flowing with it, thinking about how fast to take that next curve, and when to brake, and how the engine is running, and all the rest of it. But fright can jump right into your throat when you mess up at speed, like I did that time at Riverside. When your machine is sliding or looping, when you don't know how or *if* you're gonna come out, those are the bad times. But, Jesus! There are so many good times in racing. Like the race at Sebring. . . . That was really something. You never forget a race like that."

Located at the center of the Florida peninsula, Sebring had been a landing field for massive B-17 bombers during the Second World War. Beginning in 1950, the site became a racing circuit, host to the International Manufacturers' Championship endurance race.

In March 1970, for the twentieth running of this annual event, an all-star field of sports racing machines lined up on the starting grid. Here, facing a 12-hour grind over the tough 5.2-mile circuit, were the world's top drivers: Dan Gurney, driving a Matra, Jo Siffert and Pedro Rodriguez in Porsches, Piers Courage and Masten Gregory in Alfas, Jacky Ickx and the great Indy champ, Mario Andretti, in Ferraris.

McQueen's white Porsche 908 Spyder, codriven by millionaire sportsman/racer Peter Revson, had qualified fifteenth fastest. Race buffs looked on the entry with scorn; how could an underpowered Porsche, entered by a screen star who was foolish enough to attempt to operate the clutch pedal with a broken left foot, ever hope to compete on a professional level against the finest European cars and drivers? "I had a lot to prove out there," McQueen admitted. "In a way, it was the most important race of my life."

Steve had decided to take on a two-hour double shift at the wheel of the 908, "in order to sort myself out and see how my busted foot would hold up." He wore what he jokingly called "my Frankenstein boot," a covering of custom-made reinforced leather designed to fit over a cut-down plaster cast. A strip of sandpaper was glued to the bottom for traction on the clutch pedal.

"The Sebring observers watched me like hawks when I practiced on the circuit," related McQueen. "When they saw I could handle the car okay they qualified me for the race. But it was close. I almost didn't make it."

Under a hot, muggy sun, McQueen hobbled to his low white 908 and eased into the narrow cockpit. Inside, he fastened belts and adjusted his helmet.

In rows of two, the cars got underway behind ex-world champion Phil Hill in the pace car, then cut loose at the flag in a released sea of roaring motors as 68 determined drivers jockeyed for the first turn at the end of the pit straight.

In speed and horsepower, McQueen's 3-liter 908 Porsche was simply no match for the factory-prepared 5-liter 512 Ferraris or the fantastic 4.5-liter 917 Porsches. Even in McQueen's 3-liter class, the 650 Matras, T-33 Alfas, and the 312 Ferraris could all potentially outgun the 908.

"We were counting on the fact that many of the larger, faster machines would eliminate themselves in a twelve-hour grind by pushing too hard from the start," Steve said. "Our plan was to stick to a safe, steady pace, to keep the car in good shape, then to make our strongest bid in the closing hours."

Mario Andretti driving a fierce red 512 Ferrari battled Jo Siffert's 917 Porsche for the lead, both of them challenged by Vic Elford in another fast 917.

An hour passed on the official timing clock. Eleven to go.

Into the second hour, under the broiling Florida sun, tightly strapped into the 908's snug cockpit, McQueen threaded his way around the five-mile circuit; he passed slower Fiats and Lancias, slipped through the tricky S-turns, downshifted for the hairpin, gunned along the straights, bumping over the rutted, broken runways—smoothly feeding power to the Porsche's fuel-injected engine, learning to read each uneven stretch of grass-tufted concrete and raw blacktop. "The pain from my left leg was really getting bad," he admitted.

> The cast had split, and I didn't know if I could keep going, but I didn't want to hand over to Pete until I'd done my full two hours. Still, the pain was messing up my concentration. In a race, particularly a long endurance race such as Sebring, concentration is everything. You can't let your mind wander, because that's how crashes happen. I kept trying to tighten my concentration, but I was getting weird flashes and dingy vision on the straights. And I was so hot my skin just seemed to be burning up. I knew I had to bring in the car—so I did, and Pete took over.

Steve had his throbbing foot packed in ice, drank "about a gallon of water," and had the broken cast retaped. "Then I tried to rest," he said. "I knew I had a lot of tough driving ahead."

The race was stressing man and machine to the breaking point; an MGB had lost a wheel and flipped on the high-speed turn off the pit straight; into the third hour a 512 was hit by a Lancia in a metal-rending five-car crash near the hairpin. A 917 Porsche was caught in the tangle, shedding a wheel. By the fifth hour, another accident involved Chuck Parsons in his 312 Ferrari, and a course worker who was on the track, picking up debris. Parsons tried to avoid him—but the side of his Ferrari clipped the worker in passing; the man survived with a badly slashed leg.

At six hours, with the sun sliding down the baked Florida sky, the crowd grew excited as halftime results were posted. The Revson/McQueen 908 was running first in class and fourth overall. Only three cars were ahead of the 908, with Andretti's booming Ferrari in the lead.

A blown head gasket put Jacky Ickx out of the race. And Dan Gurney, another major threat, dropped well back with a sour engine.

Darkness closed over Sebring; cars ripped past the stands along the pit straight in slashes of light and sound. Tension mounted. "At nine hours, the three-quarter mark," said McQueen,

Andretti still held the lead, followed by Pedro Rodriguez in the 917 Porsche and Masten Gregory in the T-33 Alfa. Our 908 was running fourth, clock-smooth, and my leg pain wasn't bad. In fact, my lap times had picked up after dark; I was lapping within seven seconds of Pete Revson's time. I had a better understanding of the circuit now and of what I could and could not do on it, of how hard I could take each of the turns. Pete and I were being careful with things, not overstraining the car.

With two hours to go, Gregory's Alfa fell back—and the McQueen/Revson 908 advanced two more positions—into an astounding second overall behind the big Andretti/Marzario Ferrari.

The drama intensified: A fresh blare of loudspeakers drew the excited crowd to the fence line; eyes strained the course for sight of the leaders. Where was Andretti?

Incredibly, the lead Ferrari was *out* of the race. After ten and a half hours, Andretti's car had coasted to a stop with a blown transmission. "At that point it looked as if we might win the whole turkey shoot," recalled McQueen. "Pete was out there, driving the final shift, looking great."

With less than an hour remaining, the fourth-running 512 Ferrari, driven by Vacarella, was called into the pits and Mario Andretti quickly took over the wheel. Using the full range of his talent, and with a healthy car under his throttle foot, Andretti instantly began closing on Revson.

With 22 minutes left on the clock, he slammed the Italian machine past the 908 to regain first place. His powerful machine opened a solid 30-second lead. There seemed no chance whatever that Revson's slower 908 could catch Andretti in the closing minutes.

Yet . . .

Another blare of loudspeakers. Andretti's engine was missing, sputtering. He was running out of gas on the next-to-last lap. The crowd broke into wild shouting. Reporters and photographers converged on the McQueen pits.

"You and Pete, you've *won* it!" yelled a mechanic, slapping Steve on the back. McQueen shook his head. "It isn't over yet."

Indeed it wasn't. Andretti switched to his reserve tank and

rolled quickly into the Ferrari pits. In a few frantic seconds he was away with gas enough to finish.

Lights slashing the circuit, Pete Revson was driving all-out in the ghost-white 908, going for the lead as Mario Andretti blasted the big red Ferrari back into action.

Revson had regained several vital seconds, but the time gap was too great. The smaller 908 was just not powerful enough to overcome Andretti's Ferrari. The crowd witnessed the closest finish in Sebring's two decades of international racing, as Mario Andretti swept under the checker to cinch the race.

In finishing second overall, McQueen and Revson had brilliantly won their 3-liter prototype class, a full lap ahead of the third-place Gregory/Hazemans T-33 Alfa. Steve's most valued trophy, however, was his alone—the Hayden Williams Sportsmanship Cup, awarded him for his incredible leg-in-a-cast driving performance.

An exhausted Andretti was grateful to have pulled off the overall win: "I never drove so hard in my life, not even when I won Indy. This was the toughest race I've run and I'm lucky to have taken it."

Was McQueen disappointed?

"Hell, no," he said with a smile. "We never expected to do *anything* against all those bigger machines. We were just trying for a class win, not the overall. This is fantastic . . . just fantastic!"

As one sports writer summed up the results: "It took the sport's champion driver operating at the top of his form, in not one but *two* powerful factory Ferraris, to beat a single, privately-entered 908 Porsche co-driven by a lame film star."

14. . .

In the
24-Hours

We talked about women, about emotional and
sexual problems faced by superstars.

"Not many marriages in Hollywood last as long
as my first one did," Steve said. "Of course, Neile
put up with a helluva lot from me. She was much
stronger, emotionally, than most women I've
known, and that made the difference, I guess. But
I gave her some rough times."

"You mean with other women?"

"Mainly with the racing thing. All the broken
promises about quitting. All the dangers and
risks. . . . And, let's face it, I'm not an easy guy to
live with. I get in moods. I get spiky over things
when I'm into a picture or runnin' Solar or whatever. And I take home all my grief. The woman
I'm with, she gets it all dumped on her. Yeah,
Neile put up with a lot from me."

"But what about other women . . . don't they come
on strong to you?"

"Oh, sure they do. Shit, sometimes it gets . . ."

He grinned. "I mean, it's kinda *spooky*, the things they'll do to score...bribe their way into your hotel room, hide naked under the bed....And they're not too subtle about letting you know what they want. It can get a little embarrassing. Females can be very aggressive in this business."

"When you were making *Le Mans* in Europe, I read an interview you did with a London reporter on the subject of women. Let me run it by for your reaction, okay?"

"Go ahead."

"He quotes you: 'It's very hard to say no to these women sometimes. Some are very beautiful, and I'm no saint. Marriage is really difficult when you're in the public eye. You're exposed to so many rumors about other women.' Unquote. Care to comment?"

"Well, that's what I told this British guy—and it's true. You're always under the gun. Lots of pressure. Most marriages in the industry crack up fast, mainly due to this kind of pressure. But me, I'm no party stud. I'm with one woman at a time, and she's my lady and that's it until the ball game's over and we decide to walk in different directions. No matter what you've read in the gossip rags, I'm not a cat who sleeps around when I'm into a heavy relationship. That's just not my style." He grinned again. "Besides, my bikes keep me too busy. I mean, how many women want to go cowtrailing in the desert? That's one place they don't come after me!"

"Aren't there lady bikers?"

"A few." He chuckled. "Hell, I ran into one who forced me right off the road. I didn't know it was a gal under the helmet and leathers, so I chased her like crazy, caught up, and was all set to punch her out—until I saw her lipstick. But most lady bikers care more about ridin' than they do about chasin' guys."

"*Le Mans* really destroyed your first marriage, didn't it?"

"Well, that sure put the cap on it. I don't think Neile ever got the image of me hot-assin' that 917 down Mulsanne at 200-plus out of her mind." He drew a long breath. "I laid the whole package on the line for that one—my career, my money, my marriage, even my *life*. I went balls out on *Le Mans*."

With John Wayne and Paul Newman, Steve McQueen ranked as one of the three top box-office stars in 1970. Which probably explains why he was able to get financial backing on a film that most critics correctly predicted would be a financial bomb.

Within a week after Steve's remarkable performance at Sebring, the Hollywood trade papers were announcing that John Sturges had been signed to direct *Le Mans* and that the film was scheduled for summer production in France.

"John is perfect for it," McQueen told the trade papers. "He's into fast cars—owns a custom 911-T Porsche—and knows everything about action pictures. Which is vital to us because this one's *all* action."

In April 1970, more headlines: "McQueen to Drive Le Mans 24-Hours with Stewart." Steve had made arrangements with world champion Jackie Stewart to codrive a full-race, factory-prepared 917 Porsche in the round-the-clock, day-night contest. He and Stewart would be running officially under the John Wyer Gulf-Porsche team banner. "We'll be driving one of the fastest sports cars in the world," Steve declared, "and we think we have a good chance to take home all the marbles."

But Gordon Stulberg of Cinema Center Films, the financial arm of the new project, was appalled by McQueen's plan to compete. "He's absolutely out of his mind! We simply cannot allow this. We'll cancel the production immediately unless he reverses his position."

Steve was effectively blocked. Knowing that he would have no chance of refinancing the film with another company, he was forced to withdraw his Le Mans entry. In a cold rage, he refused to discuss the matter publicly or with friends or associates.

One of his bike pals observed: "For a week, Steve wouldn't rap with anybody. He just walked around with this touch-me-

and-I'll-kill-you look on his face. I'd never seen him so mad. Nobody went near him."

McQueen cooled down when Cinema Center agreed to purchase a new $70,000 917 factory Porsche for the film. They further agreed that he could do all of his own stunt driving on the Le Mans circuit during production. Also, they would back the entry of his 908 Porsche as a camera car for the race itself, with the clear understanding that McQueen would not be competing in it.

Steve was euphoric when he flew to Le Mans for the mid-June race. Neile and the children remained in California; they would join him later that month. For now, there was only the race.

Le Mans is in the farming country of midwestern France, 120 miles from Paris. It was here, on August 8, 1908, that the first air exhibition in Europe took place. The site gained international fame as a motor racing circuit in 1921, when American driver Jimmy Murphy won the Grand Prix of France there in a boat-tailed Dusenberg. Two years later, in 1923, a field of improbable vehicles smoked away down the straight for the first Le Mans 24-Hours—and the greatest endurance race in motoring history was born.

Running from 4 P.M. Saturday to 4 P.M. Sunday, this race was particularly hazardous (Mario Andretti called it "the most dangerous in the world"), and it had claimed the lives of many competitors. In 1955, Le Mans became the site of motor racing's greatest tragedy, as a Mercedes struck a smaller Healey and plowed into a crowd of spectators along the front straight, killing 83 of them as well as the Mercedes driver, Pierre Levegh. After the 1955 tragedy the front straight had been widened, and a steel guard rail had recently been built around the entire circuit.

McQueen encountered problems in entering the 908 Porsche (to be driven for Solar by Herbert Linge of West Germany and Jonathan Williams of England). Le Mans officials were, at first, solidly against allowing a camera-equipped car to compete. McQueen demonstrated that the three cameras were mounted to the frame and were thus an integral part of the chassis (one was fitted under a bubble in the hood); there was no chance that loose parts would fall onto the track. "We *had* to have footage from the actual race," he explained.

Otherwise, we'd have no vital point-of-view shots. At the going rate for extras, trying to duplicate the vast crowd at Le Mans was impossible. You just don't hire half a million people! We needed that in-race footage to catch the main mass of people along the length of the circuit.

Steve won his argument. The Solar entry was allowed to compete, and McQueen's pit prepared to supply cans of film as well as the usual gas, oil, and tires for the 908.

McQueen was not satisfied with the condition of the 8.4-mile circuit. Many sections were dark and drab, unsuitable for his color cameras. Therefore, with the delighted permission of the officials, he gave his crew the job of brightening Le Mans. Among other improvements, Solar workers completely re-painted the pits and added new circuit lights at key corners such as Tertre Rouge and Maison Blanche.

Le Mans 1970 lived up to its dangerous reputation. Four of the 512 Ferraris piled up in the tricky White House section, and Jacky Ickx (the 1969 winner), running second in the rain, attempted to squeeze his 512 Ferrari into a one-lane S-turn ahead of a competitor. He couldn't make it and was forced to slam on the brakes; his rear wheels locked and the red Ferrari spun into a road bank, killing a turn marshal.

It was a Porsche victory, with Hans Herrmann and Richard Attwood first under the flag in their 917. Only 17 of the 51 entries lasted the full 24 hours—but the McQueen-entered Solar 908, very capably driven by Linge and Williams, was one of the top finishers. Despite many stops for film reloads, the 908 finished second in class and eighth overall. Its three cameras, plus 16 others spaced around the circuit, gave McQueen more than 80,000 feet of full-color race footage.

Normally, after the race, Le Mans is open to traffic during the rest of the year (since it incorporates several miles of public road), but McQueen's company rented the entire circuit. Solar Village was built near the paddock area to house the 150-person production crew. The village sprawled over 100,000 square feet, and miles of electrical wiring and water pipes were laid through the French countryside. A restaurant was constructed, designed to feed up to 300 people per meal. Additionally, many professional drivers were hired to double for actors during racing sequences.

"We hired some real racing talent," said McQueen. "Mike Parkes was our consultant, and drove for us. So did Jacky Ickx, Jo Siffert, and Masten Gregory."

A carnival atmosphere is very much a part of Le Mans, and McQueen was forced to rent all of the rides and booths that crowd the infield each year to re-create the carnival atmosphere behind the grandstands. By the time Neile arrived in France with the children, Steve had rented a massive, 30-room villa in the country near the village of Le Mans. Neile found much beauty in the placid cattle and wheat-farming community but did *not* enjoy the roar of fast cars.

"She came to the circuit just once," a member of the crew reported. "I saw her watch Steve go down Mulsanne at over 200, and she looked real grim and tight-faced. Then she just walked back to her car and drove away. I never saw her there again."

Neile refused to return. Steve could take the children to the circuit if he insisted, but she'd stay at the villa during the time she was in France. And how long would that be? She wasn't sure.

On July 1, 1970, *Daily Variety* columnist Army Archerd announced that the McQueens had separated, and that Neile had taken the two children on a tour of Europe. When reporters asked McQueen about the state of his marriage he gave them a flat "no comment," but when they wanted to know about his new film he agreed to talk. "Basically," he told them,

> I want to avoid the usual phoniness connected with racing films up to now. Racing is a beautiful sport. I'm very serious about doing it justice. Sure, we'll have some crashes in the film because cars *do* crash at Le Mans. But this picture will be totally honest, with no compromises.

Steve was the only actor in the production to do all of his own stunt driving, and journalist John Skow, covering the shooting in France for *Playboy*, questioned him on why he insisted on personally risking his life. "Nobody will be able to tell *who*'s in the car," Skow pointed out.

> "Okay, so it's really you out there under the cloth fire mask and Bell helmet. So what? Who'll know?"

"The audience will know," [Steve replied.] "They expect this kind of thing from me. And, even more important, *I'll* know. What counts is playing this straight, with no cheating."

"How fast is your 917 down Mulsanne?"

"It's capable of 240—but I don't take it up to full chat. Most times I'm hitting 225 or so."

"And what does John Sturges think of your driving?"

"Johnny thinks I tend to go faster than I need to."

"And do you?"

"Maybe."

For Steve, driving the Porsche at speed provided ultimate satisfaction. Hand-assembled at the Stuttgart factory, the 917 was a true racing thoroughbred, whose rear-mounted, fuel-injected, 12-cylinder, air-cooled engine delivered a jolting 600-horsepower thrust. "I've never been in anything quite this fast," Steve admitted.

The first time I went through the Mulsanne kink—that little curve on the long back straight—at 215 miles an hour I really felt the hair on the back of my neck standing on end! In most cars you feel what's going to happen *before* it happens and you can adjust, but this Porsche is always a bit ahead of you in making up its mind about things. You need to be extremely alert to stay on top of it.

Beyond McQueen's 917, Solar had lined up what amounted to a million-dollar racing stable for the production. When Enzo Ferrari was approached regarding use of some of his factory models he asked: "Who wins in your picture, Ferrari or Porsche?"

When he was told that a Porsche wins, he refused to allow use of his cars. Solar nevertheless found some private owners who agreed to supply the needed Ferraris. McQueen also arranged to have Ferrari body shells built over two Corvette-powered Lolas for crash sequences.

Among the cars leased or purchased outright for *Le Mans* were four 917 Porsches, two 908s, some production 911s and a scattering of Lolas, Alfas, and Matras, along with five Ferraris. Each had spare engines, sets of wet and dry tires, and extra wheels. (A plane stood by during the shooting to pick up any needed parts from Stuttgart, West Germany, or Modena, Italy.) McQueen had imported Indy expert Haig Alltounian as chief mechanic.

Camera car for *Le Mans* was a modified open-cockpit GT-40 Ford, powered with a V-8 4.7-liter engine, and handled by stunt driver Rob Slotemaker. A stationary 35-mm Arriflex camera faced rearward in the center of the chassis; a second camera unit was fitted into an aluminum, foam-lined bubble seat beside the driver, in which operator Alex Barbey handled the swivel-mounted 35-mm Mitchell camera, adapted for Pan-avision lenses.

Driving this GT-40 Ford was extremely tricky, since it had to move alongside racing machines at full speed on narrow sections of road, taking an outside line through corners meant for a single car.

McQueen refused to allow any fake process shots, which meant driving at full-race speeds in front of cameras. One dangerous sequence called for him to pass a 512 Ferrari inside a turn on a wet track. McQueen described the risk:

> There was no margin for error. I had my left front tire on the white line, only about a foot and a half from the iron guard rail. I figured that if I lost it I'd try and slap the rail and ride it along rather than bounce back into the road and take a chance on getting center-punched by the camera car.

At one point in the filming, Steve came close to disaster. Roaring over a slight rise on Mulsanne in the 917, he was set to pass a car ahead at 200 mph with the camera GT riding next to him, recording the action. The three cars boomed down the long straight and cleared the rise. But in the middle of the straight, motoring serenely toward them, was a massive Solar service truck. The driver had been told that the day's shooting was over, and the last thing he expected to meet on Mulsanne was this trio of fast-charging race cars. In a panic, the driver threw his truck against the rail, while the racers ripped past, sliding and fish-tailing. Nobody crashed. Nobody hurt. But it had been close. Very, very close.

"This film is a tremendous personal risk for me on *every* level," McQueen told the press.

> If I bust myself up on the circuit, not only does this whole operation go down the tubes, but *I* go with it. The insurance companies will nail me for full production costs—and we're talking several million here. It's bad enough, losing the picture, but they can come and take away my house, my cars, all my possessions.

Steve was earning respect for his talent behind the wheel as the day-to-day filming continued. "He drives damn well," said Masten Gregory, the veteran Steve had beaten for the class win that year at Sebring. "Steve is a real pro. Maybe not top-level as yet, but he *could* be with more race seasoning." And Mike Parkes agreed: "He's an extremely good driver. Going down the Mulsanne straight we're all doing exactly what we'd do in the actual race, and Steve's right there with us all the way."

Before climbing into their cars, the drivers always inserted wax ear plugs to deaden the unmuffled roar from the full-race engines—but McQueen needed only *one*, "for my right ear. By then I was totally deaf in the left. Couldn't hear a damn thing with it."

Tension was mounting between director and star. When McQueen verbally attacked one of the drivers, ordering him off the location, John Sturges was upset.

"Why did you do it, Steve?"

"That bastard told a London paper he was doubling for me in the Porsche, that I wasn't really doing my own driving. When they printed that story I fired his ass."

"As director, I should have been consulted. Maybe he was misquoted by the paper."

"No, he said what he said, and now he's out. He's a liar, and I don't work with liars."

Further tension developed over a McQueen prank. Celebrating the Fourth of July in his own private fashion, Steve exploded a large firecracker under the director's 911 Porsche. A rising plume of smoke from the car alarmed Sturges and he rushed from his office to see what was happening. He looked over to see McQueen howling with delight. But the joke was a sour one, and the long McQueen-Sturges friendship was beginning to erode.

Sturges was also concerned about the script. The latest draft failed to satisfy him, and he argued with McQueen over it.

"Where's the *human* story?" he demanded. "It's cars, cars, cars."

"That's what Le Mans is all about, John."

"It's not enough. We *must* have a strong emotional story to carry all this racing stuff. And it just isn't here."

The worried executives at Cinema Center Films agreed with Sturges. They flew to Le Mans, looked over the latest script, and groaned at the $40,000 per day shooting expenses. (McQueen had blown the engine on his 917, which also added to the rising production costs.) After several emergency talks, a two-week shutdown was ordered. The CCF executives needed "some time to assess the situation."

One disgusted production assistant acidly termed the project

> McQueen's eight-million-dollar home movie. He's got all of us stuck out here in the middle of France just so he can play hero racer and drive his big Porsche around Le Mans. We've got thousands of miles of racing footage on cars and about an inch and a half of footage containing dialogue between people. This picture is one big joke, if you ask me!

Would Cinema Center Films cancel the production? Was *Le Mans* to go the way of *Day of the Champion?* Steve assured his crew that the film *would* be completed. CCF agreed to continue financing. The shutdown was temporary.

For John Sturges it was permanent. He declared that he no longer intended to continue working with an uncompleted screenplay. "I went looking for Steve, to have a final showdown on the script," said Sturges, "but he'd taken off for England without bothering to tell me he was leaving. That did it. I was through. I just packed my bags and booked the next plane back to the States."

In London, the McQueens were together once again. Neile had consented ("for the sake of the children, really") to a final try at resolving their marital troubles—and Steve had again impressed her with his humane actions. He had made a special point of touring the Great Ormond Street Hospital for Sick Children, moving from bed to bed through the wards, chatting with each afflicted child. He kept the British reporters away, wanting no publicity for the visit, and before returning to Le Mans, he arranged to auction off one of his antique guns as a contribution to the French Children's Fund for Orphans.

By the first week in August, with production resumed, Lee H. Katzin replaced Sturges as director. Katzin, who had made his reputation in action television dramas, was willing to go along with McQueen's view of the story.

"Steve has a very strong idea of how he wants this film handled," Katzin said. "He wants to do something very close to a pure documentary, holding characters and dialogue to a minimum and letting the race itself dominate."

Trade papers reported that Solar Productions had severed all future contracts with Cinema Center Films. The account quoted McQueen: "I've fought the establishment all my life. . . . The CCF people decided to ride the rest of the way with us on this one, but they wanted a lot more control in future films, and I said no."

As *Le Mans* continued, the natural hazards of such an undertaking began to take a toll on cars and drivers. Several members of the production crew discovered the dangers of fast motoring. So many privately owned cars were smashed up between takes that a new club was formed, described by one member as "the Le Mans Daredevil Driving and Beer Drinking Society—membership in which is earned by wrecking your car on the circuit."

But far more serious accidents occurred during the actual filming. Driver Derek Bell was throttling one of the $65,000 Ferraris down Mulsanne at over 200 mph when smoke began pouring from the car; the electrical system had malfunctioned and the Ferrari was aflame. Before Bell could stop, the gas tank exploded, bathing him in fire. A Le Mans ruling requires that all drivers wear flameproof clothing capable of withstanding the temperature of burning gasoline for 15 seconds. This ruling saved Bell's life; he was alive when pulled from the car, but his face and hands were severely burned. The Ferrari was a fire-gutted write-off.

On another afternoon of shooting, over a different section of the circuit, David Piper (driving a car identical to McQueen's 917) struck the rail, spun wildly, slamming into the rail again 325 feet farther down the track. Breaking into pieces, the Porsche threw its wheels 150 yards into a lettuce patch. Piper was rushed

to the hospital with a triple compound fracture of the right leg.
London doctors worked desperately to save the leg but were
eventually forced to amputate below the knee.

McQueen decided to duplicate this accident in the film. The
action called for Steve to come up too fast on a smaller car,
brake and lose control, spin and crash, slamming the 917 to
pieces against the guard rails on either side of the track. This
staged smashup was designed to give moviegoers the gut-sen-
sation of having crashed a racing machine at speed.

"Using a remote-controlled car," said McQueen,

> we engineered the crash, covering the action with four-
> teen cameras, three of them in slow motion, the other
> eleven from different angles. Then we cut this together
> so you could actually *see* what the driver goes through.
> You see him make his mistake; you see the car go out
> of control and crash—all in normal fast motion. As his
> machine comes to rest, the camera looks in through the
> shattered windshield at the driver's eyes, seems to enter
> his head, his thoughts, as the entire crash is relived in
> slow motion. It's totally unlike anything ever done on
> the screen.

By September, after three months of filming, and numerous
scripts from four writers, the plot of *Le Mans* was at last
finalized. McQueen was Michael Delaney, an ice-hard professional who had crashed the previous year at Le Mans and who
was trying for a comeback in a Gulf Porsche 917. He faced
his great rival, Erich Stahler (played by Siegfried Rauch) in a
512 Ferrari. Delaney's crash had claimed the life of another
driver, Belgetti, and this man's widow, Lisa, had returned to
Le Mans, drawn to Delaney, yet still bitter over her husband's
death. During the race Delaney is balked by a slower car and
once again crashes. But the Porsche team manager puts him
into another 917 and he engages Stahler in a fierce duel in the
closing stages of the event. Too far back to claim outright
victory, he nevertheless edges out Stahler in the final lap.

Young Chad McQueen, who was visiting his father at the
circuit, was thrilled by the automotive action. He'd already
mastered dirt bikes; now he wanted to try out a racing car.

At Le Mans he got his chance. Piloting a miniature Ferrari

for a special children's race, the nine-year-old McQueen did his father proud by entering the *Quatre Jours Du Mans* and defeating a dozen other competitors.

Le Mans had required five months to film (from June into November) and McQueen returned to California with 450,000 feet of film to be edited. Said Katzin:

> It took six months of looping, dubbing, splicing and cutting to get our final work print. We had to match *fifty-five* sound tracks, including one for each racing car, plus laying in the music. Footage from the actual Le Mans race had been so well integrated with staged footage that the effect was seamless.

When reporters asked Steve if this one had been rough, the star chuckled. "Rough? It was the most dangerous thing I've ever done. I'm lucky I'm still alive."

But he had achieved his goal; he had made an authentic racing film. There had been no compromises.

15...

A New Beginning
with Ali MacGraw

On the Mojave. McQueen, riding with his buddies, three small, heat-rippled dots in the immensity of the desert. Mount San Jacinto high and blue-gray along the horizon. A hot, clear sun diamond-dusting the sand. Steve throttled hard for a wash, weaving his cycle around a stand of manzanita, cleared the lip of the wash, ripped along it, full out. The other riders followed him in, but were unable to match his speed. One struck deep sand and unloaded from his bike in a racketing spill that brought McQueen and the other rider to his side.

"You okay?" Steve asked.

"Yeah. Got in too deep."

"It can happen." McQueen shrugged, gunning away once again in a fantail of sand.

When it was all done, and the other two riders had returned to Los Angeles in their pickup, we sat in McQueen's Palm Springs living room, sipping Coors.

"One of these days I'm gonna sell this place," he said. "Too many golf courses around now anyhow. They keep buildin' more every year. Used to be antelopes here, till the railroad drove 'em off. We still get coyotes and jack rabbits and ground squirrels. No more antelopes, though."

He fiddled with a zebra-skinned pillow, looked up at the mounted head of a bighorn sheep. "I don't kill things anymore. Animals kill each other and that's natural, but people have no damn business doing it. No more mounted heads for me. No more hunting."

"Are you and Neile really finished?" (This was fall 1971.)

"Yeah. We had another go at trying to make it stick but we both decided to end things for good. We separated in June . . . and she's filed for divorce. Under the California Community Property Law, she owns half of everything we've put together, right down the line. And lemme tellya, she deserves every penny. She shaped me up, made me stick with my career." He thought for a moment. "And she gave up a *lot* for me."

He tossed the pillow aside, stretched, walked to the window. "Late afternoon, when it cools down, the hawks come sailing out. . . . There's quail up there, too." He hesitated. "Funny thing about my marriage—the racing really killed it, and now I don't compete anymore. No more cars. And at 41 I'm getting too old for the cycle races. So after all these years at it, just when I finally decide to hang up the goggles, it's too late. Funny, huh?"

And he grinned at the irony.

For Steve McQueen, the racing years ended with the release of *Le Mans* and a cycle film he had helped finance, *On Any Sunday*.

This 91-minute documentary was produced, written, and directed by Bruce Brown, aided by $313,000 of McQueen's money. The production was excellent in every respect. Brown did for motorcycle competition what he had done for surfing in his *Endless Summer;* he transferred a sport to film with passion, grace, and excitement. *On Any Sunday* blended the spectacular dangers of closed-track racing with the serene beauty of open-country riding. Actual footage of Steve's 1970 run at Lake Elsinore (when he had finished tenth in a field of more than 500 riders) was integrated into a long, lyrical sequence of McQueen joyriding along back roads and over golden sands with his cycle buddies. The film was a stunning success, grossing an incredible total of $24,000,000 in box-office revenue. The satisfaction, for McQueen, was that it helped erase the Hell's Angel cycle-riding image from the public mind.

However, Steve was far from pleased with the public reception of *Le Mans* that summer. Moviegoers, for the most part, were either frustrated or bored—and most critics were hostile. Great race footage, but where was the story, the *human* conflict? In fact, where was the dialogue? As one reviewer complained:

> All we get from Mr. McQueen is a series of fierce stares at his competitors and liquid-eyed glances at his potential lady-love. He mumbles out perhaps ten lines of cryptic dialogue, about why men have to race, then climbs into his big speedwagon for two hours of vrooming and zooming. Not even a star of McQueen's magnitude can get away with this one.

The critic was right: Solar Productions and CCF sustained a crippling financial loss with *Le Mans*. Steve's vision of a one-man empire dissolved with the box-office failure of this film.

But McQueen was never a man to allow setbacks to slow him down, and he was determined to maintain his status. "I just had to take my lumps and move in a new direction," he said. "I could no longer depend on Solar alone. I needed more production muscle behind me. Which is why I joined First Artists in '71. To *get* that kind of muscle."

Under the banner of First Artists Productions, McQueen became part of a major film partnership that year with three other industry heavyweights: Barbra Streisand, Sidney Poitier, and Steve's longtime friend and box-office rival, Paul Newman. (Dustin Hoffman joined the group in 1972.)

This powerhouse combination guaranteed McQueen a high degree of creative control in any First Artists project he chose to do, and in signing he had finally abandoned his "lone wolf" stance.

"I didn't really mind," he said. "You try a thing and if it doesn't work out you try something else. The trick is to stay active, not to freeze up. In this business, you gotta keep moving."

Los Angeles Times columnist Joyce Haber arranged for an interview with McQueen that summer and was surprised when Steve called personally to tell her that his 12-year-old daughter was graduating and had won a special citizenship award. He wanted to be there for the occasion, so would it be okay to reschedule their talk? "In fifteen years of reporting," Haber said, "I've met very few people—and even fewer stars—who would bother to phone me personally to apologize for a delay. Usually, it's their press agent who revises the interview schedule. I was sincerely impressed."

In her column she also reported that

> A few seasons ago the owners of Four Oaks, a local restaurant, invited fifty black orphans for a free Thanksgiving Day dinner. They also invited several celebrities. McQueen arrived promptly on his cycle. He was the only star to show. I call that the act of a good man.

During their interview, they talked about the recent failure of *Le Mans,* and Steve admitted that he had "been wrong about a lot of things" regarding that project. "John Sturges left because the pressure was too much for him. And I don't blame him. We just didn't have a script."

What film was next on the horizon?

"I'm heading into Arizona to do *Junior Bonner,*" he said. "Sam Peckinpah is directing. I play an over-the-hill rodeo champ in this one."

He discussed his reputation as a troublemaker. "I know that I've been a big pain to the studios. I've always been a perfectionist, and that means I give headaches to a lot of people. Sam's got a bad rep, too. He's a prime hellraiser. Him and me, we're *some* combo. Cinerama is buyin' a lot of aspirin."

Was he looking forward to *Bonner?*

"Not hardly! I gotta rope steers, and ride a bull. And those rodeo bulls are big and *mean*. Horses and bulls you just can't trust. Never know what they'll take it into their stubborn animal heads to do."

Before he left for the Arizona filming, Steve had magazine journalist Robert Jones out to his Palm Springs home. McQueen's son, Chad, was along that weekend—and the 10-year-old rode wheel-to-wheel with his father on a fast dirt mini-bike of his own. "Bought it himself," Steve proudly informed Jones.

> Saved up for it out of his pocket money. Chad likes dirt riding a lot. Maybe too much. I had to ground him for two months earlier this year when his grades got sloppy. But he's shaped up nice since then. I figure that riding through clean desert in clean air has *got* to be good for the kid. Christ, I was stealin' cars at his age!

Jones liked the youngster, describing him as "a striking contrast to his father, dark and open rather than blond and curt. He wears braces over his uninhibited smile and he has none of that exasperating cocksurety so common to actors' children."

When the article was published (in *Sports Illustrated*) it was accompanied by a photo of Steve and Chad, shirts off, standing quietly together in the desert. Clearly, father and son shared the same passion for open spaces.

Steve talked to Jones about his "respect" for the desert. "It cuts you down to size. You have to understand it as a living thing." McQueen related a story to make his point. He had been with some Indians, and they had given him peyote. "They were really serious about peyote," Steve said.

> They didn't take it for kicks, to get high on...it was a *philosophy,* a way for them to deal with their environment. Anyhow, although I've never been into drugs, I did try this because they asked me to—as a kind of ritual. Well, it really hit me. Made me feel invincible. I took off across the sand on my bike, flat out, bound and determined to *whip* it. I mean, conquer the desert. I took a lot of falls, and cactus ripped me and rocks chewed on my hide. I had grit up my nose and kangaroo rats in my ears!

Finally the bike ran out of gas—and I remember just

sitting alone out there in the sand. Everything was dead quiet, with night coming on, and my bike making these little crackling noises as the metal cooled. . . . I knew then that the whole idea of trying to whip the desert was ridiculous. You don't fight it, you accept it, respect it, blend into it.

Having arrived at the Arizona location for *Junior Bonner*, in Prescott, McQueen settled into his title role. In previous films he had learned to strum a guitar, sky glide, play polo, and dismantle a ship's engine. Now, somewhat reluctantly, he was learning to bulldog a steer and stay aboard a wild bull—activities which left him "a little beat up around the edges." Indeed, after just a week of shooting, Steve had sprained a finger, gashed his nose, and suffered a possible fracture of the left wrist. "Jeez," he growled. "This is more dangerous than Le Mans, and a hell of a lot less enjoyable."

Acting, by itself, was no longer satisfying to him in a creative sense. "What I really want to do now is produce and direct," he stated. "Get *behind* the camera for awhile. There's a lot more challenge there. When it comes to acting, I've just about run out of tricks."

As usual, McQueen was underestimating his talent. In the role of Bonner, a man struggling to retain remnants of a life that had passed him by, Steve gave what critic Joanna Campbell called "one of his finest performances." Los Angeles film critic Michael Sragow went even further:

As a rodeo star past his prime, McQueen acts out faded glory without self-pity or preening. He displays just enough of his character's former vanity and power to make his current failure sting. . . . He embodies Bonner so fully, from the inside out, that when he bandages up his damaged midsection he seems to be struggling physically to repair his pride. Few mainstream American stars could pull off such a balancing act.

Steve had strong competition in the film from veteran Robert Preston, at his brilliant best as Junior's father, Ace Bonner, who dreams of leaving city life behind and becoming a sheep farmer in the vast, open spaces of Australia. (This was a McQueen addition to the script, and echoed Steve's oft-expressed desire to "just go disappear in the Australian wilds.")

During the film Steve rides a killer bull to earn enough to buy his father a plane ticket to Australia. It is, one senses, Junior Bonner's last act of triumph. We see him at the end, heading for another lonely rodeo town, but his string has clearly been played out.

On location in Prescott, McQueen's compassion for the plight of the American Indian was again demonstrated when he donated the proceeds from two benefit screenings of *On Any Sunday* to the Yavapai tribe of Arizona.

In marketing *Junior Bonner*, Cinerama enlisted the aid of a special press agent to drumbeat the film. McQueen was talked into personally inviting newspaper columnist James Bacon to a private preview at the press agent's home. Although he liked the film, and said so in print, Bacon was confused and angered by McQueen's aloofness. Steve had been rude and hostile, making no effort to cooperate on the story.

The next morning Bacon received a phone call from McQueen. "Hey, man, I don't want you to be sore at me, okay?"

"Then why did you act like such a shit last night?"

McQueen laughed. "I was teed off because those publicity guys wanted me to kiss ass to sell the picture and I guess I overreacted. I'm sorry."

Bacon accepted the apology.

"I've spent at least a third of my life being angry and not really knowing why," Steve admitted. "I try to improve, but I gotta keep watching myself. Sometimes I slip—like last night."

And Bacon wrote: "We ended up friends."

Filming on *Bonner* was completed in August 1971. McQueen returned to Los Angeles to face Neile's petition for divorce. In March 1972 it became binding; she received custody of the children and a settlement of nearly one and a half million dollars. Plus alimony and child support. Steve left the courtroom in Santa Monica shaken and grim-faced.

How did he feel about the final breakup?

"The show's all over for us and the curtain is down," he said. "Neile has to build a new life, same as I do. We said our goodbyes, but it wasn't easy. When you spend fourteen years of your life with somebody a piece of you is gone forever when you split up."

The McQueen career continued. Steve seriously considered

starring in *Roy Brightsword*, as an Arkansas hillbilly tamed by a Jewish social worker during the Great Depression, but he found another role more to his liking, that of Doc McCoy, a quick-shooting convict-crook, in *The Getaway*.

Originally, this film was to have been produced at Paramount, with Peter Bogdanovich directing, but when McQueen took over the project (from First Artists), he brought in Sam Peckinpah. Another major change was to affect Steve's personal life. For the role of McCoy's wife, Dyan Cannon was replaced by Ali MacGraw.

McQueen and MacGraw had never met until they worked together in Texas on *The Getaway*, but by the end of their first filmed love scene it was apparent that sexual sparks had been ignited. On location in El Paso, during May 1972, Ali talked enthusiastically about her new costar:

> Steve is one of two or three actors in the world I think are always fabulous to watch. Actually, he's a big surprise to me. I mean, I just wasn't prepared for his intelligence. It's not the kind you associate with books, it has to do with his enormous ability to do subtle things.
>
> He deals with people on a very straight level. He says exactly what he means and no bullshit. Some people find that kind of honesty hard to take. In this industry you play games, but Steve won't play. He makes his own rules. Really, he's a fascinating man.

The attraction was mutual; Steve found this long-legged, dark-eyed beauty to be equally fascinating. *The Getaway* was his twenty-third film, but Ali had done only two others, *Goodbye, Columbus* and *Love Story*. Both had been substantial box-office hits, yet their success had failed to erase the basic insecurity she felt about herself as an actress. To Ali MacGraw, her screen persona was, in her words, "unreal, dreamlike, not based on anything I can take pride in." She very much admired McQueen's cool control, his obvious mastery of a craft she was still trying to understand. "I really don't know quite how I got into films," she admitted. "No experience. No training. I'm a prime example of the Schwab Drug Store School of Acting!"

Alice MacGraw was raised by artist/designer parents in New York's forested Westchester County. An exceptionally bright student, she won scholarships to Connecticut's Rosemary Hall, a girls' prep school, and to Wellesley—where she majored in art history and worked as a part-time waitress to earn basic living expenses.

She met a Harvard man, Robert Hoen, and after graduation (as valedictorian, class of 1960) she quickly married and divorced him. ("It was one of those spur-of-the-moment relationships, with no real basis.") She worked as an editorial assistant for *Harper's Bazaar*, and the next step, into modeling, was an easy one for her ("except that I always *loathed* being a model"). One of Ali's commercials, for Chanel No. 5, caught the attention of an agent and resulted in a film offer.

"I categorically decided that I didn't want to be involved in this racket," she recalled. "So I said no thanks." But when she was offered the lead role in *Goodbye, Columbus* she couldn't turn it down.

"At 30, I suddenly found myself a movie star, despite the fact that I didn't know a damned thing about acting. I played that role strictly by instinct—terrified all the way."

Dynamic young Paramount tycoon Robert Evans produced the film, and he followed it by casting MacGraw as the doomed-but-gutsy heroine in *Love Story*. "For a year and a half," Evans recalled, "we had nothing to do with one another beyond a casual business relationship. I'd been married twice before, and was in no rush to get involved again with anyone. But then we took a fresh look, and discovered each other. We were married in October of 1969."

Ali moved into the Evans mansion, a lavish French Provincial estate in Beverly Hills, with pool, projection room, gardens, tennis courts, and 26 telephones. Inside, she lounged in black marble tubs, slept with her new husband on a king-sized bed paneled in calfskin, and spent most of her days wandering idly through the house, "trying to convince myself that I was happy."

In truth, her Cinderella dream life was lonely and frustrating. Evans gave her scant attention. "Either Bob was working very late at the studio or he was on location out of town," she said. "I began to think of myself as a movie widow."

Their child, Joshua, was born in January 1971, but the new baby didn't improve the fading relationship. Finally, during production of *The Getaway* in Texas, Ali decided to file for divorce. In Steve McQueen, she was convinced she had found what she had been looking for all her life—a man rooted in the here-and-now, who made his own way, and who ignored the glitter crowds and the party circuits.

"Steve is into *basics*," she told a New York journalist that summer. "He's like a tonic for me. He gives my life some solid reality—which, up to now, I've never had."

An amusing sidelight to the filming involved Ali's uncertainty behind the wheel of an automobile. She had never learned to drive, yet according to the script she was to handle the getaway car. She had been taking lessons from a driving school in El Paso, but was what McQueen termed "a slow learner when it came to anything mechanical."

Before the getaway scene, McQueen approached Peckinpah: "I think we should switch it around and let *me* do the driving. I get nervous in a car with amateurs." Peckinpah did not agree, and the sequence was filmed as written, with MacGraw roaring the getaway car through crowds of extras while Steve sat sweating in the seat beside her.

He emerged shaken, but grinning. "She was all over the place," he said. "Skiddin' left, then right, barely missing the crowds. Once we were even airborne! Now I know how Faye Dunaway felt ridin' in that dune buggy with me."

As he had done with *Junior Bonner*, McQueen paid close attention to the final shooting script. ("I sure as hell didn't want another *Le Mans* . . . all action and no story.") The film's writer, Walter Hill, was impressed with Steve's eye for detail. "He had total concentration," said Hill.

> He was concerned about every scene, down to the smallest plot point. He'd sometimes call me at 3 A.M. with a suggestion for a change. Steve tended not to like dialogue, especially long speeches, and preferred to convey thought through body language. In my opinion, he was the best actor in the last twenty-five years at getting real emotion across without having to say a word.

Steve claimed that "I almost got my ass chewed off making *Getaway*. That was at Huntsville." Peckinpah had moved the company to the Huntsville State Penitentiary for three days of location work. "I played one of the prisoners," Steve declared.

Sam had more than half a hundred of the real convicts in the film—for a sequence in the exercise yard. On our first afternoon there, when the scene was wrapped and Sam yelled "Cut!" I took off toward my dressing room for some coffee. Well, here I was, in prison duds, splitting away from all the other cons—and suddenly I'm runnin' like hell, 'cuz this pack of hounds are snappin' at my ass! They'd been trained to go after any con who broke ranks, and nobody had bothered to tell 'em this was only a movie. I barely made it outa that yard in one piece!

There were several explosive shootouts in *The Getaway*, and during the course of the action McQueen taught Ali how to handle and fire various handguns. "I'd never thought of myself as a violent person," she said, "but, with the guns, I really got into it. Doing those scenes was like being in the middle of a war."

One of the sound men connected with the production recalled an argument between Peckinpah and McQueen.

No two people hear exactly alike—and Steve and Sam just couldn't agree on how the gunshots in the picture ought to sound. Peckinpah laid in one set of gunshots and McQueen marched into the cutting room, insisting on another set. Funny thing was—a lifetime of booze had affected Sam's low-end hearing, while cycle racing had wiped out Steve's high-end hearing. He had only one good ear anyhow. So it turned out they were *both* wrong!

The Getaway, under Peckinpah's violence-prone directive hand, was a blood-soaked, action-jammed thriller in the *Bullitt* tradition. McQueen was in easy command as Doc McCoy, a man sprung from prison to mastermind a bank raid. As Carol, his scheming wife, who flees with him into Texas after the robbery, MacGraw projected a sensual believability. Their love scenes together were erotic and convincing. Critics sensed the genuine passion behind these steamy sequences. One reviewer declared: "McQueen has never heated up the screen as he does in this new thriller, and MacGraw matches him frame for frame in sexual intensity."

Their offscreen life was equally intense. Anxious to ease the pain of his recent divorce, McQueen savored this new relationship. "I may be a loner," he said, "but that doesn't mean I like living alone. I miss having a woman around. Ali is good medicine for me."

She realized that his break with Neile had been traumatic, and told reporter Liz Smith: "I don't know if Steve's divorce is the best or the worst thing that has happened to him. I think that he's just beginning to find himself. He knows now that you don't have to be a race driver in order to take big risks in life, that you can also risk your life *emotionally*."

In his new commitment to Ali MacGraw, Steve was willing to take that risk once again but wanted to be certain that his children fully accepted her. He brought Chad and Terri to El Paso during the filming that summer to introduce them to Ali. They took to her, in Steve's words, "like a couple of ducks to water."

Terri, now entering her clothes-conscious teens, appreciated Ali's sense of fashion and happily imitated her dress style; Chad responded to her basic warmth and directness. Steve visibly relaxed, knowing that "everything was going to work out. All the vibes were solid."

On the surface, their backgrounds, education, and personality indicated a basic incompatibility. Ali was an avid reader; Steve never cracked a book. She disliked machinery and blood sports; he was still heavily into cycles. She was a sentimental romantic; he was a stubborn realist. Yet the chemistry between them seemed strong enough to overcome these differences. "We are both sharply opinionated," Ali admitted.

> Steve has some very strong male attitudes, and I certainly don't buy all of them. But we understand each other and respect each other and we turn each other on. So we'll just build from there. Steve wants to start a new life and I want to share it with him.

McQueen *was* attempting to change. Having read about lung cancer, he told Ali he was giving up cigarettes. Also, he was sticking to his decision about automobile competition; racing cars were no longer a part of his future.

Another major change came about when he had given up

his Solar offices in Studio City. "I got in there over my head," he admitted.

> Found myself working 16 hours a day ... president of three corporations ... scads of secretaries, accountants, clerks ... dozens of production people. It got kinda crazy, and it was makin' *me* crazy. So I cut it. And I've lightened up on the booze, too. I was into it pretty good there for a while. I don't want to grow old in this business and die with a martini in my hand.

He talked about his increasing dissatisfaction with acting. "I have more and more doubts about it. Sure, sometimes I get that buzz going and know I'm doing good work—but the kick just isn't there most of the time. You can only go so far as an actor. There are other areas I want to explore, a lot of other doors I want to open."

16...

A Prison in Jamaica—
and a Fire in
San Francisco

Late afternoon along the Malibu coast. A spill of white foam and the muted crash of Pacific breakers. Clouded sunlight on the wide, blue-steel spread of ocean.

We were walking barefoot over the cool beach. Our subject: all the films Steve *didn't* make.

"I know all about *Day of the Champion* and *Yucatan*," I said. "But I also heard that you were set to do *Man on a Nylon String*."

"Right," said Steve. "Solar was into it. But it's lucky I never got around to that one. Probably would have broken my neck. It was about mountain climbing—and I would have been doing all the stunt climb stuff myself."

"In the middle '60s you were supposed to play a bullfighter, weren't you?"

"Yeah, yeah...Jesus, that's *another* one I'm glad I missed. My agent was setting it up for me to play the part of some famous matador... Luis somebody."

"Luis Miguel Dominguin?"

"Yeah, him. Well... ole Steve-o-reno woulda been out there in the bullring for sure, wavin' a cape over a sharp pair of horns. Man, that's a real mean trip, bullfighting."

"Then, for Sturges, some war film?"

"*The Yards at Essendorf.*" Steve nodded. "Johnny wanted me to do it in '68, but things didn't pan out."

We walked in silence for a few moments, listening to the ocean. Gulls were crying high above the beach.

"There was this film on Entebbe," said Steve. "I was gonna play Dan Shomren, Israel's head honcho who led the big raid. He commanded their paratroop and infantry forces. Schaffner was set to direct. This was in '76, after we'd done *Papillon* together. But the deal fell apart."

"Weren't you and Neile once offered *Gable and Lombard?*"

He grinned. "They asked us to do it, but we both thought it was a howl. Neile's no Lombard and I'm no Gable. That was one turkey less in my life!"

"Then there was *The Cold War Swap.*"

"Right. I was supposed to do it after *Bullitt*, in 1968. Was all set to fly to Berlin... but I ended up in Vegas for the Stardust 7-11." He shrugged.

"Others?"

"Sure... there was a western, *Applegate's Gold*, and a thing called *The Johnson County War*. I forget exactly what happened but both deals fell through. It happens."

"Of all these films, which one are you sorry you didn't make?"

"*Yucatan*," Steve said. "With all that action cycle stuff. Shit, I rode five hundred miles through Mexico, scouting locations, and Harry Kleiner did a bitch of a good script on my story idea. We figured to bring it in at Solar for under three million. Even had our start date. February 15, 1971. But *Le Mans* killed it." He shook his head. "Boy . . . the beating we took with *Le Mans* was brutal."

The sun was almost down and a sharp wind was gusting in from the ocean.

"Gettin' cold," said McQueen.

And the talking was done.

In February of 1973, the epic production of *Papillon*, based on the best-selling book by Henri Charriere, began filming in Fuenterrabia, Spain, starring McQueen in the title role and costarring Dustin Hoffman as Louis Dega.

Nicknamed "Papillon" (the butterfly) because of his implacable desire to remain free, Charriere was sentenced to life imprisonment after murdering a pimp in Paris during the early 1930s. But no prison could hold him. He escaped several times—and was eventually condemned to Devil's Island, off French Guiana in South America. He became the first man to escape from the dreaded penal colony, using a self-made raft of dried coconuts. He found refuge in Venezuela and became a prosperous citizen there, eventually writing his memoirs as *Papillon*. His book detailed 13 harrowing years of captivity.

The screenplay had been in preparation for two years and was still not completed. Four writers had been hired and fired by the time director Franklin Schaffner brought in Dalton Trumbo to work on the final shooting script.

"Our main problem has been the book itself," said Schaffner. "Damn thing's five hundred pages long, and it was tough to know what to leave in and what to take out, but I think that with Trumbo we've finally got the proper handle on it." McQueen was Schaffner's first choice for the starring role. "Steve embodies Charriere's passion for personal freedom," said Schaffner, "and this is the heart of our story. Charriere's need, like that of the butterfly tattooed on his chest, is to fly free."

Dustin Hoffman brilliantly portrayed Dega, a bespectacled, physically weak counterfeiter who pays Charriere to protect him from the other convicts. A close friendship develops, and Papillon ends up saving Dega's life. (McQueen received

$2,000,000 for his title role; Hoffman got $1,250,000.)

The bulk of the filming took place in Jamaica, where a huge prison set was constructed. (The 600 "French prisoners" were actually German-descended farmers recruited from the island.)

Charriere himself visited the set in Jamaica and was stunned, finding it identical to the actual prison in which he'd been confined as a French convict. "I shiver, standing here," he said. "It seems that at any moment a guard will appear to lock me up again. . . . It is all too realistic."

Shooting on the island became a grueling ordeal. For three months the cast and crew labored under a humid, oven-hot sun in thick jungle and along rocky shores, bitten by insects and menaced by crocodiles.

In the film McQueen escapes twice before being sent to Devil's Island. He emerges from his final five years of solitary confinement gaunt and white-haired, but still fiercely determined to escape.

Charriere's intense study of the waters around the island is rewarded when he discovers that every seventh wave carries the current back to sea. He constructs his small raft and, to the amazement of Dega who never believed such a plan could succeed, dives from the high rocks into the waters below. The film ends with a triumphant Papillon riding to freedom on the seventh wave.

Originally projected at $4,500,000, the film actually cost Allied Artists almost three times that amount, but nevertheless earned a substantial profit—with critics praising the sensitive, meticulously crafted performances of McQueen and Hoffman. Again, in an extremely difficult and demanding role, Steve McQueen had reaffirmed his ability to bring strength and conviction to the screen.

Ali MacGraw had accompanied Steve on location, and he admitted that her presence in Jamaica had "saved me from going around the bend. Those three months on the island would have been sheer hell without her. When things got rough she was right there beside me and that *counted*. I value her a lot. We're good for each other."

Their relationship deepened into a full commitment that July, when they drove into Cheyenne, Wyoming, with marriage in mind. Steve's two children and Ali's young son, Josh, were with them, but no reporters were aware of their plan.

Steve reached Justice of the Peace Arthur Garfield by phone at the local golf course, telling Garfield that he had Ali MacGraw with him, "and we want you to marry us." Garfield was startled, and it took some talking to convince him that the phone call was genuine. He finally agreed to meet them at the county courthouse.

But Steve said no, that he and Ali wanted to be married under a big shade tree, "with lots of green grass around."

In Holiday Park, on July 13, 1973, under a canopy of tall cottonwood trees, with their children as witnesses, Steve McQueen and Ali MacGraw were married. At 43, he had taken a second wife ten years his junior.

The press asked Neile Adams McQueen to comment on the wedding. Was she upset by the news? "It's not news to me," she replied. "Ali's my friend. In fact, the day before they left for Cheyenne she and Steve were at my place to tell me they were going to marry. I gave them my blessing."

And how did she feel personally about Steve?

"It took a couple of years for us to become good friends again after our marriage ended, but now we're family to each other. He's the father of my children . . . why *shouldn't* we be close? I love Steve and he loves me—and that's forever."

In her new role as Mrs. Steve McQueen, Ali MacGraw decided to put her film career "on the shelf for awhile." She was ready for a try at being a housewife and mother. "I needed to settle down and raise my son," she said.

> I didn't want to go on dragging Joshua from one movie location to another. When I married Steve my son was just two and a half, and Chad, who stayed with us, was twelve. [Terri lived with Neile.] Children as young as Joshua and Chad need the stability of a solid family life. To me, that meant being home with them, creating a sense of security in their lives after the trauma of our two divorces. God knows, that need took priority over my film career.

After a honeymoon in Yellowstone National Park, the McQueens settled into a modest ocean-front house at Trancas Beach, along the California coast just north of Malibu. "We liked Trancas," Ali said. "A lot less smog there . . . miles of safe beach for kids . . . good schools. I felt a great sense of peace, living there."

To retain her figure, Ali arranged for regular workouts at Ron Fletcher's Studio in Beverly Hills. "Steve likes his women slim, and I worked hard to stay that way."

After the rigors of *Papillon,* McQueen was in no hurry to sign for another film. He told his agent: "No out-of-state locations for the next one. Gotta be right here in California. And I want some fat percentages. That's where the heavy bread is, in a solid percentage deal. Get me one."

Steve's agent did exactly that, arranging what McQueen termed "a sweetheart deal" for a starring role in *The Towering Inferno,* to be shot in San Francisco and at the 20th Century-Fox studio lot in Los Angeles. Steve would receive $1 million for the film, plus a hefty 7.5 percent of box-office gross. (As McQueen observed: "They can kill you on net, but on gross you make out like a bandit!")

The project had a complex history and involved a conflict between 20th Century-Fox and Warner Brothers. Each studio had purchased rights to novels dealing with disastrous fires in high-rise buildings. Fox had paid $400,000 for *The Glass Inferno* by Frank M. Robinson and Thomas Scortia; Warners had shelled out $300,000 for rights to *The Tower* by Richard Martin Stern. Each studio announced major production plans.

"They were like two big buffalos, going head to head," reported one of the agents active in the transaction. "An insane situation, since the studios knew it didn't make sense to produce *two* films on the same subject, each in direct competition with the other. That's when Irwin Allen came into it."

Fresh from his world triumph with *The Poseidon Adventure,* Allen had a powerful reputation for producing money-making disaster films—and he now talked Fox and Warners into combining their resources in the production of a high-budget film encompassing the primary plot elements from *both* novels. This idea was unprecedented in the industry—the merger of two major studios to produce a single motion picture. Allen's plan obviously made solid commercial sense, and a final agreement was reached in October 1973.

By the following spring, an all-star cast had been assembled: McQueen, Paul Newman, Faye Dunaway, William Holden, Fred Astaire, Robert Wagner, Jennifer Jones, Richard Chamberlain, and Robert Vaughn. In May, location shooting began in downtown San Francisco.

McQueen was at his best in a fluid action role that allowed him to be tough and heroic by turn. He was Fire Battalion Chief Michael O'Hallorhan, who is called in to confront a murderous blaze that threatens to consume the entire upper section of a new 138-story skyscraper. Several dozen party-goers are trapped on the top floor's huge Promenade Room, and it is McQueen's job to save these people before the ram-paging fire reaches them.

Veteran scriptwriter Stirling Silliphant adapted both novels into a tense screenplay, short on original character development but powerful in its handling of heart-in-the-throat action se-quences.

McQueen made it clear to both Fox and Warners that he would grant no interviews during the 70-day production of *Inferno*. "I don't need the publicity and I don't want it," he told them.

And despite the fact that he was relaxed enough to share between-scenes jokes with Newman (whom he called "ole blue eyes"), Steve's basic insecurity again surfaced.

He counted the lines of dialogue in the final shooting script and determined that Newman had 12 more lines than he did. Steve immediately phoned the producers and demanded that 12 more lines of dialogue be added to his role.

"We had to send out a boat to reach Silliphant who was at sea for the weekend," said a Fox executive. "McQueen insisted that Silliphant come back to shore that afternoon and write the 12 lines. So he did. Which satisfied Steve. But I can tell you, Silliphant wasn't too happy about having his trip ruined."

Newman and McQueen were working together for the first time since Steve's screen debut as a bit player in *Somebody Up There Likes Me*. The financial contrast, for McQueen, was truly astonishing. In 1956, he had been paid $19 a day for his work; for *The Towering Inferno*, with his up-front payment and his 7.5 percent of the gross profits, he would eventually earn a staggering $12 million!

Commenting on this, critic Charles Champlin wrote: "McQueen's fire captain in *Towering Inferno* left no doubt why he was worth every penny of the millions he earned. He brought to that role an authority that few other actors could touch." And film historian Derek Elley praised McQueen's taut, pragmatic playing. He completely dominates every scene. His performance is one of the most authoritative of his career—echoes of the obsessive, ruthless anti-heroes of *The War Lover* and *Hell Is for Heroes,* but modulated by age and greater expertise. Once again, amid a starry cast, McQueen emerges as the outsider, existing within his own set of principles and beliefs.

Newman was equally well cast as Doug Roberts, the building's architect, who joins McQueen and his fire crew in a series of dangerous rescue attempts inside the flame-ravaged skyscraper.

One sequence called for Steve to make a perilous descent down an elevator shaft to reach a trapped family. As usual, he insisted on doing the stunt work himself, handling it with cool proficiency.

In another jolting sequence he is lowered by helicopter to the roof of an outside scenic elevator. Blown from its moorings, the cage, with its terrified occupants, is on the verge of plunging to the street below. Steve attaches a steel cable to the elevator, then rides it down as the helicopter lowers the wildly swinging cage to safe ground. During the entire scene, Steve is gripping the wrists of a desperate man who has slipped from his perch on the elevator's angled roof.

For the film's spectacular climax, McQueen rigs a series of explosives to shatter the building's main water storage tanks, releasing a million-gallon deluge that douses the flames in the Promenade Room just before they reach the trapped partygoers.

The action sequences were filmed at the 20th Century-Fox lot back in Los Angeles. A four-story section of building was constructed at the Fox Ranch for outside camera work in the scenic elevator sequence. Matte paintings and model work were added to make it appear that these four stories loomed high above San Francisco streets.

A record number of 57 sets were built at Fox on eight large sound stages to represent the interior floors. When a set was burned for a scene, and something went wrong with the action, the entire sequence often had to be reshot. But how does one reshoot on a fire-gutted set?

Director of photography Joseph Biroc had the answer: "Our crew would hop into action, replaster and repaint, bring in new carpeting, furniture, and matching drapes and clean everything up. In twenty minutes we'd be ready to shoot again."

The walls and ceilings of each set were fireproofed. A large part of the budget went into these elaborate sets. The Promenade Room alone cost $300,000. It occupied 11,000 square feet and was surrounded by a 340-foot cyclorama of the San Francisco skyline. This entire set had to be built eight feet above floor level so that some 8,000 gallons of water could run off freely in the final storage tank explosion sequence.

City fire fighters were standing by during each scene. There were strict rules for the use of fire, the intensity allowed, and the length of time it could burn. "The fires were all propane-fed from one-inch valve-controlled hoses," Biroc explained. "While the gas was running full force through these hoses the flames and build-up of heat could be enormous. These 'full burns' were usually limited to no more than half a minute."

Outdoor location shooting took place in downtown San Francisco, with the Hyatt-Regency doubling for the script's fictional skyscraper. McQueen worked with nearly 100 of the city's off-duty fire fighters and almost 3,000 extras. Twenty-five stunt actors were required to "die" for the cameras in breathtaking dives through the upper windows and down elevator shafts and stairwells. They wore lightweight, nonflammable Nomex body suits (originally developed to protect Indianapolis racing drivers). These were coated with a mixture of benzine and alcohol. When ignited, they produced a chillingly realistic "human torch" effect.

One of the more harrowing and spectacular sequences involved an elevator crowded with a dozen partygoers trying to escape the holocaust. Script action called for the buttons on the elevator's control panel to be activated by heat, causing the doors to open directly into a flame-filled hallway. "As the doors opened we turned on a propane jet," said Biroc, "and the effect is that of a ball of fire swooping into the elevator. The fire was actually stopped by a thick sheet of clear plastic. On film, however, the illusion is extremely real. The people appear to be totally engulfed by the flames. It's a shocking scene, but it just might teach people *not* to use elevators during a fire."

In the picture's final moments, after the blaze has finally been extinguished, McQueen and Newman grimly face each other, as O'Hallorhan tells Roberts that architects had best consult with fire fighters *before* designing their buildings to prevent future disasters of this nature. The scene and dialogue are overly simplistic, but McQueen's intensity gets the message across.

A special Los Angeles fire fighter had been assigned to each member of the cast. Despite the hazards, not one actor was injured.

In August 1974 McQueen was made an "honorary Los Angeles fire fighter" in an official ceremony at City Hall. The title was no empty one for Steve, since he had actually helped battle a real fire. Earlier that year at Fox, McQueen had been discussing technical details of his *Inferno* role with Los Angeles City Battalion Chief Peter Lucarelli. An emergency call came through: Stages 3 and 4 were afire at the Goldwyn Studio and flames were threatening to engulf the production offices. Lucarelli told Steve he'd take him along. "Maybe you can learn something."

When they arrived at the Goldwyn lot a large crowd had gathered—and some 200 fire fighters, representing two dozen city units, were battling the flames.

McQueen and Lucarelli entered the fire area, and Steve donned a heavy jacket, boots and regulation helmet, then followed Lucarelli into one of the buildings through a lower floor window.

The ceiling was afire, burning fiercely, and McQueen joined several other fire fighters who were attempting to hose down the flames. One of them stared at him: "Shit! My wife will never believe this." Steve grinned, blinking back raw smoke. "Neither will mine."

With all fires out, real and cinematic, McQueen returned to his reclusive beach life in Trancas—but by early 1975, rumors were spreading. The relationship between Steve and Ali MacGraw was coming apart at the seams. After less than two years, McQueen's second marriage was in serious trouble.

17...

The Ibsen Challenge

Again, we dealt with the ever-haunting subject of his father.

"Maybe if I'd known him I'd be able to forget he ever existed. It's the *mystery* of a thing that keeps bringing you back...you want to solve it." Steve hesitated. "But that's one mystery I'll never solve."

We were in an after-hours bar in Santa Monica. Quiet. Dimly lit. A place for reflection. A place to think about the past.

"Here I am, doin' what *he* did," said McQueen. "Flyin' these ole biplanes...the same kind he barnstormed in the '20s and '30s. Leather helmet and goggles. Open cockpit. Wind in your face....Yeah, I know now why he was a pilot. Great feeling, up there in the sky. Just you and the plane, humming along free and easy."

"Didn't Chad take some flying lessons?"

"Yeah, but I think he prefers the bikes. He's a lot like me in some ways...even *spooky* ways. I

168

look at him next to me and he's holdin' his arm
down loose, with his hand kind of away from his
body, fingers half open, exactly the way I stand.
Identical posture. And that's spooky, lookin' at him
and seeing myself in his gestures. Know what I
mean?"

"I think so."

He took a quick swallow from the drink in his
hand. "Now he tells me he wants to be an actor,
and I tell him it's a tough life. Tough if you don't
make it—and tough if you *do*."

"What about Terri? Think she'll go into show
business?"

"I doubt it. She's into prelaw now. Says she's
gonna be a Supreme Court judge." He chuckled.
"When she was a little girl I taught her how to
ride a cycle, and she thought it was just the greatest. Told me she wanted to become the country's
first lady motorcycle champion."

"From what I've heard—you've been a good
parent to your kids."

He sighed, slowly turning the glass in his hand.
"I tried to be . . . Man, I really tried to be."

And the long years of fatherhood were there.
In his eyes.

During the entirety of 1975 McQueen remained away from
motion picture cameras, turning down every script. As a result,
by year's end, he had dropped to ninth position among world
film favorites.

When producers wanted to know why they couldn't reach
him, Steve's agents had no answer. "Just the way he is these
days. Stays in Trancas. Won't talk to anybody. Won't see
anybody. Most of the time he won't even answer the phone."

There was speculation that Steve's increasing deafness had
caused him to withdraw from social contact, and that he had
been trying acupuncture to improve his hearing.

Magazine writer Marie Brenner reported on the McQueen/
MacGraw lifestyle for *Redbook:* "Last June, Ali and Steve
trekked off to his house in Palm Springs and plastered and

wallpapered it. . . . At their beach house, Ali makes tuna fish salads and broils steaks. She does most of the housework, with the cleaning woman in just once a week, and seems content to stay at home."

In truth, Ali was growing progressively discontented with her role as a Trancas housewife. She was frustrated by McQueen's stubborn attitude toward her screen career. When her agent, Sue Mengers, would call with a film offer, Steve would grab the phone and curtly remind the agent: "My wife works only with *me,* on a project I'll choose for both of us!"

McQueen seriously considered starring in another film with Ali, *Fancy Hardware,* but as she reported, "Steve broke a bone in his left foot practicing karate and called off the picture."

Ali was now visiting a Beverly Hills psychiatrist four days a week in an attempt to understand why she was so unhappy. She was greatly upset at various gossip items that were circulating about her marriage: "I kept reading things that were totally untrue," she declared.

> About how Steve had made a "house slave" of me and forced me to live like a hermit . . . that he'd even *beaten* me! Sure, we had our arguments, but he never batted me around. Not once. Not ever. As for the hermit stuff, that was as much my choice as his. Essentially, I'm a shy person, a kind of fanatic about my privacy, and I was doing exactly what I wanted to do in living away from the social whirl at the beach. The idea that we were hermits came from the fact that we wouldn't do interviews. At that time, Steve literally didn't want to talk to anybody, and neither did I. We both wanted to stay *out* of the public eye.
>
> But, after a while, I began to miss big-city life. I *do* love New York when I'm in a certain mood for it—and I found myself missing that kind of hyperenergy. . . . I began to question this whole withdrawn response to life. I began to rebel at my own shyness, at the isolated existence I'd chosen. That was one reason why I felt the need to see a psychiatrist.

McQueen was undergoing his own discontent. Bored and rootless, uncertain of what career goals to pursue, and angry over his eroding marriage, Steve began drinking heavily. He was also smoking again (up to three packs of cigarettes per day). He would sit for hours in front of the television set, downing endless cans of beer—or he would aimlessly ride one of his cycles along private roads near Malibu.

When he did venture out for an occasional business meeting in Beverly Hills, reporters were caustic in their descriptions: "McQueen strolls through the room [the Polo Lounge] in a faded work shirt tucked into dirty beige jeans, his feet in Chukka boots, his beer gut leading the way."

Steve's temper was on a short fuse, and he began to argue with his beach neighbor, Keith Moon, regarding several flood-lights on the Moon property. McQueen told him they were "too damn bright," that they kept him awake. When Moon refused to turn off the lights Steve shot them out in a repeat performance of the streetlight shootout in Hollywood years earlier. "He also argued with our neighbors over parking space," Ali said. "And about noise from his motorcycles and Lord knows what else. It got a bit frantic."

That September, disturbed by restrictions in state cycle laws, McQueen sent an open letter to *Cycle News:* "We can save the future of motorcycling by working toward a sane solution to bike safety. Together, we can win the respect our sport deserves." Steve felt that safety must be self-regulated by the cyclists themselves, state to state, without government control.

With his career at a standstill, machines and machinery had now become a way of life, the one area where he could be "in control." These months were "Steve's truck farm period," Ali said. To a magazine interviewer she claimed that

> if you parked them in a line, bumper to bumper, Steve's trucks would stretch from here to South Dakota. Seven of them are parked on the street right now outside our house. I get up in the morning and Steve's on the phone to someone in Arkansas, setting up a deal to buy a 1921 model truck he just can't live without.

Since she had grown up in a world of classical music, theater, and literature, it was difficult for her to adjust to McQueen's world of machinery. "Trucks don't really thrill me at all that much," she told the journalist.

Ali did manage to talk Steve into taking her to the ballet at the Dorothy Chandler Pavilion in downtown Los Angeles, but he grew restless and stalked out in the middle of the performance. ("We conducted a public shouting match in the lobby," she recalled.) At Trancas, according to Ali, they set up dual systems of entertainment:

> Our bedroom is wired with separate earphones to our own TV and stereo sets. That way we don't have to deal with each other's choices. I can watch a program on classical dance while he tunes in the latest football game. There are a lot of areas Steve and I just don't share in common.

McQueen's desire for privacy deepened with each passing month; when agents and producers continued to send unwanted scripts to his Trancas address he uprooted the mailbox and pitched it into the ocean. Thereafter, he had all of their mail delivered to a Gulf gas station on the Pacific Coast Highway, where it often remained uncollected for several days.

But as an actor, Steve was still very much in demand. Francis Ford Coppola sought him for the lead role in *Apocalypse Now*. In December 1975 Coppola offered $1,500,000 and Steve said that he would accept that sum, but only as "front money." He wanted the *same* amount upon completion of the film. McQueen would therefore agree to sign for *double* Coppola's initial offer, a guarantee of $3 million.

"I thought that over very carefully," said Coppola. "We had a series of meetings on it—and when Steve finally decided he didn't want to spend several months on location I offered him a smaller role he could handle in three weeks."

"Okay," Steve told him, "but my price still stands."

Coppola was shocked. "You mean three million for just three weeks?"

"Right. Million a week. Take it or leave it."

"I left it," said Coppola. "That price was totally unreal. And he didn't seem to give a damn whether I said yes or no."

McQueen instructed his agent to inform producers that his fee was now $50,000 simply to *read* a script.

"They won't pay it, Steve," the agent declared.

"Great. Then I won't have to read any more lousy screenplays."

For the first time in his life McQueen allowed himself to gain an excessive amount of weight. Beer and an intake of rich Mexican food swelled him from a taut-muscled 150 to a corpulent 210 pounds—and his daily workouts were a thing of the past.

"Hell, man, I've had it with exercise," he told a cycle buddy. "Why should I kill myself liftin' weights...screw that jazz! If I want to get fat that's *my* business. I'm not plannin' to enter any beauty contests."

In April 1976 Ali was celebrating her thirty-seventh birthday with some friends at the exclusive Le Bistro in Beverly Hills when a roaring engine shattered the intimate quiet of the restaurant. It was McQueen, weaving his motorcycle between tables, heading straight for Ali's party.

"McQueen was obviously drunk," a witness recalled, "bearded, dressed in tattered jeans and a grease-stained shirt. He'd bought a birthday cake somewhere and was trying to deliver it on his cycle when the manager rushed out with a couple of big waiters and hustled him back to the street." Ali was furious. She gave him an ultimatum. Either he would "straighten out his life," or she would take Joshua and leave immediately. She accused him of living like a drunken beach bum.

McQueen did not argue the point. Her description was accurate. He admitted that it was time for him to resume his career. "I told her that I'd found a project I wanted to do," he recalled. "It would be the biggest risk of my life." He wanted to produce an Ibsen play. "I've been into a lot of his stuff, and I've picked out something I want to do."

"You mean...you want to do a classic play by Henrik Ibsen?"

"Yeah, that's it. But not for the stage. I want to do his *Enemy of the People* as a film. And not just act in it, I also want to produce and direct. The whole bag. That's why I've been growin' this beard—for the role."

Indeed, as Ibsen's Thomas Stockmann, a doctor whose fight against pollution made him "an enemy of the people," McQueen intended to change his entire physical appearance. The weight would be part of it, since he felt that Stockmann, as an older man, would be heavy as well as bearded. Also, he intended to wear wire-rimmed spectacles and long, curling hair to complete the alteration.

That summer McQueen formally announced the new film, telling *The Hollywood Reporter:* "I'm lucky that I'm in a position to do it. I can afford to fail now, so I want to try this. Up to now, I've never wanted to tackle anything I could fail at. Artistically, I've been a coward."

During 1976 McQueen turned down several million-plus offers on other projects. "I'm not backing away from the Ibsen," he said.

> That's my next picture, no matter what. I've taken a lot of flak about it from agents and industry people who tell me I've gotta be nuts. And maybe they're right. Maybe I'll fall flat on my duff. But I'll never know if I don't try. The chips are down and I'm playing out the hand.

Steve decided to abandon his plan of directing to concentrate on acting and executive production. Under a First Artists' agreement, Warner Brothers would finance the new film (projected at a "tight" $2,000,000), although they were less than delighted with McQueen's choice of material. "They want me on the screen with a gun in my hand," he said.

> The full macho bit. McQueen the rebel, the cool killer. Same crap I've been into for years. But this time I'm goin' in a different direction. When you get right down to it, though, I'm *still* playing a nonconformist, because that's what Stockmann is. He's a guy who won't back down when the whole town's against him. He stands alone for what he knows is right, and he's *strong* because of that. Sure, it was written nearly a century ago, but the theme ties right in to the problems we face today with polluted lakes and poisoned air and chemicals in all our food. That's what attracted me to this play, the message it carries—that we need to take personal responsibility for what's happening around us. That's what Ibsen was saying.

Henrik Ibsen, a pioneer of realism in the theater, wrote *An Enemy of the People* in 1882. His play celebrated the courage of Thomas Stockmann, a doctor in a small Norwegian village, who discovers that the so-called "healing waters" of the community springs have been polluted by wastes from a nearby tannery. Stockmann informs the villagers. Led by their mayor, they turn against him. In their view, the pollution should be ignored, considering the fact that substantial tourist income will be lost if the truth becomes known. Monetary greed has overcome their concern for health standards. When Stockmann will not back down, the mayor destroys the doctor's credibility—and in a drama-charged town meeting, Stockmann is branded "an enemy of the people." His home is stoned, his wife is insulted, his daughter loses her teaching job, his sons are teased and assaulted—but Stockmann prevails. As the play ends, the point is made that the truth *will* be told and that Thomas Stockmann will endure to tell it.

McQueen chose George Schaefer to direct the production. Among many honors, Schaefer had won eight television Emmys and four Directors Guild of America Awards. Quality drama was his trademark, and he had established the prestigious *Hallmark Hall of Fame* series on NBC. Since Ibsen's *A Doll's House* had been a Schaefer production for Hallmark, McQueen felt that he was "just the right guy" to direct *An Enemy of the People*.

Steve chose two equally distinguished talents to costar in the film. Bibi Andersson, famous for her intense dramatic roles in several Ingmar Bergman classics, would play Stockmann's wife, Catherine. The doctor's brother, Peter, would be played by the highly respected character actor Charles Durning.

Before production began, McQueen issued a statement to the press:

> We don't have an auto chase to sell in this one. What we *do* have is dignity and truth. If the people who see it leave the theater feeling enriched, they're going to tell their friends—and an audience will be created. But I'm not doing this picture to make bucks. I'm doing it because I want to have something I can be proud of, a film that is *pure*, that is done with total quality in mind.

Three weeks of rehearsals began in early August on a sound stage at MGM, rented for this production by Warners. McQueen insisted on the rehearsals, since he wanted to be fully prepared before stepping in front of the camera. Actual filming did not begin until the first week of September 1976.

In facing his assembled cast, McQueen was blunt concerning his lack of classical training: "This is *your* world, not mine," he told them. "I'm a little out of my depth here, but I can promise you I'll give this the best I have in me. If I fail I won't blame anybody. The fault will be mine."

There were no outdoor locations for *An Enemy of the People;* the entire production was filmed on sound stages, where the 1880 locale was created in careful detail. The sets and costumes were authentic. Even the printing presses used in the film were actual period pieces dating back to the middle of the nineteenth century.

Rumors of fresh trouble in the McQueen marriage circulated when Steve rented a hotel room at the Beverly Wilshire, leaving his wife and children in Trancas. Ali replied to the rumors: "Steve wanted to be closer to the studio. He's not used to long dialogue scenes and he needs to be alone to study his lines. It takes a lot of courage to do what he's doing—and he knows I'll be here when he comes home."

After shooting all day at MGM, McQueen would usually stop by the hotel's El Padrino Room for an "ease down" drink or two. No one recognized this heavy, bearded figure, and Steve enjoyed the rare anonymity. If his drinking companions asked who he was he'd tell them, "My name's Joe. I run a construction crew." The men he drank with had no idea they were sharing bar space with an international film star.

The role of Thomas Stockmann was indeed demanding, and McQueen struggled to master long speeches in several key scenes. During one particularly difficult afternoon in October, after delivering a complex, emotionally charged three-page monologue on the set, Steve was delighted to have the entire crew break into applause.

"He's as happy as a kid with a lollipop," Charles Durning reported. "Steve feels that he's really *acting* in front of a camera for the first time in his life, and he's greatly stimulated by it."

At a rough-cut screening of the work print that winter, Warner executives were shocked, declaring that the film was "completely out of touch with today's market." One executive was openly hostile. "It's a goddam embarrassment, a piece of *junk!* Who wants to see Steve McQueen—at 210 pounds, for Christ's sake!—running around in granny glasses and a Santa Claus beard?"

Ali, however, was impressed. "Steve's brilliant in it. He made me cry. The truth is that behind his tough-guy image he's the most sensitive man I know. I'm very proud of him."

Before the year ended McQueen received news of a very special award: He was made an honorary member of the Motion Picture Stuntmen's Association, cited as "an actor who has the courage and ability to perform his own stunts." Steve was touched by the citation, being well aware that this group of professionals rarely bestowed such honors on anyone outside their dangerous profession. "I'm happy that you feel I deserve this," he told them. "It means a great deal to me and I thank you for it."

McQueen wanted to follow *An Enemy of the People* with another filmed play, a version of Harold Pinter's *Old Times,* but First Artists refused. A conflict developed; there was talk of legal action, but early in 1977 the dispute was settled when Steve agreed to put aside his plans for *Old Times* in favor of an action-adventure film, *Tom Horn,* based on true incidents in the life of this famed gunslinger.

"Actually, I'd been planning to do Horn's story," McQueen said. "It was just a matter of activating the project a little sooner than expected. Horn and I shared common experiences and I related to him on many levels."

Certainly their lives paralleled to a remarkable degree. Both were raised on Missouri farms. Both were beaten boys, Horn by his father, McQueen by his stepfather. Both were loose-footed wanderers, seeking adventure where they could find it. In fact, had McQueen been born in 1860 instead of 1930, he might well have followed many of the same wild trails.

Tom Horn was a teamster for the Santa Fe Railroad, rode shotgun for a stagecoach line, became a rodeo champion, a deputy marshal, a Pinkerton detective, and a Cavalry scout. He tracked down the great Apache chief, Geronimo, and arranged for the Indian's surrender to government troops. During the Spanish-American War, Horn was one of Teddy Roosevelt's Rough Riders. He worked his own silver mine and eventually drifted into Wyoming to become a hired gun for a cattlemen's association, hunting down rustlers. It was this final period of Horn's life that McQueen planned to film.

"But, as it turned out, we were still two years away from production when I decided to take on the project in March of '77," Steve said. "I had a lot of other things to worry about, such as my marriage. It was really breaking up, and this time there was no saving it. I think we both knew things were over that summer."

Ali MacGraw has openly discussed her marital problems during this time, admitting to a reporter:

> I became awful to live with. I really was a horror. Very negative, very judgmental. I'd become a sort of monster.
>
> Steve and I were both born under the sign of Aries, the Ram, which means we were both very aggressive and opinionated. We clashed a lot, head on. One thing about Steve, he didn't like the woman in his life to have balls!

Ali tried to lose herself in housework, cleaning out closets, polishing silver, creating endless flower arrangements, cooking and gardening—but all this activity failed to improve her state of mind. By 1977 she was thoroughly frustrated.

"I got tired of waiting for Steve to pick out a movie for both of us to star in—so I just went ahead and signed to do *Convoy*, with Kris Kristofferson," she related. "That did it. That ended our marriage."

Steve moved out of the beach house in Trancas to an apartment of his own and replaced Ali with a *Playboy* bunny. ("I thought I'd give the 'sweet life' a spin!")

Columnist James Bacon reported:

> I once talked to this young lady about Steve, and she told me she didn't know what to think about him. He'd suddenly turned into an avid reader of classics! "I guess it started with that Ibsen," she said. "But he's reading every classic he can get his hands on, Shakespeare, Chekhov—I don't know all those names—but just *everything!*" She seemed mystified at this new McQueen, and I couldn't blame her.

In his deepening search for privacy and his desire to "get back to the land, to the wild places," McQueen purchased a five-acre spread in Idaho, just outside Ketchum, in North Fork. He called it "Last Chance," and commissioned an architect in the area to build a massive log cabin on the site. "Steve insisted

McQUEEN

With Ed Sullivan as passenger, McQueen demonstrates his Solar-designed dune buggy in October 1968.

With his 1905 Winton Flyer bogged in a mudhole, McQueen hops out to check the damage in *The Reivers* (1969). (Cinema Center Films)

In the Chevy-powered Baja Boot during a rugged cross-country event. (William F. Nolan)

At the International 12-Hour event at Sebring, Florida, in March 1970, where he drove a spectacular race despite a broken left foot. (Wide World Photos)

On his way to a class victory, McQueen slides his 908 Porsche (#48) into the "S" turn at Sebring, just ahead of a faster Ferrari. (William F. Nolan)

At Le Mans, overlooking the front straight of the famed French circuit, during the production of his racing epic, *Le Mans* (1971). (Cinema Center Films)

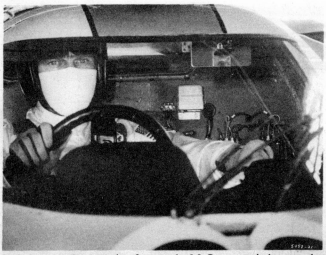

In helmet and protective fire mask, McQueen switches on the engine of his 917 Porsche. (Cinema Center Films)

McQueen's 917 Porsche (#21) follows two Ferraris through a turn on the Le Mans circuit. (William F. Nolan)

Chad McQueen, at 9, ready to climb into his mini-Ferrari at Le Mans, in 1970. He won this event for young drivers. (Wide World Photos)

As a fading rodeo champion in *Junior Bonner* (1972). (ABC/Cinerama)

Chained be-
tween guards for
his difficult role
of a man no pris-
on could hold in
Papillon (1973).
(Allied Artists)

With costar Ali MacGraw and director Sam Peckinpah in a between-scenes shot on *The Getaway* (1972). (National General)

Sharing a between-scenes joke with Faye Dunaway and Paul Newman in *The Towering Inferno*. (Courtesy of Twentieth Century-Fox. Copyright © 1974 Twentieth Century-Fox Film Corp. All Rights Reserved.)

In full fire-fighting gear for his role as Battalion Chief Michael O'Hallorhan in *The Towering Inferno* (1974). (Peter C. Borsari Photograph)

An exhausted McQueen in *The Towering Inferno*. (Courtesy of Twentieth Century-Fox. Copyright © 1974 Twentieth Century-Fox Film Corp. All Rights Reserved.)

With Ali MacGraw observing, McQueen tells a newsman, "Sorry, I don't do interviews." (Peter C. Borsari Photograph)

In 1975, Ali talked a reluctant McQueen into taking her to the ballet in Los Angeles. (Peter C. Borsari Photograph)

A tangle-haired, straggle-bearded McQueen during his reclusive period in Trancas, 1976. (Peter C. Borsari Photograph)

Facing questions from a student audience at a special UCLA showing of *An Enemy of the People* in August 1978. (Peter C. Borsari Photograph)

Barbara Minty hands Steve a beer during a Rolling Stones concert at Anaheim, California, in 1978. (Peter C. Borsari Photograph)

McQueen's beautifully restored classic, the 1931 Pitcairn PA-8 bi-plane, once flown as part of the U.S. Mail Service by famed WWI ace Eddie Rickenbacker. (Douglas Dullenkopf)

Proudly wearing his 1929 flying suit, McQueen poses in front of
the Pitcairn with pilot-friend Mike Dewey at California's Santa
Paula Airport in August 1979, a month after he earned his license.
(Douglas Dullenkopf)

Arriving with his third wife Barbara Minty McQueen at Oxnard, California, for a press preview of *Tom Horn* in March 1980, eight months prior to his death. (United Press International Photo)

A teenaged Chad McQueen. (Peter C. Borsari Photograph)

Mother and daughter; Terri with Neile Adams McQueen. (Peter C. Borsari Photograph)

on having each log 'antiqued,' to give the place a properly weathered look," an Idaho neighbor said. "Then he had a large shed put up behind the cabin to store antique furniture. When the cabin was done he intended furnishing it with real period stuff."

That year in Idaho, while he was supervising construction, McQueen met the woman who would become his third wife. "Barbara Minty owned a horse ranch down the way from the 'Last Chance'—'bout half a mile," related McQueen's neighbor. "She'd ride by his place in the afternoons—and one day Steve introduced himself. They hit it off right away."

Minty was in her early 20s, a brown-haired, brown-eyed beauty who had posed for the covers of *Vogue* and *Harper's Bazaar* as well as having done Cole of California swimsuit commercials. She was already a top fashion model when Steve met her, but her real passion, like his, was for the land, for clear-sky, green-grass country. She took special pride in her horses, breeding and training them as a hobby at her Idaho ranch. Intense, athletic, and independent-minded, she enjoyed riding cycles and horses—and, when she was with Steve in California, delighted in racing over Malibu backroads in the sidecar of McQueen's bright red Ace, one of the many antique motorcycles he was restoring.

When word of McQueen's ever-expanding stable of machinery reached the Los Angeles *Herald-Examiner*, the paper sent out a reporter that fall with an odd assignment—to count all of Steve's cars, trucks, cycles, and Jeeps. He came up with a grand total of 53 vehicles, including a ten-ton World War II Army half-track with iron treads and armor plating that Neile had given to Steve one Christmas.

"I had a lot more than that," Steve chuckled. "This guy didn't know about my whole warehouse full of antique bikes. He just counted what he found."

In late November 1977 McQueen filed for divorce, and Barbara moved in with him. ("We've decided to share our life together," she was quoted as saying. "Steve needs me. He cares about me.") A friend who knew both of them remarked that "Barbara was a lot more into Steve's world than Ali ever was. Instead of asking him to take her to the ballet, she got tickets to a Rolling Stones rock concert in Anaheim. She and Steve were 'birds of a feather.' That old saying really fit them."

And what was Ali MacGraw's attitude about the breakup of her third marriage?

"For the first time, I'm really happy," she told a reporter. "With Bob [Evans] and with Steve I was constantly trying to be some person other than myself; I was living out a fantasy. The years with Steve helped me discover who I really am. In that sense, they were valuable. And it may be corny to say so, but Steve and I are still pals."

18. . .

From Open Range
to Open Sky

"Funny, the things that can hurt you most."

McQueen was talking about pain as we sat over cups of black coffee on a cold, windy Arizona morning in 1979. He was filming *Tom Horn*, and I was visiting the location, the western movie town of Mescal, some 15 miles south of Old Tucson over roads rugged enough to make me glad I owned a Jeep.

"When I talk about hurt I don't mean broken bones," Steve said. "What happened with *Enemy of the People* hurt me more than almost anything I can remember. I put my heart and guts into that film and when it got the reaction it did, I was wiped out." He lowered his head, tugging thoughtfully at the wide, weathered brim of his sombrero. Under it, his hair was gray and thick-curling against the fur collar of his heavy sheepskin coat. "I never expected it to be any blockbuster hit, that's for sure—but when most of the critics dumped on it, and Warners refused to put up the distribution money... well, that was hard to take. It was just..."

He stopped in mid sentence, finished his coffee in silence, and stood up. "Horn was 43 when they hanged him. But he looked younger. Me, I'm 49, and I look older. But, shit..." He smiled tightly, without warmth. "I was old at 17."

And he picked up his long-barreled Remington rifle, squared his shoulders, and walked resolutely across the deep, rutted mud street—back into the life of Tom Horn.

During March and April 1978 Warner Brothers conducted "a prerelease test" with *An Enemy of the People*. They booked the film into eight U.S. cities, backed by a $400,000 newspaper ad campaign designed to remind moviegoers of McQueen's past box-office hits:

> In a time when people say there are no more heroes—there is still STEVE McQUEEN. You cheered him in *The Great Escape*, prayed for him in *Cincinnati Kid* and held your breath with him in *Bullitt* ...
>
> Now Steve McQueen portrays the most striking hero of them all—the man they called... AN ENEMY OF THE PEOPLE.

When the two-month test showings ended, and results were tabulated, the studio's worst fears were confirmed. Audiences were unable and unwilling to accept McQueen the lean-bodied modern action star as a bulky, bewhiskered doctor in a talky period melodrama.

Critical reaction was equally negative. Arthur Knight claimed that the film "has no juice, no life to it at all. McQueen lacks the voice and authority to sustain Ibsen's intense confrontation scenes." *Variety* spoke of the "obvious miscasting of McQueen... in a film that is lost in a sea of verbiage." A third critic condemned McQueen's "casual, laconic style. He mumbles into his beard... playing Christ-in-a-muffler."

Warners made a decision unheard of with regard to a new motion picture starring an international favorite—they shelved it. "After careful consideration of distribution costs, we have chosen not to release *An Enemy of the People*," they announced. The expenses in distributing the film would have amounted to its full budget, costing Warners an additional $2,500,000 to make prints and mount a national campaign. They did not intend making such an investment. McQueen was stunned. He immediately threatened to sue for the film's release.

"Don't try it, Steve," his lawyer warned him. "You'll lose. There's no way to force them into spending more money on it. They have the legal right to do anything they want with the picture. It belongs to them."

Given no choice, McQueen accepted the studio's decision. Actually, he had been spared even deeper hurt—as proven by a later New York test release (after his death) in the summer of 1981.*

Deeply discouraged by the film's initial reception, Steve sought the advice of his agent.

"He told me to do another big film," Steve said. "He claimed it was vital to prove that I was still a world superstar." McQueen agreed: "But let's make it *really* big. It's gotta knock their socks off. I want a contract that will guarantee headlines."

The deal his agency arranged late in 1978 met these requirements. Trade headlines trumpeted that Steve McQueen was to receive more money for his next film than any screen star in history: $1 million for merely signing the contract, to be followed by step payments that would total another $4 million, *plus* 15 percent of the gross after the film's break-even point.

He would portray Dick Struan, leader of the British colony in Hong Kong in an epic adaptation of James Clavell's dynastic novel, *Tai-Pan*, set in 1849. Swiss exhibitor Georges-Alain Vuille, financial backer of the project, declared that "McQueen is worth more than any actor in the world. We're delighted to have him as our star."

In November the Los Angeles *Herald-Examiner* printed a

The Village Voice wrote of "a grizzled, leaden McQueen . . . [As Stockmann] he's hopeless." The *New York Times* claimed that he was "obviously very uncomfortable with his dialogue . . . in this frail and uncertain production."

news story concerning an 8-year-old boy who was dying of a cancerous brain tumor. Since he was not expected to live another month, the family planned a Christmas party for the youngster on Thanksgiving Day. McQueen immediately phoned the boy's parents and arranged for a two-day trip to Disneyland by limousine for the boy and his family. He also reserved a suite for them at the Disneyland Hotel and had special gifts for everyone waiting in the room when the family arrived.

The boy's grandmother told a reporter about McQueen's gesture and it made the papers. "I was real upset about that," Steve said. "It was just a little something I wanted to do quietly. I didn't want anyone but the boy's family to know."

By the end of the year Barbara insisted that Steve see a doctor about a persistent cough. He claimed it was "the damn cigarettes." But he would check it out. McQueen's doctor assured him that the cough was not serious. "Just a case of some dust build-up in the lungs." He told Steve to stay away from dirt riding for awhile and give his lungs a chance to clear. "Or wear a filter mask if you *do* ride." McQueen accepted this diagnosis, more amused than alarmed. He even allowed his cycle pals to call him "Dusty."

The coughing eased, and McQueen was feeling better by the time he was ready to begin his next film, *Tom Horn,* in mid January 1979, in Nogales, Mexico. (A screenplay for *Tai-Pan* was at least a year from completion.)

When Steve originally announced his intention to produce and star in this project, Don Siegel had been signed to direct. Siegel's deal went sour, and Elliot Silverstein took his place— but further delays in the production caused Silverstein to withdraw in 1978, and James Guercio became the director. At the same time, McQueen withdrew as line producer in favor of Fred Weintraub.

Three writers had already drafted screenplays, none of which completely pleased McQueen. He now assigned a fourth writer, Bud Shrake, and worked closely with him in shaping the final shooting script. It covered the last three years of Horn's life, when the veteran gunslinger was hired by cattlemen as a "range detective" to eliminate rustlers in Wyoming. "We shifted the dates around," said McQueen.

> Horn actually had finished off most of these rustlers by 1900, but we started in 1901 to reflect the changes that

were taking place in the Old West as the new century began. We *did* stick to 1903 as the year he was hanged. That was based directly on what happened.

The real Tom Horn was convicted of murdering the teenaged son of a sheep rancher. The primary evidence against him was a drunken confession made in the office of a Deputy who fed him whiskey to loosen his tongue. Whether Horn actually killed the boy is doubtful, but he was nonetheless hanged for the crime on November 20, 1903, in Cheyenne.

Guilty or innocent, there was no doubt that Tom Horn was a practiced killer; one historian wrote: "In those closing years he turned rotten. There wasn't anyone Horn wouldn't kill for the right price." But in filming his story, McQueen chose to follow the famous words of director John Ford: "Given the truth, and given the legend, film the legend." Steve intended to portray the *legendary* Tom Horn, representing him as a man who embodied a vanishing code of honor in a dying era, "the last true hero of the Old West."

In McQueen's cinema version the gunman is framed for the boy's murder by the same cattleman who hired him as a range detective. Horn has become too dangerous, too headstrong, and independent; he poses a threat to his politically ambitious employer and is thus eliminated by the false murder charge.

McQueen's film celebrated the old, open-range way of life vs. the political encroachment of a mechanized civilization in conflict with the loner who lived by his own rules.

Arizona doubled for southern Wyoming, and after a few scenes were completed in Nogales, the cast and crew headed north into the back country beyond Tucson for another month and a half of location work. "Every shot was real," said producer Fred Weintraub.

We didn't shoot anything on a studio set. We were out there in those Arizona wilds, in mud, sleet, wind, and rain, during one of the state's worst winters, and there were times—a lot of times—when I wondered if we'd ever be able to finish the picture. But Steve wouldn't allow any faking. He wanted the real look and feel of the Old West, and we slogged through a lot of mud to get it.

Following a heavy rain, the narrow dirt roads leading to these new wilderness sites created a major problem in transport. The massive camera cranes and other heavy equipment had to be trucked in with four-wheel-drive vehicles. Mike Rachmil, the production manager, recalled one colossal bog-down.

> We tried to pull a vehicle out of the mud with one twice as big, but that one got stuck too. Another bigger vehicle was brought in, but that one also bogged down. . . . Soon we had an entire line of a dozen vehicles completely mired in the mud! We had to bring in some U.S. Army Engineers with huge trucks and tractors to pull us out.

Ice was another problem. Weintraub's Jeep slid off the edge of an icy mountain road and rolled several times. "I was thrown clear," he said. "But it was a helluva scary experience."

McQueen's personal force and enthusiasm kept cast and crew at a high performance level. "Steve set the pace for all of us," said Rachmil. "His energy level was incredible. When somebody got stuck, he'd be right out there with the crew, knee-deep in mud, helping to pull them out. There was no part of the film he didn't personally oversee. In fact, during the second week or so, he even tried to direct it."

Ten days into the shooting, McQueen fired the starting director, James Guercio, and took over the film himself, but stepped down in favor of William Wiard, who was brought in to replace Guercio. (Thus the tangled directorial sequence on *Tom Horn* had progressed from Siegel to Silverstein to Guercio to McQueen to Wiard.)

In his demand for authenticity, McQueen employed the talents of costume designer Luster Bayless who provided the proper "used" look for this turn-of-the-century production. He clothed the cast in baggy pants, long "duster" coats, ill-fitting shirts, and weathered headgear appropriate to the period. "I came up with this huge old felt sombrero for Steve," he said.

> Then we worked out his chaps-and-suspenders look. Scruffy, but real. And no fancy gun rig, just a Colt jammed into his belt at belly level the way a lot of the old westerners used to do it. Also, in those days, a man might wear two or even *three* shirts, one over the other,

to keep warm. We studied a great many photographs of the era, and followed those basic styles.

McQueen's horse and rifle were equally important, since Steve was required to fire from the saddle while in hard-riding pursuit of rustlers. "We found a horse so well trained he could have starred in his own act," Steve related. "He could walk backward, sideways, rear up on command...and his gallop was smooth and steady."

Horn's rifle in the film was a .45-.60 Remington single shot, and Steve became expert at sighting and firing the heavy weapon while at full gallop. ("I steered with my knees, like you do on a polo pony.") Since his beginning days on a horse with *Wanted—Dead or Alive*, McQueen had become a superb rider, despite his continuing aversion to four-legged steeds.

One of the main location sites for *Horn* was the Sharp Ranch in the San Rafael Valley, close to the Mexican border. Important sequences were filmed there and in the surrounding country. This richly scenic area was characterized by rolling hills, with mountains along the horizon—a perfect double for Wyoming. "We also re-dressed the movie town of Mescal outside Tucson," Rachmil said. "Made it totally faithful to the period."

The cast included McQueen's pal, Slim Pickens, as the Sheriff who befriends Horn, but who must hang him. Linda Evans played a school teacher in love with the gunman. "I didn't wear any makeup," she said.

> Steve wanted a "natural" look. He even had me wear a fake gold tooth because people had them back then. Steve projected all this toughness, but he was really a warm, caring man and a very open actor. He'd try anything to help make a scene better.

Aside from a scattering of professionals, almost all of the supporting roles were given to local cowboys. "They were there on the ranches, so we put them into the picture," said Weintraub. "They added a lot in the way of realism because the one thing a cowboy can play is a cowboy."

By March, with shooting completed, Steve returned to Los Angeles, pleased with his work in *Tom Horn*.

At the film's release, the *New Yorker* praised McQueen as "a wonderfully worn-looking old soldier cowpoke," and gave him high marks for "an intensely visual performance." The *New York Times* also commented on the quality of his performance, adding that "McQueen rises to heroic stature."

An ad campaign aimed at distributors stressed that "McQueen is back—in the kind of action role he was born to play." But the campaign failed, and *Tom Horn* had a brief run. Westerns were not generating box-office dollars. Even star names didn't help. *Horn* suffered the same drear fate as Marlon Brando's *The Missouri Breaks* and John Wayne's *The Shootist*.

A California critic summed it up: *"Tom Horn* suffered from public antipathy toward the genre. In an earlier decade, this lyrical, deeply felt little film would have been hailed as a classic." Film historian Derek Elley agreed: "The picture was sadly under rated. *Tom Horn* has a moody grace which seems to sum up the McQueen persona. It is a film of quiet bravura, framed by stunning Panavision photography."

With *Tom Horn* completed, McQueen turned his full attention to a new obsession. Throughout Steve's life, the pain of his father's abandonment had haunted him. The need for a personal resolution grew stronger as McQueen grappled with the emotional pressures of middle age. A biplane had taken William McQueen away from his son. Now, at this pivotal stage of his life, Steve felt that if he could understand and share his father's passion for flying, then some of the pain might be resolved.

Santa Paula Airport is 50 miles north of Los Angeles. Early in 1979, McQueen showed up at the "Antique Plane Capital of the World," and announced that he wanted to learn to fly a Stearman. Mike Dewey, ex-stunt pilot and air racer and now in the aircraft sales business at Santa Paula Airport, was amazed. "No student I ever knew started out cold in an antique biplane."

One veteran pilot described the Stearman as "a hefty bird that you can count on . . . sometimes rough and sometimes gentle. It takes a good pilot to get all she has to offer, but there's never been a biplane built like her. She's a real thoroughbred." Still heavily utilized in low-level crop dusting, the Stearman had been basic trainer for more than 60,000 military pilots in World War II and was as tough and reliable as any modern aircraft.

Dewey recalled that "Steve was told to contact Sammy Mason, who knows as much about flying Stearmans as any man alive." Mason told McQueen that he was retired and no longer accepted beginners. "But he just wouldn't take no for an answer," Mason said. "He kept phoning me nightly until I agreed to meet him. When I did, I was struck by his sheer intensity and sense of purpose. I found myself telling him, all right, I'd teach him to fly. But he had to have his own plane."

McQueen paid $35,000 for a bright yellow PT-17 Stearman at the Camarillo Airport that March. Built in the 1940s for the U.S. Navy, the biplane was powered by a newly overhauled 220-hp Continental radial engine and was in excellent flying shape.

In white-haired Sammy Mason, Steve found the ideal flight instructor. With over 40 years of experience behind him, Mason's background included stints as a charter pilot and engineering test pilot for Lockheed; Mason had formed his own touring air show, had worked as a stunt flier in Hollywood films, and was a specialist in aerobatics, being the first pilot to perform the dangerous feat of looping a helicopter.

"Steve purchased a hangar at the airport and set up his living quarters there," said Mason. "He wanted to stay close to his Stearman. Between our flying lessons, he worked in the hangar with an airport mechanic, learning everything he could about the engine and the plane itself. As I said, he was very intense."

Most students fly with their instructor once a day, for an hour—but McQueen insisted on going aloft three times each day, averaging two hours for each session. "He was making real progress," said Mason.

> But he could be impulsive, and he got into a very bad habit. He tended to overshoot his landings, pulling the nose of the plane up much too sharply, which you simply cannot get away with in a Stearman.
>
> One day, after such a landing, I looked him straight in the eye and said, "Keep this up, and you'll kill yourself." He nodded—and after that Steve was outstanding, taking extreme care with his landings. Some news magazine reported that he survived "countless crackups." Nonsense. He never put a scratch on that Stearman during the entire time he flew it.

McQueen soloed on May 1, 1979—and obtained his private license in late July. By then he had purchased a 15-acre ranch in Santa Paula, across the river from the airport. "Barbara brought in her horses," recalled a fellow rancher. "And Steve brought in his antique motorcycles. They furnished the place in Early American. I remember, Steve and Barbara were real happy. He told me, 'I love old bikes, old furniture, old planes and *young* women!' And even though he enjoyed the ranch, he still spent most of each day at the airport."

Barbara also began flying—taking lessons in a new Bellanca Super Decathlon, a closed-cabin monoplane that McQueen bought for her from Mike Dewey's Screaming Eagle Aircraft. She was an adept pilot, and put aside her career as a model to join Steve in the sky. "I never saw Steve fly that Bellanca," said one of the pilots at Santa Paula. "The antiques were with Steve. He had absolutely no interest in modern aircraft."

Early each morning, as the sun rose, Steve could be seen jogging along the main runway at Santa Paula "just to get my juices started." Then he would zip up his 1929 flying suit, wheel out the yellow Stearman, and roar off into the dawn sky, savoring the special sense of freedom achieved by flying. "When you're up there with nothing but clean space around you," he said, "it's like being alone at sea, or far out in the high desert . . . you're away from everything and everybody . . . no longer bound to the Earth."

"Steve eventually owned five planes," said Doug Dullenkopf, partnered with Mike Dewey in Screaming Eagle.

> In addition to the Bellanca he bought a 1946 L-4H Piper from us—and had an out-of-state firm restore another Stearman for him. This was a beautiful custom job in black and silver. He paid over $60,000 for it. But the real jewel was his 1931 Pitcairn PA-8 biplane, called a "Mailwing." It had once been part of Eastern Airlines and had been flown early on by Eddie Rickenbacker, the leading American ace from the First World War. It had been a scheduled U.S. mail plane, the last of a breed you might call the "Pony Express of the Air" back in the 1930s, when the pilot wore a pistol at his belt and carried the mail in a big canvas sack in the open front cockpit.

The dark green Pitcairn had been meticulously restored and bore the original U.S. Air Mail markings along its side. With its rugged 420-hp Wright Whirlwind engine, the PA-8 was truly a flying treasure, the only air-worthy model of its kind in the country.

"Steve didn't fly it much," Mason recalled. "He was keenly aware of its place in history as a pioneer aircraft, and he was never able to relax in it as he did with his Stearmans."

Engrossed in flying (he called the Santa Paula Airport "*my* kind of country club"), and with world proceeds pouring in from his percentage of *The Towering Inferno,* McQueen was in no hurry to make another film—relieved, in fact, when the second installment check for *Tai-Pan* failed to arrive on schedule that summer. McQueen instructed his lawyers to inform Georges-Alain Vuille that because of this breach of contract, he was withdrawing from the project.

Vuille was shocked. He had amassed financial guarantees of $18 million on the strength of McQueen's name as star. He assured Steve that a check *would* be forthcoming. Could McQueen be persuaded to change his mind? "You didn't keep your word," Steve informed Vuille. "So the deal's off."

His life in Santa Paula was idyllic; Steve and Barbara liked the town and its people. With its quiet streets and Victorian homes shaded by tall trees, the town reminded him of Slater, Missouri. On his ranch, as in the Stearmans, he was, in effect, returning to his boyhood roots.

Nestled under South Mountain, in rich citrus and grazing country, the ranch became proof of Barbara's love for animals. In addition to her horses, there were cats, rabbits, goats, chickens, and geese. The hard-working ranch foreman, Grady Ragsdale, doubled as a mechanic, helping Steve keep his Stearmans in flying condition. McQueen's generosity surfaced again when Ragsdale experienced heart problems that required expensive medical treatments. "Don't worry," McQueen told him. "Just have 'em send the bills to me." Sammy Mason recalled another striking example of Steve's personal kindness.

> There was this afternoon when he showed up at the airport driving a beautiful, cream-colored 1950 Hudson Hornet. He saw my eyes bug, and asked me if I'd like to try it out. Well, I'd driven one just like it many years ago, and this car was every bit as great as I'd remembered it to be.

I handed it back to Steve, and that was the last I saw of it—but about a week later he comes driving up in another Hornet, same model, this one a gleaming black and equally well restored. "I got no room for this darn machine," Steve tells me, "so why don't you just store it here at the airport for me. And you can drive it anytime you want, okay?" I said sure, and I *did* drive it a couple of times. Great car! Few weeks later Steve tells me, "Sam, I think you ought to buy this thing since you seem to like it so much." I told him I'd *love* to buy it, but that there was no way I could afford the price. Steve pretended to be shocked. He scowled, "Well now, I'm *real* disappointed in you, Sam. Too cheap to pay a dollar for a genuine 1950 Hudson Hornet!" I stared at him, and he grinned. "I mean it. The car's yours for a buck." I happily handed him the dollar, and he signed over the pink slip. That was the kind of man he was.

Another film project drew Steve's attention during 1979, and he began planning its production; *The Hunter* would be his twenty-eighth motion picture.

McQueen had no way of knowing it would be his last.

19. . .

Full Circle

"You don't smoke, do you?" McQueen asked.

"No," I said. "Never started."

"Well, you're smart." He nodded. "I'm always givin' the damn things up, then I end up smoking again. I get nervous."

Steve held an unlit cigarette in his hand. He looked at it, frowned, broke it in half, and flipped the two ends into an ashtray.

"I smoked cigars when I played Tommy Crown," he said. "But I didn't inhale. Cigarettes you inhale."

We were sitting in a small cafe near MGM Studios in Culver City. McQueen looked tired, and I told him so.

"Guess I been workin' too hard," he said with a faint grin. "At least I got rid of all the fat I put on for Ibsen." He scrubbed at his clean-shaven chin. "Kinda miss havin' a beard though. I think

I'll grow it back. Keep it trimmed.... At least the weight's off."

We sat over our coffee, neither of us speaking.

McQueen sighed. "I do feel kinda tired a lot of the time lately," he admitted.

On the street outside, we shook hands. "Take care of yourself, Steve," I said.

He looked a bit surprised. I'd never said that to him before.

"Sure... sure. You too."

And he walked away.

I never saw him again.

The Hunter marked a full circle for Steve McQueen. He had first attained stardom in the role of television bounty hunter Josh Randall; now, some two decades later, he was about to end his career portraying another bounty hunter, Ralph "Papa" Thorson. But the two characters were different. Randall operated in the Old West and was fictional; Thorson operates in today's world and is real.

Author Christopher Keane had written a biography of Thorson, and Steve read it in a single evening, fascinated by the man's incredible exploits. In the course of his dangerous career, Ralph Thorson had tracked and captured hundreds of fugitives, had been shot twice, stabbed three times and, in his words, "slugged so many times I've lost count." His base of operations was a large, rambling bungalow in North Hollywood, California, stocked with the tools of his trade—rifles, handguns, and a potent variety of automatic weapons.

Thorson brought in his first wanted man in the late 1940s, while attending the University of California at Berkeley. Thereafter, he switched from the study of criminology to the active pursuit of fugitives, tracing the legal sanction for his bizarre occupation back to a U.S. Supreme Court decision handed down in 1872, granting what Thorson calls "certain extraordinary rights" to bounty hunters. These include the right of forced entry.

"Actually, I hate to break down doors unless it's absolutely necessary," he said. "I've stood in hallways for an hour telling

guys, 'Oh, hell, Charlie, this is a nice door. I don't want to
break it down, and you're going to have to come out eventually,
so why waste everyone's time?'"

Thorson sets his pay rate, per fugitive, at "up to fifty percent
of the bail recovered by the bondsman." The job is hazardous,
often exhausting, "but never dull."

McQueen phoned the bearded, 52-year-old bounty hunter
and met with Thorson to discuss his life story. The two men
established an instant rapport, and Steve contacted his agent
after the meeting, telling him to set up a deal. "I want to play
Ralph Thorson," he said. "There's a hell of a picture here."

McQueen's acting fee for *The Hunter* was set at "three
million, plus percentage," with Paramount financing; Peter
Hyams was assigned to the project as director/writer. But by
the time production began in Chicago on September 10, 1979,
Hyams was out and Buzz Kulik (known for fast-action television dramas) had replaced him as director. "I actually wanted
to direct it myself," Steve admitted, "but I was stopped by the
Directors Guild on a rules situation. We had to bring in another
guy, so I picked Kulik. We knew each other. Buzz had directed
me in an old *Climax* TV show way back in '58."

Steve arranged for his son, Chad, to work as a production
assistant on *The Hunter* "to let him gain a little film experience."

One of the main action sequences began with a rooftop
pursuit, turned into a street chase and ended aboard a speeding
elevated train—which explained the Chicago location. A seven-
car unit was rented from the Chicago Transit Authority, with
the clear understanding that it be kept in motion during production. "It was one of 135 trains on the tracks," McQueen
explained. "We had to keep it moving so's not to mess up the
schedules of the other 134."

Ten days of shooting (and 800 miles of track travel) were
required to film the dangerous sequence. The script called for
Thorson to exit from a window of the coach and climb to its
roof in his pursuit of the crazed gunman.

Loren Janes was the chief stunt actor on *The Hunter*, and
now he prepared to double for McQueen during these scenes
on top of the speeding train. "No good," Steve told Kulik. "I'll
hack this one myself." With the camera rolling, McQueen slid
through a window and pulled himself to the roof, wearing tennis

shoes to maintain a better grip on the swaying top of the fast-moving elevated express. "The stunt required nerve and perfect timing," said Janes. "But Steve handled it beautifully."

Another wild script chase called for McQueen to pursue a fugitive's car into the huge Marina Towers parking facility. On the 16th-floor ramp the fugitive loses control and smashes through the railing. The car's 16-story plunge into the Chicago river provided one of the film's visual high points.

A dilapidated apartment building in a poverty-ravaged section of the city was used for a follow-up sequence.

Kulik needed another extra to fill out the scene, and Steve nodded toward a teenaged girl at the edge of the crowd. Her name was Karen Wilson, and after the scene was over, McQueen asked how she planned to spend the small check she had earned: "I'll give it to my Mom. She's real sick."

McQueen learned that the girl's mother was suffering from cancer, and he visited her at the hospital. Mort Engelberg, the film's producer, recalled the incident.

> The woman told Steve that her one regret, in dying, was that Karen would never get a decent education, that she would probably never be able to leave the slums. Steve promised that he'd see that the girl got her chance. He had a legal arrangement worked out. After her mother's death, 16-year-old Karen was enrolled in an expensive private school in Ojai, California, not far from Steve's ranch. He paid all costs. On weekends, Steve and Barbara had Karen with them, and they treated her just like their own child.

Clara Bailey, a seamstress with her own shop in Santa Paula, recalled seeing young Karen shopping in town with Barbara. "I asked her, 'Is this your mother?' And she shook her head. 'No, my mother's dead. Barbara is my *second* mother.' And there was real love in her eyes when she said it."

Stuntman Janes revealed that

> Steve was worried about some reporter finding out about the help he'd given Karen. . . . He was constantly doing this sort of thing, helping kids in one way or another. He'd see some youngsters in a poor section of town,

playing with an old battered football. . . . Next day, he'd
show up with a brand new ball for them. Stuff like that
was natural with him, but he considered it as very personal, and always kept it out of the papers.

After a month's shooting in Chicago, the production unit
moved to Kankakee, Illinois, for additional action scenes. "We
needed a Nebraska corn field," said Kulik.

For a chase sequence where Steve jumps into this big
threshing machine and uses it to run down a couple of
wacko brothers who are pitching sticks of dynamite at
him. We were able to double the Nebraska location with
a corn field we found right there in Illinois.

On the last day of October the cast and crew returned to
California for another month of shooting on the lot at Paramount. McQueen was visibly affected by the weeks of location
work. He was short of breath and his cough had returned—
but he attributed his condition to "a cold I caught in Chicago.
I just haven't been able to shake it."

At Paramount, Ralph Thorson's house had been built on
two large sound stages. These sets included all of the home's
inside rooms, plus the outside porch, yard, and two-car garage.
Among the interior items, a $200,000 collection of 750 antique
toys. "We thought it would help 'humanize' Thorson if we had
him collecting these old toys," explained Kulik.

McQueen's love interest in the picture was 29-year-old
Kathryn Harrold, playing his pregnant live-in girlfriend. "I
wore padding under my clothes for most of the production,"
she said.

This was a plot gimmick. The real Thorson has a wife
and two children, but that wouldn't have worked for our
story. The idea was that *our* Thorson didn't want to bring
kids into what he claimed was a rotten world. This provided conflict—when his girl wanted to have a baby and
he didn't.

Harrold and McQueen discovered they had both attended
the same acting schools in New York: "I studied with Sanford

Meisner and Uta Hagen, just as Steve did, and that gave us a special bond."

Thorson himself played a cameo role early in the production, as a bartender in a scene with McQueen. After the day's shooting they went out to a real bar for a drink, and Steve observed that Thorson was a poor driver, who had problems parking his car. This led to a running gag in *The Hunter*. "We had Steve in an old dented Chevy," said Kulik. "Had him constantly bumping curbs and fenders.... After all of his racing films, Steve *loved* the idea of playing a lousy driver."

As production wound to a close, what McQueen called "my Chicago cold" had progressed to chills and fever. Antibiotics were prescribed, and once again McQueen's health seemed to improve. But by the time the $10,500,000 production was completed at the end of November, Steve admitted to Barbara that he was feeling "really beat."

Despite a promise to "take a long vacation," Steve was soon discussing other film projects. He met with writer/director Charles Bail on a script called *The Last Ride*, about a cross-country motorcycle race in the 1950s — and after meeting Mary Hemingway in Ketchum, Idaho, he announced plans to star in the life story of her late husband, famed Nobel prize-winning novelist Ernest Hemingway.

But his agent seriously doubted McQueen's desire to do more films.

> Steve set a price after *The Hunter* that just didn't make sense. Told me that he wouldn't do any picture unless he could get a minimum guarantee of $5 million against 15 percent of both domestic *and* overseas gross! He actually turned down a firm offer from Carlo Ponti amounting to $4 million.

In December, McQueen was back in the news — but not for a film deal. He had collapsed at the ranch, coughing and gasping for breath. His doctor in Santa Paula took X-rays of Steve's chest but could not determine the cause of his illness. He recommended a full battery of tests at Cedars-Sinai Medical Center in Los Angeles.

McQueen checked into Cedars-Sinai on December 18, registering under a false name to avoid publicity. Over the following week and a half, doctors at the Center conducted an extensive series of tests. When Steve left the hospital three days after Christmas he looked pale and shaken.

His friends were concerned. What had caused his collapse? "I had a touch of pneumonia," he told them. "But I'm fine now. Just need a little rest."

But he was *not* fine. He had lied. The tests at Cedars-Sinai revealed a shocking fact: Steve McQueen had a malignant tumor in his right lung. Prognosis: Terminal.

20. . .

A Test
of Courage

For those afflicted with terminal cancer, the decision to remain within medically approved boundaries or to venture beyond these limited areas in search of new treatment is extremely difficult. In 1980 Steve McQueen was forced to make this decision.

The facts behind his year-long struggle to survive have been wildly distorted by the press. Magazines and newspapers deliberately slanted their accounts of his illness toward sensationalism and exploitation, treating McQueen's desperate fight against cancer as a kind of one-man circus act. And when he finally sought a cure outside the United States—one involving holistic and nutritional therapy—his sanity was questioned, and his doctors openly condemned by the American Cancer Society and other members of the conservative medical establishment.

Reports of his treatment were biased and fragmented. Lurid updates on McQueen's illness were geared to hype magazine sales. Factual errors and contradictions abounded. Until now, the true—and detailed—story of those last months has not been told—yet Steve McQueen's case marks an important milestone in the history of a disease that ravages millions each year.

In rendering this first full account, I have attempted to be objective about the controversial treatment he received during the final months of his life. It was, and still remains, highly unorthodox, and others, more medically qualified, must judge its ultimate validity.

One clear truth emerges: McQueen's battle against lung cancer was a demonstration of personal courage and fortitude that eclipsed all of his screen heroics. This final, tragic, real-life role was surely his most dramatic.

In the summer of 1979, several months before the shocking December discovery of terminal cancer by doctors at Cedars-Sinai, a trachea lung biopsy had been performed on McQueen. It failed to reveal a malignancy. At that stage, his cancer had rooted itself in the pleura (the lining between lung and chest wall), an area this earlier biopsy had not monitored.

A first appearance in the pleura is characteristic of mesothelioma. This deadly form of lung cancer is directly associated with extensive, long-term exposure to asbestos—a substance used in the brake linings of cars, as in insulation for studio sound stages, and as a lining in the protective, fireproof clothing worn by racing drivers. In fact, asbestos was present, in some form, on most of the vehicles McQueen used throughout his life (including the tanks he drove in the Marines). If mesothelioma is discovered in a late growth stage, as it was in McQueen's case, no cure is possible within the canons of approved medical procedure. Surgery was useless.

When Steve worked with Ralph Thorson on *The Hunter*, he learned of the bounty man's abiding interest in astrology. Steve phoned Thorson and asked that a planetary chart be done on him. "I don't really dig all this stars-and-planets stuff,"

McQueen admitted. "But I'm curious about what you'll come up with, okay?" Thorson agreed to cast the horoscope.

He prepared a full chart on McQueen, in all planetary aspects, and was disturbed by the results. "Steve's birth chart, with Jupiter in a bad position in Gemini, showed that he would suffer lung and chest problems," Thorson declared. "It just didn't look good for him."

In the years since their divorce, Steve and Neile Adams had remained close. "And not just because of the children," a mutual friend reported. "He used to call Neile all the time for advice. Steve wanted her opinion on everything. And she did the same. Neile took the man she planned to marry, Al Toffel, to meet Steve that winter."

"We're going to be married in January," Neile told him. McQueen grinned. "How 'bout that! Us too, me and Barbara. Looks like everybody's gettin' married in January."

Indeed, on January 16, 1980, just three days before Neile's wedding, Steve and Barbara were married at the ranch in Santa Paula. The ceremony was brief and private. Sammy Mason and his wife, Wanda, were the only invited guests. Doctor Leslie Miller, of the Ventura Missionary Church, conducted the service. Nina Blanchard, the head of Barbara's modeling agency, told the press that the new bride was "deeply content. She's a perfect wife for Steve—with both of them into ranching and flying."

McQueen issued his own innocuous statement: "Barbara and I have already found a lot of happiness together, and now we want to increase that happiness. She means everything to me." Barbara echoed his joy: "Ranch life is great. Each day I go out to the chicken coop and gather fresh eggs for breakfast.... And I ride all the time. Horseback riding is terrific exercise."

But, behind these sunny press statements, the reality of Steve's illness darkened their life together.

In late February, a month before his fiftieth birthday, Steve returned to Cedars-Sinai for further medical tests. He was told that the disease had progressed and that he now had only a 5 percent chance of living out the year. The doctors suggested radiation in the slim hope that it might slow the cancer's rate of growth, and Steve agreed to the treatment. "Researchers are working all the time on cancer cures," McQueen told Barbara.

"Maybe, if I can last long enough, they might find one for what I've got."

Flying became his escape. He would wake early, in the predawn hours, and drive to Santa Paula Airport. As the sun rose, Steve would be in the sky to meet it, goggled and helmeted in the open cockpit, winging through the early-morning air, caught up in the sheer exaltation of flight. Here he could put aside all thoughts of disease and death.

For the first time in decades, Steve was no longer considering new film projects. When an agent inquired about acting plans he declared himself out of the business. "Tell 'em I've retired. Tell 'em I'm a flying rancher." No mention was made of his illness.

In mid-March, however, the well-kept secret of McQueen's cancer exploded across the sensationalized pages of the *National Enquirer*. A full-color picture of Steve appeared on the cover, and the gaudy, mass-market tabloid declared that, in December, McQueen's doctors had operated on him, implanting radioactive cobalt in his chest and had "sewed him up, leaving the cobalt inside." The article further claimed that when doctors reopened his chest two months later "there was no regression [so] they stitched him up again." Nameless doctors were quoted as saying that his case was hopeless and that he would be dead "very soon."

McQueen was greatly disturbed by the lurid coverage, and when friends began calling him, in shock over the story, he told them to "forget it," and that he was going to sue the paper.

Bud Ekins recalled visiting McQueen shortly after the *Enquirer* piece appeared. "Are you really okay, Steve?" he asked. "Hell yes, I'm fine." McQueen pulled off his shirt, showing Ekins an unmarked chest. "Do I look like I've been under the knife?" Ekins saw no scars. "I took Steve's word that he was okay. He didn't want me to know about the cancer right then— and the part about his being cut open *was* false reporting."

McQueen denied the entire story. "I felt it was the right thing to do—for the sake of my friends and family," he later explained. "I didn't want them hounded by the press. A flat denial took off the pressure, at least for awhile. And a lot of that damn story *had* been bullshit!"

Despite this heated denial, rumors of his disease persisted. To offset them, Steve attended a press preview of *Tom Horn* that March, in Oxnard, California. Photos taken at the preview show him in apparent good health, smiling and trim-bearded, arm in arm with Barbara. Yet several reporters noted the gauntness in his face. And although he told them, "I'm fine!" they were skeptical.

During the first week of April, McQueen received more alarming news from his doctors at Cedars-Sinai. Radiation treatments failed to slow the cancer's growth. The tumor in his right lung was spreading rapidly.

When actor-pal Slim Pickens phoned to ask about his condition, Steve told him that he was having "some bad lung trouble." Pickens revealed that doctors had discovered pneumonia in one of *his* lungs—and that he had gone into a hospital for surgery. "Had a third of my right lung removed. Everything's fine now."

McQueen told him he was happy to hear that, but surgery was not the answer in his case. "Then what *is?*" Pickens asked. "I dunno," admitted Steve. "But I'm sure lookin' around for alternatives."

McQueen had been investigating unconventional cancer therapy, perusing medical magazines, talking to various doctors, but he had not come up with anything that satisfied his personal standards. In the *Journal of Health Science,* however, an article on William Donald Kelley captured his attention.

Like McQueen, Kelley was a rebel against the establishment, a medical nonconformist whose unorthodox cancer-fighting program had been outlawed by the American Cancer Society. In 1965, as a practicing dentist in Texas, Kelley was stricken with cancer of the liver and pancreas. Doctors pronounced his case terminal and gave him a maximum of two months to live. Recalling his courses in nutrition at Baylor University, where he had studied orthodontics, Kelley began a rigorous treatment involving the intake of large quantities of nutritional liver and pancreatic enzymes. He also used numerous coffee enemas to detoxify his body.

"What I was doing," he recalled, "was activating my natural immune system as an arsenal against the disease. My tumors dissolved, and the cancer vanished. I'd provided my body with the weapons needed to defeat an invading enemy."

Kelley launched into an intensive study of enzymes and vitamins as vital elements in stimulating the body's defense against cancer. His findings indicated that a high dosage of enzymes appeared to attack the cancer cells directly, and that vitamins A and C, along with thymus extract, helped bolster the body's immune system.

He called this "ecological therapy," and in 1969 wrote a book, *One Answer to Cancer,* outlining the program. When some of his patients in Grapevine, Texas, consulted him on aspects of this therapy, state medical authorities claimed that Kelley was "practicing medicine without a license." (Although he had earned his academic credentials in dentistry and orthodontics and held degrees in biology, biochemistry, and philosophy, he was not, in fact, an M.D.)

A court injunction temporarily stopped publication of Kelley's book—and in 1976 the state dental board suspended his license to practice dentistry in Texas for "exceeding the bounds of his profession." However, his license was reinstated in 1981.

These legal actions failed to deter him. Kelley became fully involved in cancer research and developed his "theory of metabolic subtypes," in which cancer patients are computer-classified according to body type and treated individually.

By 1980 he had become the nation's leading authority on non-toxic cancer therapy, having established the International Health Institute, a privately endowed consulting firm in Winthrop, Washington. Kelley also owns an organic research farm in Winthrop, and it was here, in April, that McQueen met him. "I didn't want to show up at his office," Steve said. "That would have alerted the press. The farm allowed us some privacy. Kelley outlined his whole program to me at that time."

McQueen was impressed but still cautious regarding a full commitment. He did agree to try a special "body-cleansing" diet when he returned to his ranch in California; he promised to keep in touch by phone with weekly dietary reports. For the moment, that was as far as he was willing to go with Kelley's program.

At his marriage, in January, Steve promised Barbara a honeymoon cruise to Acapulco on the *Pacific Princess.* Now he kept that promise and they boarded the big luxury liner in late April for the two-week voyage. The trip was not a success. Weak and short of breath, Steve spent most of his time in their cabin, while Barbara dined alone each evening in the ship's salon. They left before completing the voyage, and a dockside photo of McQueen revealed his obvious weight loss. He looked thin and exhausted.

"As sick as he was, Steve was still determined to keep flying," said Sammy Mason.

> I got a phone call from him in late June, asking me if I'd meet him at his hangar. "I want to fly the Stearman, Sam, but you'll have to help me into the cockpit. I can't make it alone. I need you, okay?" I told him sure, I'd be glad to help—but he never made it to the airport. He just didn't have the strength.

McQueen's final film, *The Hunter*, was released in July, and critics commented on his surprising lack of energy. "He lacks zip," said Andrew Sarris. And Michael Sragow, in the Los Angeles *Herald-Examiner*, found him "way off stride . . . McQueen's once-crisp physical reflexes look shot." The *Village Voice* rated him "a tired daredevil . . . all used up."

By the time these reviews appeared McQueen had returned to Cedars-Sinai for another cancer checkup. The news was dire. Malignant tumors had completely engulfed his right lung and had spread to other areas in his chest and neck. The doctors gave him just two weeks to live.

Steve phoned Kelley from the ranch. "What can you do for me if I go *all* the way with your program?" Kelley would make no predictions as to a cure, given the advanced stage of McQueen's cancer, but he did urge him to get into total, around-the-clock therapy. He warned that every hour counted. McQueen told him he'd make up his mind soon.

In a final act of defiance, Steve arranged a dinner party at Hollywood's exclusive Ma Maison restaurant. During the evening he seemed to be enjoying himself. Reported columnist Robin Leach, who was among those attending: "When the crowd applauded him, McQueen stabbed a foot-long cigar in the air as a gesture of joy. Everyone at the party believed he was celebrating a return to health and a new movie contract."

Actually, the affair was his way of saying goodbye to many of his friends, "just in case I don't make it," as he told Barbara. "He didn't want them to remember him as a weakened cancer victim," she said. "Steve wanted to be remembered as the man he once was, and that night he acted the part beautifully."

But McQueen's strength was diminishing. Barbara urged him to accept Kelley's treatment. The doctors at Cedars-Sinai had given up on him. What other choice did he have? "Yeah," Steve said. "I guess it's time to bite the bullet."

Kelley was a consultant at the Plaza Santa Maria, a newly opened private clinic near Rosarita Beach in Mexico, some 30 miles south of the international border. He made arrangements for McQueen to be treated there. Santa Maria's 100 acres sprawl across a high cliff overlooking the Pacific Ocean. Designed to accommodate 110 live-in patients, the estimated cost, per patient, was then $10,000 a month.*

Cameron Stauth, who worked with Dr. Kelley on his book of basic therapy, *The Kelley Anti-Cancer Program,* recalled McQueen's arrival: "When he checked into the clinic on July 31, he was gaunt, could barely walk, and was in enough pain to require the use of some 30 grains of codeine each day."

To avoid press attention, McQueen registered under the name of Don Schoonover. Barbara had come with him to Santa Maria, and they were assigned a small private bungalow on the grounds of the clinic. When Kelley examined his new patient he expressed regret that McQueen had waited so long to begin his program. "He was in bad shape," said Kelley. "He had a blood clot in his arm and a tumor in his neck the size of an apple. He could hardly breathe, and he had no appetite. He also had fluid in the abdomen, where the cancer had spread."

McQueen wanted to know what chance he had to survive.

Kelley admitted that it was impossible to say, and that he preferred to begin treating patients at a much earlier stage. "The treatment is rigorous," Kelley told him. "We'll need your fullest cooperation."

"That's what I'm here to give."

Kelley knew that they were fighting an uphill battle. In medical establishment journals there had been no recorded recoveries from McQueen's form of cancer.

Kelley's basic healing philosophy involved "simultaneous whole-body treatment," calling for massive dosages of enzymes and vitamins to neutralize toxic agents placed in the blood-

*It should be noted that as of December 1980, the Plaza Santa Maria changed management and is no longer connected in any way with Dr. Kelley, his program, or his associates.

stream by malignant cancer cells. Patients are fed minerals and various glandular extracts. The body is detoxified by gall bladder flushes and kidney cleansing, using diuretics and fruit juices, and by coffee enemas, in which the caffeine, traveling through the portal vein directly into the liver, greatly stimulates its functions.

Kelley was subject to caustic and derisive attacks for using this latter method as part of his therapy. It has been called "Kelley's crazy laxative." Actually, coffee enemas are a standard medical procedure dating back to the early 1900s, and are fully documented in medical literature. This method of treatment garnered particular attention in the 1940s, when utilized by New York M.D. Max Gerson. Gerson believed that a tumor mass could be successfully treated only by restoring the body's total metabolism. According to Gerson, coffee enemas stimulate bile secretions, which first detoxify the liver and then the rest of the body. The restored metabolism, he claimed, "boosted by massive infusions of raw vegetable and liver juices, then gets rid of the tumor without the aid of toxic drugs."

Kelley asked McQueen to fill out a detailed questionnaire relating to dietary habits, prior body condition, and overall life pattern. "Patients fall into one of ten metabolic subtypes related to their personal biochemistry," said Kelley.

> The answers from this questionnaire are evaluated by a computer, along with blood and urine samples. In McQueen's case, we determined that he was a Type IV metabolizer, and we worked out a program of therapy tailored to his specific problems and body type.

A therapist at Santa Maria described McQueen's daily regimen:

> He was awakened at 7 A.M. to a high-fiber natural food breakfast. At mid-day he had a high-protein drink made from crushed almonds. Dinner was at 6 P.M. It generally consisted of soup, whole-grain bread, and fresh garden-grown vegetables. Fish was also served and beef was added twice a week. At intervals during the day, Mr. McQueen was given a total of more than 50 pills—vitamins, minerals and supplements—to restore his body balance.

He also received a Japanese extract of bacilli Z, laetrile, enzyme implants, thymus extract injections, coffee enemas, injections of sheep embryos, chiropractic manipulation, saunas, body massages, and mental exercises designed for full muscle relaxation. He was usually asleep before midnight. The next morning we began the whole process again.*

McQueen was under the personal supervision of the clinic's directors, Dr. Rodrigo Rodriguez, an M.D. with a postgraduate degree in nuclear medicine from the University of Mexico, and Dr. Dwight McKee, an M.D. from Colorado.

When Neile found out what type of treatment Steve was undergoing she reacted in shock, publicly branding Kelley and his staff as "charlatans and exploiters." But McQueen himself was convinced the treatment had merit, and after six weeks of intensive daily therapy, he had gained weight and strength and was able to take short walks along the high cliff overlooking the ocean. He was allowed to break his diet by treating himself to some Häagen-Dazs ice cream, brought to him from Los Angeles by a friend. Each evening, in their bungalow, he and Barbara would watch video cassettes of his old films.

"Barbara was being very brave about the situation," reported a family friend. "She'd always *hated* being around anyone who was seriously ill; it frustrated and depressed her. But, in Steve's case, she stuck with him all the way, demonstrating the depth of her love and commitment."

Curious about his sudden disappearance from California, reporters from the *National Enquirer* traced him to Plaza Santa Maria—then wrote a sensationalized cover story condemning his treatment there. Declaring that "McQueen has put himself in the hands of quacks who run a phony cancer clinic in Mexico," the paper quoted Helene Brown, chair of the American Cancer Society National Public Education Committee in Los Angeles: "This metabolic treatment is the craziest stuff you ever heard of in your life . . . it's really a fraud."

One of the inside sources involved in the *Enquirer* story was Robert DeBragga, who had been a patient at the clinic and

---

*Laetrile and DMSO were used in treating McQueen. Although not part of the Kelley program, these were prescribed by the doctors at Santa Maria.

who credited Kelley's program for his survival from lung cancer. DeBragga had agreed to help the *Enquirer* on the promise of "an accurate and fair appraisal." He later claimed that he had been "double-crossed" by the tabloid. "In the original draft of their story, read to me over the phone, the writers took a basically factual position," he stated. "Then, next thing I heard, the editors had decided to go for a totally negative approach. Based, one would assume, on the sad fact that lurid controversy outsells straight truth."

No longer able to conceal his treatment at Santa Maria, McQueen issued a statement to the press: "My body may be broken, but my heart and spirit are not. I'm going to continue to fight this thing every inch of the way." Dr. Rodriguez told the press that McQueen

> has stabilized considerably. He has shown no new tumor growth and there is clear shrinkage of existing tumors. He no longer receives pain-killing drugs, has a much better appetite, has gained weight and has even been swimming in our pool. He is still, without question, a very sick man, but we now have definable, objective cause for optimism.

"Steve *wants* to live," added Kelley. "He doesn't have an ounce of give-up in him. I now believe that his chances are excellent."

In a public interview with a reporter from Televisa, Mexico's national television network, McQueen praised the care he was receiving. "Mexico is showing the world this new way of fighting cancer through metabolic therapy. Congratulations—and thank you for saving my life." He added, in a strained, tired voice: "And I would hope that the cheap scandal sheets will not try to seek me out, so that I can continue my treatment." Barbara McQueen commented further:

> The press has treated Steve with cruelty and ignorance. When you're a public figure people think they can use you to fill whatever needs they have, regardless of ethics. Steve's doctors have warned us that such sensationalized stories can have a negative impact upon his chance for survival. They must *stop!*

But of course they did not. Widespread media interest in McQueen's case prompted an international press conference on October 9th at the Los Angeles Press Club. DeBragga was also involved here (as he had been with the *Enquirer* story), helping to bring together a dozen ex-cancer patients who credited their complete recovery to Kelley. Several brought full medical pathology records to back up their claims. "More than 80 world journalists came to the conference," said DeBragga.

> But they totally ignored the other patients in favor of the McQueen story. They didn't interview a single *one* of them! Each case was a cover story in itself, but these reporters weren't interested. They didn't care about the fact that here were twelve people alive and well five years after being on the Kelley program. All the press gave a damn about was McQueen.

This same sensationalistic approach was taken on NBC's influential *Today* show in mid-October. A California gynecologist branded Kelley's therapy as "rank quackery." The host of the show, Tom Brokaw, was equally hostile, caustically (and incorrectly) referring to the use of "coffee enzymes." Kelley responded:

> We have never claimed any kind of "miracle cures." Our therapy is designed to allow the body to cure *itself*, using its own immune system.
>
> We have a good, scientific program, based on many years of medical research. Steve McQueen has upset the establishment by coming forward to challenge the chaotic medical care system in our country. When he came to us, Steve had been sent home to die. We have already extended his life by some two months beyond maximum predictions.
>
> We are *not* at war with the medical community. We are ready and willing to match our program on degenerative diseases against any other program endorsed by the National Cancer Institute, or the American Medical Association. But the truth is, it's a closed shop, and they want to keep it that way.

Peter Chowka, an editor with *New Age* magazine, firmly agreed with Kelley.

> If present trends continue, one in four of us will get cancer and one in six will die of it, yet there is active resistance to all new ideas and therapies that are not spawned within the conventional establishment. Only three methods of treatment are presently allowed: surgery, radiation and chemotherapy. Over the years, scores of nontoxic, alternative treatments have been proposed— involving diet, the immune system, and psychology— but since these approaches lie outside the narrow paradigm of conventional treatment, they are automatically designated as unscientific and worthless. There is a blacklist, distributed widely by the American Cancer Society, that prevents their testing and use.

Senator Orrin Hatch of Utah echoed this charge: "The establishment's vested interest, amounting to billions of dollars in government research grants each year, keeps innovative methods from being investigated."

Chowka also bitterly protested McQueen's loss of vital months in 1978 and 1979 when his illness grew unchecked, pointing out the fact that useless antibiotics and tranquilizers had been prescribed, "masking the real disease and allowing the cancer to seat itself deeply in McQueen's system."

As he grew stronger, Steve's natural impatience began to assert itself. The close confinement of the clinic made him feel, in his words, "like a prisoner." In late October he asked Dr. Rodriguez how much longer he would have to undergo treatment at Santa Maria. Rodriguez estimated at least another four months. McQueen claimed that he could not continue without a break. He had been under treatment for nearly 12 weeks and was going "stir crazy." He intended to drive back to the ranch.

McKee and Rodriguez were greatly disturbed by McQueen's announcement. They attempted to change his mind, but he was stubbornly determined to leave, even though he felt the Kelley therapy *had* saved his life. In a statement to the press, Rodriguez expressed his disappointment:

> Mr. McQueen is much improved. His primary lung tumor shows definite shrinkage, and his other abdominal meta-

stases have stopped growing. But he is far from cured. We were achieving steady progress, and I wanted to take advantage of this progress and keep going in our present direction. By leaving at this critical stage, I think Mr. McQueen is making a serious mistake.

Kelley told the press that "Steve wanted a little vacation . . . he wanted to get back to his ranch—but we expect him to return soon and continue his therapy." Kelley claimed that "his right lung is much improved. His left lung had several hard tumors, and these are almost gone. What's left of the tumor mass is light, like cotton candy. The X-rays show that they have been disintegrating."

Stateside doctors challenged Kelley to prove these claims, and he obliged by releasing data representing independent confirmation. Blood samples from McQueen had been submitted on two occasions (in early August and late October) to Emil Schandl, Ph.D., director of the CA Laboratory-Center in Dania, Florida. Schandl conducted extensive laboratory tests on the blood and was amazed at the results. "Our tests allow us to monitor a patient's response to therapy," Schandl said. "This applies to whatever type of treatment the patient receives— chemotherapy, radiation or, in this case, metabolic therapy."

At the time the blood samples were submitted to Schandl they came to him under the name of Don Schoonover. Only later did he learn that the patient was Steve McQueen.

The first time this patient was tested, he had three markers that were quite abnormal—very abnormal. But when I tested his blood the second time, some eight weeks later, all the markers were negative—that is to say, in the normal range. It was totally unbelievable for me to see such a tremendous clinical biochemical improvement.

On October 24, with Barbara beside him, McQueen drove his Mercedes through the high iron gates of Plaza Santa Maria and out along the new two-lane blacktop Ensenada highway, heading back to his Santa Paula ranch. He talked about his "improved quality of life" and of how happy he was "to be free again."

Four days later, when therapists from the clinic visited Steve at the ranch to check his condition, they were shocked to find him drinking beer, smoking, and eating junk food. They warned him that his health was still far too fragile to permit such self-indulgent excesses, that he was being very foolish and reckless. "I feel a lot better," Steve told them. "I figure I can afford to ease off a little."

McQueen was deluding himself; his condition remained extremely critical. He soon found he was having difficulty urinating. Steve phoned Kelley, who conferred with Rodriguez and McKee on the problem. "With the dead tumor in the abdomen being as large as it was," Kelley said,

> it had put pressure on the tubes running from kidney to bladder, and this caused a urination blockage. We were afraid of toxicity from the tumor mass. An operation was the only answer, despite the risk involved. We explained this to Steve and recommended surgery.

Since the Santa Maria clinic was not equipped for major surgery, Kelley suggested that the operation be performed by Dr. Cesar Santos Vargas, a heart and kidney specialist with the Santa Rosa Clinic in Juarez, Mexico, directly across the Rio Grande from El Paso, Texas. There were no guarantees. Kelley knew that complications could arise, but he felt that the gamble must be taken.

At this point, 11 days had passed since Steve had left Plaza Santa Maria, and he was growing progressively weaker; his breathing was labored and the urination problem remained to be dealt with. He agreed to the operation.

Travel arrangements were made. The bed in McQueen's camper was outfitted with an oxygen unit, and Steve was driven to Oxnard Airport where he boarded a waiting Learjet with Barbara. When he said goodbye to Sammy Mason, he was calm: "However it goes, Sam, I'm ready. I've made my peace with God."

Another family friend, who had known Steve and Barbara for several years, remarked on McQueen's "religious change" in the last months of his life, activated by his wife's background and beliefs. "Behind all of her model's sophistication, Barbara is still an Oregon farm girl," he said.

As a child, she had a strict religious upbringing on the farm and it stuck. While they were at the ranch, she regularly attended the Ventura Missionary Church and Steve often went with her. He'd never been religious, but he loved Barbara a lot, and she exerted a strong influence on his state of mind during those final months.

On the afternoon of November 4th, under an assumed name, Steve McQueen was admitted to the Clinica de Santa Rosa in Ciudad Juarez, Mexico. "He was walking with a cane," recalled Dr. Santos Vargas, "and his abdomen was noticeably swollen." Chad and Terri McQueen were at the hospital, and Steve told them not to worry, that he would "get through this okay."

On November 6, 1980, after a cardiologist's examination certified that his heart was strong enough to withstand major surgery, Steve was wheeled down the corridor to the small clinic's main operating room. Santos Vargas recalled that McQueen had gripped his hand. "He made a signal with his thumb up, showing his confidence."

During the operation, having reached the diseased area, Santos Vargas found that the abdomen contained three tumors.

According to Peter Chowka, who described McQueen's surgery for *New Age* magazine, "both Kelley and Dr. McKee were present during the 45-minute operation. Tumors weighing over three pounds were removed." He quoted Dr. Kelley: "Most of the tumors in his abdomen were no longer attached. They were dead masses, and were lifted out easily. One, however, was attached to his liver, and Dr. Santos Vargas cut it away, removing a small lower section of the liver."

McQueen was in good spirits following the operation and was talking coherently. "He gave me another thumbs up sign," said Santos Vargas, "and said in Spanish, 'Lo hice!' . . . 'I did it!'"

These were his last recorded words. Fourteen hours later, early on the morning of November 7th, while sleeping under sedation, Steve McQueen suffered a sudden heart seizure. Then, minutes later, a second attack shook his body. This one was fatal.

According to a reporter, when Dr. Vargas broke the news to Barbara McQueen she began to sob deeply, repeating the words, "He belongs to God now . . . Steve belongs to God now."

For William Donald Kelley, McQueen's death was a deep, personal blow. "But any time you do surgery," he said, "even a simple tooth extraction, you face the chance of an embolism, or blood clot, developing. This can lodge in the patient's heart, causing death. It's a major risk with all surgery—and that's what happened to Steve."

Critics of the Kelley program were quick to respond. On the morning following McQueen's death, a statement appeared in the *Los Angeles Times* under the heading: "Doctors Warn Against Unorthodox Treatment." Dr. Edward Zalta, president of the Los Angeles County Medical Association, issued a stern warning.

> We don't want people who have a chance to be cured by conventional methods to feel that these [unorthodox] techniques or combination of therapies are the answers to their problems. I don't fault Mr. McQueen for doing what he did—but I wouldn't want my family victimized by my desire to stay alive a while longer.
>
> We sincerely hope that others who find themselves in the position of making a choice between orthodox and unorthodox therapy would not choose unproven therapies which may, indeed, hasten their deaths.

And Dr. Eugene Frankel, head of the cancer center at the University of Texas, claimed that "while nutrition is an important part of managing cancer, seeking a magical or unusual cure is a serious risk."

The implication was clear: McQueen had died prematurely at the hands of quacks.

Kelley responded with an attack of his own.

> Cancer therapy in America is a scandal. It's a swamp of politics, greed and fear. Changing medical protocol is the slowest ordeal imaginable. Doctors are steeped in fear of change. They feel they must protect their myth of infallibility. Right now, over two billion dollars a year is being spent on conventional therapy, yet two out of three patients treated conventionally will die. The cancer cure rate has risen only 2% in the past 25 years! Steve called it a "shameless racket," and told me that he in-

tended to take on the whole medical establishment in order to reveal the truth about conventional cancer therapy.

Far from having his death hastened by our therapy, Steve lived three full months longer than his Los Angeles doctors claimed was possible. He has dramatically changed the course of medicine by bringing alternatives to the attention of the public. Steve showed that hope can exist even when doctors tell you the situation is hopeless. There's no doubt in my mind that had he survived the operation, and continued his therapy, Steve *would* have recovered. A heart attack killed him, not the cancer. We had it beaten.

Neile McQueen was impelled to write a letter to *People* magazine: "Through treatment in Mexico, Steve was offered a glimmer of hope . . . but I feel it would be a tragedy if people who are being medically treated under a doctor's care and who have average resources were to flock to similar programs without carefully considering all the alternatives."

Peter Chowka countercharged that "McQueen was actually a victim of conventional medicine. For two years his 'orthodox' doctors totally misdiagnosed his killing disease, even though they had all the opportunity in the world for early detection." Robert DeBragga added his opinion: "I believe with all my heart that if McQueen had gone to Plaza Santa Maria on the day he left that Los Angeles hospital in December of 1979, and not wasted seven vital months, he'd be alive today."

Media response was heated. Magazine reader P. Brooks, writing in *Newsweek* (November 17, 1980) expressed a strong personal opinion: "Why is it that conventional cancer therapy, which leaves the victim without organs, limbs, hair, energy, or defense against other disease (including more cancer) is considered normal and acceptable, while cancer therapy that leaves the patient not only intact, but in good health and better educated about keeping his or her body free of disease is called 'a strange form' of therapy?"

McQueen's case *was* responsible, in part, for a fresh appraisal of mesothelioma by the medical profession.

Dr. Stephen Levin, of the Department of Occupational Medicine at the Mount Sinai School of Medicine in New York, declared: "There is evidence that the individual's own immune system *can* retard development of mesothelioma as long as that system remains effective. However, once the body's defense breaks down, the disease grows unchecked."

Many conservative members of the cancer community now share Dr. Levin's view, conceding that the body's immune system is indeed the best weapon against cancer and that our state of mind and body determines the best chance for survival. Santa Maria's Dr. Dwight McKee expressed hope for a medical breakthrough:

> I think that the 1980s will mark the beginning of the end of our present impasse, this useless, destructive conflict between the conservative establishment on one hand and all of us who follow unconventional pioneering medicine on the other. We are coming into a change of national consciousness that is going to have a profound effect on our lives—and on our medical health care system.*

A Learjet carried Steve McQueen's body back to Los Angeles for cremation. He had wanted no burial and had asked Barbara, in the event of his death, to have his ashes scattered over the Pacific Ocean.

Two days after this was done, a private memorial service was held at the Santa Paula ranch. All three of Steve's wives were there, Neile, Ali, and Barbara—and McQueen's two children also attended the memorial, as did four of Steve's best friends: Sammy Mason, Bud Ekins, Pat Johnson, and Elmer Valentine. In his will, McQueen left the Mercedes to Johnson, his karate instructor, and the classic Pitcairn Mailwing to Mason. The ranch had gone to Chad and Terri—and through the McQueen Children's Trust Steve had left $200,000 to the Boys Republic at Chino.

The friends and family members gathered on the lawn for an outdoor ceremony conducted by Dr. Leonard DeWitt, pastor of the Ventura Missionary Church. At its close, a group of vintage biplanes from Santa Paula Airport flew over the ranch in a cross formation. "In the center of the formation was Steve's

---

*Doctors McKee and Rodriguez are no longer associated with the Plaza Santa Maria, and have resumed private practice.

yellow Stearman," one witness observed. "His flying buddy, Larry Endicott, was at the controls, and Larry dipped the wings in final salute. It was a stirring tribute, a fond farewell to a fellow pilot who loved the sky."

Bud Ekins recalled a trip he'd taken with McQueen eight months earlier.

> I didn't know about his illness then, so I was surprised when Steve said, "Bud, in case something happens to me, I want you to have all my bikes, okay?" I didn't know what to say. By then, he'd collected well over a hundred classic motorcycles and had restored about fifty of them to showroom condition. They were worth quite a lot.
>
> When I didn't reply, Steve asked, "Well, wouldn't *you* do the same for me?" And I said no, that I'd leave the collection to my kids. He thought about that for a moment, then nodded. "Yeah, Bud, you're right. That would be the thing to do." And he did—except, in his will, Steve left me "any two bikes" of my choice. I have my own large antique bike collection, and Steve figured there'd be a couple of his I'd really want. All the others went to his kids.

McQueen's death garnered remarkably few printed tributes in comparison to the usual display of public grief surrounding the passing of an international celebrity. Only Jacqueline Bisset, James Garner, Faye Dunaway, and Slim Pickens expressed their sorrow on the printed page. McQueen's close friends and family refused to issue statements; the long ordeal was over, and they had nothing to say to the press. They knew that this was what Steve would want; he had openly expressed his distaste for "the usual goddamn hoopla and razzmatazz they bury people with in this town."

Any final assessment of Steve McQueen must begin with his films. The best of them will continue to be shown and enjoyed around the world by audiences young and old. The luminous screen characters he created in full dimension are still very much alive for us: the Cincinnati Kid...Junior Bonner...Nevada Smith...pilot Buzz Rickson...sailor Jake Holman...rollicking Boon Hogganbeck...Battalion Chief Michael O'Hallorhan...Detective Lieutenant Frank Bullitt...Vin, of the magnificent seven...ruthless Doc McCoy ...suave, romantic Tommy Crown...Hilts, the cooler king...Eustis Clay, a grinning soldier in the rain...Papillon, the man who would be free...and Dr. Thomas Stockmann, who stood strong and alone against injustice.

These memorable characterizations form a solid legacy of entertainment. McQueen gave a part of himself to each of them, investing each role with his dignity, his honor, his sense of artistic truth.

The man himself remained a risk taker who lived a far more dangerous and adventurous life than most Hollywood actors ever dream of; he matched the heroics of his screen persona with real offscreen heroics. There were no headline scandals in his life, no shocking revelations, no hidden "monster behind the mask"—but he was far from saintly.

McQueen could be cruel, cold, abrasive. He made more enemies than friends and was capable of misusing the power of superstardom. He felt that he had to be number one, the winner, the best, the top dog—and he fought hard to achieve and maintain that position. He savored the drama of business conflict as much as he savored desert combat on a cycle. He hated to admit he was wrong about his career choices, or his life choices, and his temper was violent and quick-flaring.

Yet, always, there was the *other* McQueen—a man whose often-awkward and frustrated attempts to find the love denied him as a child reflected the depth of his need for human intimacy, a man sensitive to outcasts, to the dispossessed, to young people in trouble, a man whose charity was apparently limitless.

Steve McQueen ended as he began, a rebel outside the establishment, a man who had preserved his fierce sense of unwavering integrity against all odds, who had gone through the fire, and who had found, at the end, a deep personal peace within himself.

He died as he had lived—with courage.

Appendix:
Steve McQueen's Feature-Length Films, Television Appearances, and Stage Performances

---

- **Feature-Length Films**

SOMEBODY UP THERE LIKES ME *(MGM, 1956)*. Screenplay by Ernest Lehman; based on the autobiography of Rocky Graziano (with Richard Barber). Produced by Charles Schnee. Directed by Robert Wise. With Steve McQueen, in a bit role (as Fidel), Paul Newman, Pier Angeli, Everett Sloane, and Sal Mineo.

NEVER LOVE A STRANGER *(Allied Artists, 1958)*. Screenplay by Harold Robbins and Richard Day; based on the novel by Robbins. Produced by Harold Robbins and Richard Day for Caryn Productions. Directed by Robert Stevens. With Steve McQueen (as Martin Cabell), John Drew Barrymore, Lita Milan, and Robert Bray.

THE BLOB *(Paramount, 1958)*. Screenplay by Theodore Simonson and Kate Phillips; based on an original story by Irvin Millgate. Produced by Jack H. Harris for Tonylyn Productions. Directed by Irvin S. Yeaworth, Jr. With

Steve McQueen (as Steve), Aneta Corseaut, and Earl Rowe.

THE GREAT ST. LOUIS BANK ROBBERY *(United Artists, 1959)*. Screenplay by Richard Heffron; based on an actual case file of a St. Louis bank robbery. Produced by Charles Guggenheim for Guggenheim Associates, Inc. Directed by Charles Guggenheim and John Stix. With Steve McQueen (as George Fowler), David Clarke, and Graham Denton.

NEVER SO FEW *(MGM, 1959)*. Screenplay by Millard Kaufman; based on the novel by Tom Chamales. Produced by Edmund Grainger for Canterbury Productions. Directed by John Sturges. With Steve McQueen (as Bill Ringa), Frank Sinatra, Gina Lollobrigida, and Peter Lawford.

THE MAGNIFICENT SEVEN *(United Artists, 1960)*. Screenplay by William Roberts; based on *Seven Samurai,* a film by Akira Kurosawa. Produced by John Sturges for Mirisch-Alpha Productions. Directed by John Sturges. With Steve McQueen (as Vin), Yul Brynner, James Coburn, Charles Bronson, Robert Vaughn, Horst Buchholz, Brad Dexter, and with Eli Wallach.

THE HONEYMOON MACHINE *(MGM, 1961)*. Screenplay by George Wells; based on *The Golden Fleecing,* a play by Lorenzo Semple. Produced by Lawrence Weingarten for Avon Productions. Directed by Richard Thorpe. With Steve McQueen (as Lieutenant Fergie Howard), Jim Hutton, Brigid Bazlen, and Paula Prentiss.

HELL IS FOR HEROES *(Paramount, 1962)*. Screenplay by Robert Pirosh and Richard Carr; based on an original story by Robert Pirosh. Produced by Henry Blanke. Directed by Don Siegel. With Steve McQueen (as Reese), Bobby Darin, Fess Parker, and Nick Adams.

THE WAR LOVER *(Columbia, 1962)*. Screenplay by Howard Koch; based on the novel by John Hersey. Produced by Arthur Hornblow, Jr. Directed by Philip Leacock. With Steve McQueen (as Buzz Rickson), Robert Wagner, and Shirley Anne Field.

THE GREAT ESCAPE *(United Artists, 1963)*. Screenplay by James Clavell and W. R. Burnett; based on the book by Paul Brickhill. Produced by John Sturges for Mirisch-Alpha Productions. Directed by John Sturges. With Steve McQueen (as Virgil Hilts), James Garner, Richard Attenborough, Charles Bronson, and James Coburn.

LOVE WITH THE PROPER STRANGER *(Paramount, 1963)*. Screenplay by Arnold Schulman. Produced by Alan J. Pakula for Pakula-Mulligan Productions. Directed by Robert Mulligan. With Steve McQueen (as Rocky Papasano), Natalie Wood, Edie Adams, and Herschel Bernardi.

SOLDIER IN THE RAIN *(Allied Artists, 1963)*. Screenplay by Maurice Richlin and Blake Edwards; based on the novel by William Goldman. Produced by Martin Jurow for Cedar and Solar Productions. Directed by Ralph Nelson. With Steve McQueen (as Sergeant Eustis Clay), Jackie Gleason, Tuesday Weld, and Tony Bill.

BABY, THE RAIN MUST FALL *(Columbia, 1965)*. Screenplay by Horton Foote; based on his play *The Traveling Lady*. Produced by Alan J. Pakula for Pakula-Mulligan Productions. Directed by Robert Mulligan. With Steve McQueen (as Henry Thomas), Lee Remick, and Don Murray.

THE CINCINNATI KID *(MGM, 1965)*. Screenplay by Ring Lardner, Jr. and Terry Southern; based on the novel by Richard Jessup. Produced by Martin Ransohoff for Filmways and Solar Productions. Directed by Norman Jewison. With Steve McQueen (as Eric Stone, the Cincinnati Kid), Edward G. Robinson, Karl Malden, Tuesday Weld, and Ann-Margret.

NEVADA SMITH *(Paramount, 1966)*. Screenplay by John Michael Hayes; based on the character created by Harold Robbins in his novel, *The Carpetbaggers*. Produced by Henry Hathaway for Embassy and Solar Productions. Directed by Henry Hathaway. With Steve McQueen (as Max Sand, alias Nevada Smith), Karl Malden, Brian Keith, and Suzanne Pleshette.

THE SAND PEBBLES *(20th Century-Fox, 1966)*. Screenplay by Robert Anderson; based on the novel by Richard McKenna. Produced by Robert Wise for Argyle and Solar Productions. Directed by Robert Wise. With Steve McQueen (as Jake Holman), Richard Crenna, Candice Bergen, and Richard Attenborough.

THE THOMAS CROWN AFFAIR *(United Artists, 1968)*. Screenplay by Alan R. Trustman. Produced by Norman Jewison for Mirisch Corp. and Solar Productions. Directed by Norman Jewison. With Steve McQueen (as Thomas Crown), Faye Dunaway, and Jack Weston.

BULLITT *(Warner Brothers/Seven Arts, 1968)*. Screenplay by Alan R. Trustman and Harry Kleiner; based on the novel *Mute Witness* by Robert L. Pike. Produced by Robert Relyea for Solar Productions. Directed by Peter Yates. With Steve McQueen (as Frank Bullitt), Jacqueline Bisset, and Robert Vaughn.

THE REIVERS *(Cinema Center, through National General, 1969)*. Screenplay by Irving Ravetch and Harriet Frank, Jr; based on the novel by William Faulkner. Produced by Irving Ravetch for Duo and Solar Productions. Directed by Mark Rydell. With Steve McQueen (as Boon Hogganbeck), Sharon Farrell, Rupert Crosse, and Mitch Vogel.

LE MANS *(Cinema Center, through National General, 1971)*. Screenplay by Harry Kleiner. Produced by Jack Reddish for Solar Productions. Directed by Lee H. Katzin. With Steve McQueen (as Michael Delaney), Siegfried Rauch, and Elga Andersen.

ON ANY SUNDAY *(Cinema 5, 1971)*. Screenplay by Bruce Brown. Produced by Bruce Brown for Solar Productions. Directed by Bruce Brown. With Steve McQueen (as himself), Mert Lawwill, and Malcolm Smith. (This was a documentary, partially financed by Solar.)

JUNIOR BONNER *(Cinerama, 1972)*. Screenplay by Jeb Rosebrook. Produced by Joe Wizan for Wizan-Gardner and Solar Productions. Directed by Sam Peckinpah. With Steve McQueen (as Junior Bonner), Robert Preston, and Ida Lupino.

THE GETAWAY *(National General, 1972)*. Screenplay by Walter Hill; based on the novel by Jim Thompson. Produced by David Foster and Mitchell Brower for Solar-First Artists. Directed by Sam Peckinpah. With Steve McQueen (as Doc McCoy), Ali MacGraw, Ben Johnson, and Slim Pickens.

PAPILLON *(Columbia/Allied Artists, 1973)*. Screenplay by Dalton Trumbo and Lorenzo Semple, Jr.; based on the autobiography of Henri Charriere. Produced by Robert Dorfmann and Franklin J. Schaffner. Directed by Franklin J. Schaffner. With Steve McQueen (as Henri Charriere—"Papillon"), Dustin Hoffman, and Victor Jory.

THE TOWERING INFERNO *(20th Century-Fox and Warner Bros., 1974)*. Screenplay by Stirling Silliphant; based on two novels: *The Tower* by Richard Martin Stern and *The Glass Inferno* by Frank M. Robinson and Thomas Scortia. Produced by Irwin Allen. Directed by John Guillerman and Irwin Allen. With Steve McQueen (as Michael O'Hallorhan), Paul Newman, Faye Dunaway, William Holden, and Fred Astaire.

AN ENEMY OF THE PEOPLE *(Warner Bros., 1977)*. Screenplay by Alexander Jacobs; based on the play by Henrik Ibsen as adapted by Arthur Miller. Produced by George Schaefer for Solar-First Artists. Executive Producer: Steve McQueen. Directed by George Schaefer. With Steve McQueen (as Dr. Thomas Stockmann), Bibi Andersson, and Charles Durning.

TOM HORN *(Columbia/Warner Bros., 1980)*. Screenplay by Thomas McGuane and Bud Shrake; based on Tom Horn's autobiography, *The Life of Tom Horn, Government Scout and Interpreter*. Produced by Fred Weintraub for Solar-First Artists. Executive Producer: Steve McQueen. Directed by William Wiard. With Steve McQueen (as Tom Horn), Linda Evans, and Slim Pickens.

THE HUNTER *(Paramount, 1980)*. Screenplay by Ted Leighton and Peter Hyams; based on the book by Christopher Keane and the life of Ralph Thorson. Produced by Mort Engelberg for Rastar-Engelberg Productions. Directed by Buzz Kulik. With Steve McQueen (as Ralph "Papa"

Thorson), Kathryn Harrold, Ben Johnson, and Eli Wallach.

● **Television**

THE CHIVINGTON RAID for *The Philco-Goodyear Playhouse* (NBC), March 27, 1955. BRING ME A DREAM for *The U.S. Steel Hour* (CBS), January 4, 1956. THE DEFENDER for *Studio One* (CBS), in two parts: February 23, 1957 and March 4, 1957. AMBUSH for *West Point* (CBS), March 8, 1957. FOUR HOURS IN WHITE for *Climax* (CBS), February 6, 1958. BILL LONGLEY for *Tales of Wells Fargo* (NBC), February 10, 1958. THE BOUNTY HUNTER for *Trackdown* (CBS), March 7, 1958. WANTED—DEAD OR ALIVE (CBS); from September 6, 1958 to March 29, 1961. HUMAN INTEREST STORY for *Alfred Hitchcock Presents* (CBS), May 24, 1959. MAN FROM THE SOUTH for *Alfred Hitchcock Presents* (CBS), January 3, 1960. THUNDER IN A FORGOTTEN TOWN for *The Dick Powell Theatre* (NBC), March 5, 1963. THE COMING OF THE ROADS (KABC-TV); documentary with McQueen as narrator, September 17, 1966.

Apparently, McQueen appeared on *The 20th Century-Fox Hour* and *The Armstrong Circle Theatre* in the 1950s, but definitive data are unavailable. He also made guest appearances on the Bob Hope, Ed Sullivan, and Perry Como shows.

● **Stage**

PEG O' MY HEART (1952). Staged by a small theater company in Fayetteville, New York; starred Margaret O'-Brien, with McQueen in a minor role.

MEMBER OF THE WEDDING (1952). McQueen appeared (with star Ethel Waters) in a road company production in Rochester, New York.

TIME OUT FOR GINGER (1952). A small role in the national road company with star Melvyn Douglas.

Two Fingers of Pride (1956). Summer stock in Maine with star Gary Merrill.

A Hatful of Rain (1956). McQueen's Broadway debut, replacing Ben Gazzara in the role of Johnny Pope.

Acknowledgments

Biography is always a collaborative endeavor. In writing this book, beyond the extensive talks I had with Steve himself, I drew upon a number of other individuals—producers, writers, artists, designers, directors, editors, actors, racing drivers, cinematographers, stuntmen, doctors, publicists, agents, critics, teachers, pilots, members of the clergy, business executives, and friends—all of whom entered the life of Steve McQueen.

Among them: Neile Adams, Ed Adamson, Irwin Allen, Mario Andretti, Army Archerd, Jane Ardmore, Trevor Armbrister, Richard Attwood.

James Bacon, Clara Bailey, George Barris, Joan Barthel, James Bax. Luster Bayless, Jim Beaver, Harrison Bemis, Joseph Biroc, Jacqueline Bisset, Nina Blanchard, Mary Blume, Tony Brenna, Marie Brenner, Helene Brown, Peter Bunzel, Henry Burn.

Jean Calvin, Joanna Campbell, Charles Champlin, Peter Chowka, Ann Cinquina, Paul Ciotti, Frank Conroy, Francis Ford Coppola, Frank Corsaro, Richard Crenna.

Robert DeBragga, Stephen Decatur, Mike Dewey, Doug

Dullenkopf, Faye Dunaway, Charles Durning.

Bud Ekins, Hillard Elkins, Derek Elley, Mort Engelberg, Linda Evans, Robert Evans.

Vince Fennelly, Peter Flint, Eugene Frankel.

Arthur Garfield, Richie Ginther, Gina Glaze, Jackie Gleason, Frank Graves, Chris Greenwood, Masten Gregory.

Joyce Haber, John Hallowell, Kathryn Harrold, Ernest Havemann, Donald Healey, Walter Hill, Jim Hoffman, Dave Holeman, Michael Housego.

Robert Johnson, Loren Janes, Robert F. Jones.

Stuart Kaminsky, Michael Katz, Lee H. Katzin, William Donald Kelley, Judy Klemesrud, Dan Knapp, Arthur Knight, Buzz Kulik.

John Lachuk, Abe Lastfogel, Robin Leach, Stephen Levin, Bill Libby, Peter Lucarelli.

Ali MacGraw, Sy Marsh, Sammy Mason, Wanda Mason, Malachy McCoy, Dwight McKee, Sanford Meisner, Gary Merrill, Edwin Miller, Mike Miller, Barbara Minty (McQueen), Stirling Moss, Robert Mulligan.

Paul Newman.

Susan Oliver, Bill Ornstein, Katie O'Sullavan.

Mike Parkes, Sam Peckinpah, Slim Pickens, James Powers.

Mike Rachmil, Jack Reddish, Robert Relyea, Frank M. Robinson, Rodrigo Rodriguez, Betty Rollin, Ron Rosenbaum, Ken Rudeen, Mark Rydell.

Bill Sanders, Andrew Sarris, Jo Scalzo, Franklin Schaffner, Emil Schandl, Heinz Schneider, Mark Schorr, Edouard Seidler, Michael Seiler, A. B. Shuman, Don Siegel, John Skow, Liz Smith, Michael Sragow, Cameron Stauth, Gordon Stulberg, John Sturges, Nicole Szulc.

Tedd Thomey, Ralph Thorson, Mike Tomkies, Vincent Tubbs.

Cesar Santos Vargas, Carol Veazie, Georges-Alain Vuille.

S. Wallace, Wayne Warga, Fred Weintraub, Karen Wilson, Robert Wise.

Peter Yates.

Edward Zalta.

My debt to all is gratefully acknowledged. Each has made his or her contribution to this book. I also wish to express my gratitude to the Library of the Academy of Motion Picture Arts and Sciences and to the International Association of Cancer

Victims and Friends, Playa del Rey, California.

Special thanks to Peter Chowka for his permission to quote from an exclusive interview with Robert DeBragga; to my wife, Kam Nolan, for her loyal support, her objective editorial counsel, and her expert typing; and to Tom Congdon and Marilee Talman for their continued support of this book.

William F. Nolan
Agoura, California
1983

Index

231

Glittering lives of famous people!
Bestsellers from Berkley

★ ★

____	**JANE FONDA: HEROINE FOR OUR TIME** Thomas Kiernan	06164-7—$3.50
____	**BRANDO FOR BREAKFAST** Anna Kashfi Brando and E.P. Stein	04698-2—$2.75
____	**MISS TALLULAH BANKHEAD** Lee Israel	04574-9—$2.75
____	**MOMMIE DEAREST** Christina Crawford	07289-4—$3.95
____	**MOTHER GODDAM** Whitney Stine with Bette Davis	07507-9—$3.95
____	**MY WICKED, WICKED WAYS** Errol Flynn	07996-1—$3.50
____	**NO BED OF ROSES** Joan Fontaine	05028-9—$2.75
____	**RICHARD BURTON** Paul Ferris	07374-2—$3.50
____	**RITA HAYWORTH: THE TIME, THE PLACE AND** **THE WOMAN** John Kobal	07170-7—$3.50
____	**SHADOWLAND: FRANCES FARMER** William Arnold	06992-3—$2.95
____	**SUSAN HAYWARD: PORTRAIT OF A SURVIVOR** Beverly Linet	07509-5—$3.95

Prices may be slightly higher in Canada.